THIS
BOOK
BELONGS TO

Dramatic Imagination

By
Jerneral Cranston

Interface California Corporation • Eureka

Library of Congress Catalog Card Number 75-7845.
ISBN 0-915580-01-2.
Published by Interface California Corporation
1806 E. Street, Suite B
Eureka, California 95501

AUTHOR'S PREFACE

This book is intended to be useful for teachers at all levels from pre-school through 12th grade and beyond to beginning acting classes in college. During my career I have worked with students of all ages from pre-school through college. The ideas in this book are an outgrowth of my experiences as an elementary school teacher for six years and a college professor for nearly six years.

Our society has a singularly unique combination of problems demanding solutions, yet American cultural offerings deny us the opportunity or choices necessary to obtain a balanced existence between mind and body. Fads on changing one's state of consciousness have allowed no religion, including Satanism, to go untapped. Their many forms include growth centers, trips to the guru, purifying and cleansing the body with garlic, and the list goes on. Drugs that range from aspirin to psychedelics send their users into blissful reaches of existence or down a chamber of horrors.

To say that there is a lot of seeking, some of it illegal or superficial, is an understatement. The experiences of instability are more than apparent among youth. Yet, during the last twenty years, few significant changes have been made within the school curriculum.

I remember my son's first day at school. I was on yard duty as a teacher, and I could see him across the field. He looked small and excited about having a new adventure. The glow of school being an adventure lasted through most of his elementary school experience. Fortunately, he was exposed to some teachers that allowed for creative expression. The school has become, and is still, the most stable institution for pursuing social as well as personal integration in society.

In many schools today, teachers view skill, or information subjects, and the arts on two different levels: Work and play. By about the fourth grade, the information subjects begin to crowd out time allotted for creative expression.

While I was supervising some college students teaching Creative Dramatics in an elementary school, the principal called me into his office, told me that sensitivity training would have to stop, and that "play" activities should not be carried on during morning hours reserved for "solids." After talking to the student instructors, I learned that one class had been exploring an exercise called the Blind Walk. The other was conducting a space exercise in which each child moved within his own imaginary bubble.

When confronted by restrictive attitudes, some teachers seem able to forge through, and find a way to coordinate "play" and "work." Students in their classes learn history by approaching it as a fascinating story, find ways to relive an epoch by integrating crafts, drama and the arts.

I continue to teach and visit many schools. I notice only a slight difference in the system today compared with the system when I entered kindergarten 36 years ago. With the exception of a few dedicated people connected with teaching who foresee needed change and often generate it, our schools are still starving children on the same curriculum, according to the same criteria, that was in vogue during our educators' childhoods. However, change is beginning to take place. As Dr. Frederick P. Cranston, speaking at a Humboldt State University commencement, said:

> **We know that. . .education is in the process of great change, and either we help guide the change or outside elements will force change upon us. . .Thus our University should provide the opportunity for man to expand his humanness in ways which weren't possible in the past. This expansion, it seems,. . .is going to require a greater concentration of our efforts in the Liberal Arts and Sciences. . .Many more people will be painting pictures, throwing pots, writing poetry, acting in plays, performing in concerts, and even solving Physics problems for fun. Our new University must provide the opportunities for man to free himself.**

My own experience with children and teaching leaves me with a vision that has haunted me for years: I see lost looking children, victims of cultural or sociological circumstances who could not compete. The environment of these children did not provide the soil from which they could grow. There were few outlets in their prison for personal discovery, and the only means of communication remaining appeared through vocal or facial expressions.

During the educational reforms of the 1950's and 1960's, the curriculum was never viewed as a whole. As Dr. Charles E. Silverman described in his book, *The Open Classroom Reader* "An important result of the reformer's failure to consider the curriculum as a whole is the fact that they left one of the most critical areas of the curriculum almost completely untouched: namely, the Arts."

Creative dramatics can provide a focal point for retaining the arts, movement, and creative involvement in our curricula. The factor described by Richard Courtney in *Play, Drama, and Thought* as "spontaneous creativity" is based upon sense experience. It is in this awareness of environment that creative dramatics becomes important.

Some elementary schools set aside one day out of the year for an event called "Exploration Day." As one pupil described it, "It's just like kindergarten." At such events, children are often alive and rush from one activity to another as though afraid that in some way they will miss out. The same approach is occasionally experimented with in secondary schools, when various changes in scheduling are tried. With few exceptions, such experiments are unsuccessful; the students have been frustrated too often and refuse to participate fully. I've asked some high school students why they go to school, and most reply without thinking, "Because I have to." Some say, "So I can get into college." Occasionally, the response is, "Because I can learn," but with suprising frequency we hear, "Because I can see my friends there." Dropouts may be, in some respects, the most active learners. They remain highly sensitive to their own needs and feel that the goal is not to "learn" or to be gorged with isolated facts to which they are unable to relate.

Disadvantaged children are a case in point. In *The Effect of Sociodramatic Play on Disadvantaged Pre-School Children*, Sara Smilansky noted that young boys from this group frequently have a disadvantage in developing the male role, since no models exist at the father-parent level. More pressure is placed upon the boy to be "a man" than corresponds in girls to adopt their role as women. In classrooms, identity problems are ignored in the quest for skill knowlege. Expressional forms such as dance and singing are de-emphasized because of negative student reactions.

The link that is missing, of course, is the connection of the learning process to the students themselves. Creative dramatics can help put them in touch with those things or interests they feel are important.

Drama, in which dance, mime, and creative expression would all be aspects of curriculum, has been completely overlooked as a viable subject for inclusion in the Fine Arts program of most schools. More than any other of the arts, it requires that individuals work together in groups, reflects common or universal experiences, and contains workable inclusions of most other art forms. In addition, creative dramatics can become an extension of abstract thought. How, I frequently ask myself, may we ask children to believe in the abstractions of history, literature, mathematics or geography if their own reality is denied them?

A recently-published language series states that its purpose is to teach the child to read with more accuracy and sensitivity. More time, however, is spent having the child look up words in the dictionary than participating in exercises dealing with the senses. A statement included in the series explains that "appreciation is a private matter," assuming that the child is on his or her own when relating to the poem through personal experience.

The difficulty frequently encountered when distinguishing between cognitive and affective learning must become a matter of great concern to educators today. The intelligence displayed by one child's sensitivity about a poem might far outweigh the understanding of another child whose penchant for dictionary definitions enables him to translate the meaning of the poem verbally with great accuracy. Both children display cognitive skills, but the dictionary buff's I.Q. score would soar, while the other child's might appear average. However, no one has successfully designed an accurate test for depth of understanding.

In order to gain the needed commitment from children involved in creative dramatics, the teacher or leader must himself be totally involved and commited. Several years ago, another teacher and I were leading a class of 37 children in summer school creative dramatics. Our goal for the class was that the children would enjoy themselves in a new way which hopefully would include a greater degree of involvement between all domains of learning.

One day, my partner-instructor took those children who hadn't become involved over to another part of the room, leaving the remaining students with me. He told his group of the day his dog had died, and noticed their reaction to his story. After bringing their feelings of concern into the discussion, he told them the story was not really true. He then let them discuss whether the emotion they had felt was real, even though he had made the situation up. In this way, we were able to introduce the problem of an actor's belief in his role, and discussed this with them. The actor must first believe, or the audience certainly will not. One technique, of course, is to think about how one might feel in a similar emotional situation.

Belief is not only the problem of the actor, but of the instructor as well. If children are to become involved, certainly the teacher must first be involved. The pin-drop stillness created by music, understanding, or immersion in a new experience is a powerful moment because all psychic energy is directed. To attain this level of delight requires a high degree of concentration. Concentration is likewise necessary for successful drama, because so much energy is frequently involved in active group participation that it should be channeled.

Questions form an ideal method of channeling such energy. The children are given a focus that helps them obtain their objectives as the teacher states questions in the best manner to properly guide them. "Can you see the objects being handled?" "See if you can imagine what kind of place this is!" "Can you tell what kind of person this is by how he walks?"

Learning is frequently more observable in the classroom when activities that interest the child are included. Those that come immediately to mind are conducting experiments, learning games, stories and the like. Sometimes, the situation involves strange tales about real incidents. However, in such cases if distortion of reality is included, a little exaggeration frequently goes a long way. If excessive exaggeration is sensed by the children, the spell of belief and trust may be broken and disrupt the learning process. Whether the motivation is provided by a story, an experiment or a game, the explanation should be attached closely to the children's realm. Only within the familiar surroundings of childhood can the enjoyment of "stretched" imagination occur, with its connection, hopefully, to discovery learning. In presenting a concept, the teacher must decide whether best results will be obtained by telling a story, by giving an example from real life, by drawing a diagram, or by establishing a relationship that may be personalized. The conditions of learning are not determined as much by age or subject matter as by the manner of pursuit and strategy.

Likewise, true play contains discipline and direction. In his book, *Play, Dreams and Imitation*, Piaget describes play as allowing a repetition of a discovery. By repeating the discovery, children are able to solidify their experiences and enjoy them for the pleasure gained. A child will frequently substitute a pie pan for a cup, or even drink from a cup that is not there. This higher level of play is characterized by rules that the children establish themselves, organizing for the teacher their own involvement. Rules and planning such as this are frequently adaptable to, or a starting point for, drama.

The exercises and lessons provide a route, in which any player may play the game in any style he wishes, as long as he abides by the basic rules. Children are freed to create alternative routes as long as they remain involved in working toward the objective. There is no need for competition, but ample room for discovery of the many ways open to reach a common goal.

The exercises and lesson plans contained in chapters Three and Four, along with their associated appendix, provide profitable starting points for teachers experimenting for the first time with creative dramatics. Beginning with common physical actions, and leading to actions based upon situations or circumstances in a sensible progression suitable for use with any age group, these exercises and lessons are adaptable to situations which are unique to your group.

We have all experienced a classroom at this point of learning. There may be absolute silence among the children, or a healthy background of noisy activity, but in either case, rapt attentiveness and concentration toward the task at hand. All outside distraction has ceased because of the child's overwhelming fascination and pursuit of his goal. It is this feeling of awe, this "golden moment," that I hope to provide instructors of Creative Dramatics through my book.

Jerneral Cranston
Arcata, California

to Larry

and the Larrys of future generations

Acknowledgments

I wish to thank the following persons who have assisted me in the preparation of this book: Candace K. B. Matzke for initial editing and suggestions; Jane Epperson for reading the manuscript and making valuable and unique suggestions; the Centering School; the teachers and students at Jacoby Creek School and Arcata High School for participating in many of the creative dramatics activities; Lou and Linda Agliolo for their inspiration and dedication to helping adolescents; Principal Clyde Patenaude and the teachers and students of Blue Lake Elementary School who were receptive to the philosophy inherent in Creative Dramatics; Sally Palmquist and Zora Dolezal for proofreading; John Pauley and Charles Myers for their gift of time; Peggy Holliwell, Eliza Donlon, Linda Duglay, and John Kilbourne who taught me by their own development what children needed; and my own teachers, especially Jack Cook, Donald Bissett and Sue Vallance, who inspired me in this direction.

Special thanks are merited by Bob and Genelle Dolezal for their perseverance in editing and developing the final format of the book. Peter Palmquist and Helen Hofsted deserve special praise for preparation of the photographic material. And finally, to my husband who, through his hard work, encouragement, and inspiration, helped unfailingly.

TABLE OF CONTENTS

Introduction

1: History of Creative Drama 1

2: Use and Purpose of Creative Drama 9

3: Exercises 21

Senses 25
Space 35
Imagination 39
Plots 47
Character 53
Mime 61
Abstract Mime 71
Speech 77

4: Lesson Plans 85

The Drowning Giant 97
The Peddler and the Monkeys 101
The Selfish Giant 107
A Sacrifice 115
The Fuzzies 117
The Cave 119
The Party 123
The Hare that Ran Away 131
Trip to Earth 137
Haunted House 141
The Problem 145
Moon Monster 149
The Brahman, Tiger and Jackal 155
Roast Pig 161
Javelin Throw 169
Pandora 179
Norwegian Winter 187
Little Miss Muffet 191
Town Planning 195
Role—Playing 197

5: Improvisation 201

Exercises 207
Scenarios 220

Appendix
Glossary
Bibliography and Music

INTRODUCTION

In ancient times primitive man strove to ally himself with those supernatural forces he could not control or understand. Threshing floors and hillside slopes became the first theaters where man expressed the overwhelming forces of his environment. Instead of being dominated or overpowered by nature, man became one with its forces.

Children are like primitive man, who needed little training in order to communicate their experiences, express emotional concerns or project their imaginative life by using their bodies as a medium. A child's emotional needs are often varied and complex. Unless a channel exists for creative release, confused feelings may become a disruptive force to society or their own well-being. This book describes and evaluates the use of mime and creative dramatics for children. Its program is equally suited for use in elementary, secondary or university-level instruction, and aids students in keeping their child-like attitude towards learning.

Mime and creative dramatics should be included as legitimate parts of the school curriculum because of their unique advantages to children. Teachers may use both creative dramatics and mime in most classrooms to lead or direct students in expressing themselves with actions. As an approach to learning about living, creative dramatics employs exercises presented in an imaginative and dramatic framework. One example involves stories told by the teacher, made up by the children, or focused on nearby incidents and objects. Working in a group, each story is amplified by the students and motivates movement around a central theme which follows established dramatic structures.

Creative dramatics and mime may also serve the objectives of emotional and sensory awareness, psychomotor development, and mental and aesthetic experience. Within the creative dramatics structure which the teacher or leader provides, imaginative thought may be extended and developed, guiding the child toward understanding and maintaining his own self-discipline.

An example is provided by the use of music during creative dramatics instruction. Music may lead to many varied emotional and aesthetic discoveries. An intense interplay of emotions may find expression through movement while reacting to music which is calm yet dramatic. Lyrical music can instill beauty of form and purity of line that may be relived many times over by memory of the emotional and physical response envoked. Creative dramatics may become a medium to resolve conflicts within the child's personality.

In addition to its aesthetic advantages, creative dramatics and mime can provide an improved balance in the child's emotional health. His newly-experienced stability often influences his sensory perceptions and capacity for knowlege. As a result, learning may more directly apply to the child's environment, allowing him a greater understanding and respect for the strengths and weaknesses in living things.

Emotional catharsis may be achieved through experiencing pity or fear in response to a stimulus. In classical Greek tragedy, the word *purging* was used to describe the result of this catharsis. The intention of those dramas was to cleanse through re-experiencing the emotion. The processes of releasing and re-experiencing are synonomous; a release cannot be conducted without sufficient stimulation or channeling of emotion. Using a structure for the release of emotions allows them an existence in time and space and allows for purging. An emotional spectrum is represented when the rhythm of motivation, stimulus, and involvement is considered. If feelings are expressed superficially, then motivation, stimulus, involvement, and release do not result in a re-experiencing of fear, wonder, awe, and finally a release into sadness and joy. Much of the misuse and distrust of drama in schools is the result of a superficial level of involvement or the fear of too much emotional involvement. In the first instance the emotions are not considered, and activity is overly structured; in the second, emotions are encountered that the teacher cannot channel. The hoped-for outcome is to reach a balance between emotional motivation and its release. Catharsis and guidance of the emotions result in artistic form and personal satisfaction. If the leader's own belief is strengthened through practice, the children may be guided to achieve this experience. Sometimes the experience occurs in ten minutes; sometimes not for ten months.

In comparison to teachers in England, the understanding of emotional growth among Americans has been pushed aside to make room for the need to become more competitive. This competitive drive has replaced a need to grow emotionally. For those children who do not compete, growth has become stifled; and for those children who do compete, growth has also become stifled. The emotions are inhibited, have become disconnected from reality, and may be released in anti-social ways.

In the typical learning process which demonstrates the mind-body connection, the infant goes through the stages of physiological reaction to stimuli many times before a psychomotor reflex pattern is established. Activities such as these might occur over a period of many years and be stored sequentially in the child's memory. Not until the mind needs to transform these signals into psychological meaning does a symbolic transformation take place as an idea or action. For example, if a young child has been confronted by a multi-media environment and has had to make choices between alternate stimuli, the experience of making a commitment to a single task later on will not seem difficult.

Learning, as in the process described above, often occurs as a reaction to fear or as a protective device. The opposite can occur when the body repeats an action for the sake of pleasure. A new connection between mind and body is formed, and the pleasure of movement becomes a second step on the level of play.

In much the same manner, if dance and movement forms have been handled in relation to young children's play and learning, their memories will store this relationship between their body and the environment. Such memories frequently reappear at a later date, transformed to an idea or action through the internal pattern of movement. The reaction to learning and the search for truth also includes a personal search that is often overlooked. By not providing scope for individual direction, the mechanical aspect of learning is frequently emphasized.

The process of learning, in which the learner is wholly involved would integrate and focus his experiences. Such a relationship of the cognitive, psychomotor, and affective domains requires participation in activities which allow the mind-body processes to function, and to pull together otherwise unrelated details on a personal plane first. The amount of flexibility and sensitivity needed by teachers and children requires a thought process that is divergent and unique, not just conventional steps leading to a single "right" answer.

The teacher must approach the classroom flexibly, providing a creative atmosphere for learning. If the teacher's motive is to get the children to learn a specific lesson, then it is unlikely that their enthusiasm will spread to any larger learning situation. Learning, therefore, is a product of its stimulant: the teacher. Learning cannot exceed the boundaries of situation. Unless the openness and flexibility of the teacher allows the student to go beyond the immediate situation, growth — and learning — will necessarily be inhibited.

In this book, importance has been placed upon the value of movement exercises, games and involvement techniques. Ideas and lesson plans for stimulating movement, including the use of props, music, and percussion instruments, are included for instructor convenience.

In its introductory section, background information on creative dramatics and mime as a representative folk art explores spontaneous drama throughout history. Examples of the ways in which mankind channeled his exuberance, phrased his questions about the unknown, and celebrated his life through creative dramatics are included.

Most of the book is designed to serve teachers and leaders as a handbook for instruction in the classroom. Lesson plans, detailed exercises, and explanatory material is presented in a usable program of discovery learning. An appendix aids instructors in tailoring lesson plans and exercises to age levels, intended use, and objectives.

A complete section on Improvisation is also included, providing a goal for teachers with students interested in further development of creative dramatics and mime skills.

"One can keep on looking and not know why. . ."

1: HISTORY OF CREATIVE DRAMA

Informal drama, whether creative dramatics, mime, or improvisation, can be traced to prehistoric attempts by early man to understand or control his environment. Man's earliest attempts to communicate were in the form of gesture. His child-like logic led him to communicate emotionally by creating gestures that would influence or beg favors from the gods of nature that he did not understand. He reached toward the sky in order to appease the rain god, or hurled his crudely-made weapon toward an element of nature that threatened him.

Frequently early man devised a process of "sympathetic magic" that included dance. He imitated the movements of plants and animals and interpreted the rhythm of wind and water. By joining with others in a rhythmic chant, his magic became still more effective. His dancing grew into a circle of bodies turning and crying in unison, concentrating their efforts. Voices and bodies soon reached a frenzied pace, and the "spell" grew in both stature and ritual. Since understanding the forces of nature was impossible with early man's limited knowlege, these elaborate rituals reassured, protected, and finally made him nature's equal.

From magic rituals, man quickly developed a better understanding of self-expression. He began to dress up in costume and assumed the role of a character. Frequently, several men spoke in unison in response to their leader, thus linking themselves to the altar and its deity. Settings, first in the form of sacrificial offerings and later as decorations, became important. The Greek god Dionysus, for example, was represented by the vineyard, a symbol of his fertility. His shrine became one of the structures important to the developing, formalized theater. As gods and idols became secularized, other structures took the place of original tombs and shrines. The proscenium and orchestra pit were built to separate the actor from the chorus, and the nonparticipants, or audience, became further divided from actions "on stage."

Because both formal and informal drama developed from primitive ritual, little information leading to the exact origin of mime within drama can be traced, except in the form of semi-legend. By going back to these partly imaginary, partly factual tales, it is possible to conjecture a few probable origins of informal drama. The need which ancient man may have felt for burlesqueing the gods and heroes of early formal drama, together with a trend for satirizing domestic and national events, may have provided the impetus for improvisation.

Informal drama, more closely allied to creative dramatics, has been been obscured by close association to ritual, dance, celebrations, and festivals. All such activities have in common the childlike need for harmonious self-expression between man and his environment. If, in tracing the historical development of creative dramatics and mime, a broad definition such as that described above is applied, its appearance in fertility and puberty rites can be traced back to ancient times.

Mime may have developed from formal drama as Thespis stood apart from the other actors and led the crowd in antiphonal chants, frequently using masks and gestures to convey different characters. By Roman times, however, it is relatively certain that Livius Andronicus was responsible for rediscovering mime as an art form. Legend suggests that, in 240 B.C., Andronicus lost his voice on stage, and through inspired improvisation and gesticulation was so captivating to his Roman audience the mime was born.

From these beginnings, mime was used as an interlude or epilogue to more serious plays. In the same way that Thespis expanded his role as an actor, the single mime player from Rome soon became able to include more themes. For their story-line mimes frequently chose events with political allusions. The art form traveled across Europe as Roman armies of conquest expanded the empire. The entrance of Roman pantomime art into England probably occurred with the conquest of Julius Caesar in 52 B.C.

During the Middle Ages, wandering players or *jongleurs* roamed through villages engaging in buffoonery and providing a brash, extemporal kind of entertainment. A procession of players who continued to satirize contemporary events kept the spirit of extemporaneous acting and improvisation alive in the Byzantine Empire after the Roman Empire collapsed.

The church created a simple four line playlet form of its own that made up liturgical drama. Within these simple plays, mime became a part of church ritual and made the stories from the Bible seem as real as had been the Dionysiac festivals celebrating the growth, maturation, and death of the vine.

As more people came to see the plays, the drama moved outdoors and onto the steps of the church. The church authorities became aware that the symbolically-created drama was growing in intensity. New roles and longer themes were included. None of the prohibitions which the authorities placed upon the performances seemed to be taken seriously. Into these plays, or *cycles*, crept humorous episodes about heaven and hell, suggesting that humor provided a welcome release for pent up emotions concerning fear and damnation.

Many of the rituals have become lost, but because of a few that still exist, folk drama can be traced to ceremonies in which dialogue was chanted. Celebrations during this period, continued in forms similar to the modern Mummer's and Passion plays, for which a single town was responsible. Such forms are popular even today. Many towns continue to reenact their own history, inspired by ritualistic needs for identification. Among such presentations are dramas of Appalachian communities that have tried to maintain the unique elements of cultures which might otherwise have faded or become extinct.

The performers are members of the community and usually are known to the audience. In some cases, players rotate from year to year, and audiences and performers are exchanged in much the same way as is common in creative dramatics. As soon as the form becomes popularized, the cast remains stable, more performances are given, and (in order to make a living) the players may become like those of the middle ages who toured from village to village. Unlike formal drama, both folk drama and popular drama can be performed anywhere. Relationships between the audience and players provide a spontaneous medium for interaction. Responses from the audience may be built into the action at some point.

Seen in this way, folk drama has continued to exist in a form somewhere between festivals (such as Mardi Gras), and ritual (such as many Easter ceremonies). Creative dramatics includes both areas, however, and does not tie individuals to distinct roles as is common in both ritual and formal dramatics.

As the formal church dramas moved from the altar to the marketplace, they became part of the village festivals which celebrated the arrival of spring and harvest. The May Day celebration has always been representative of those holidays which entreat the sympathies of Nature. Drama connects the modern May Day ceremony with the former practice of sacrificing the king. In both ceremonies, the killing of a material body symbolized its seasonal, and therefore limited, life on earth. The purpose of this dramatized killing was to enable the true riding spirit to escape and be revived in a stronger, yet more youthful, form.

In a similar manner, the Feast of Fools developed as a result of the difference in days between the solar and lunar year. In order to have the same number of days in the solar year, as many as 5 to 12 days were added at the end of the year. It was generally an occasion for changing rulers and satirizing the staunch traditions which preserved order during the year. Such foolishness as introducing an ass into the church under a gold cloth led to re-enactments of the biblical flight into Egypt, and finally to the dramatization of indecent farces outside the church.

The Feast of the Innocents was a replica of the Feast of Fools, and was celebrated on the 28th of December. Nuns and their pupils exchanged parts and roles. Another aspect of the Feast of the Innocents involved the ceremony in which a boy Bishop reigned until Saint Nicholas Day, the holiday observing the patron saint of children. The boy Bishop was led with song and dance from house to house as he blessed the people who offered him their benediction.

Beside religious ceremonies, which are a passive form of creative dramatics, many seasonal festivals are still celebrated today. They include May Day, Halloween, Guy Fawke's Day, and the Mardi Gras of mid-winter. These ceremonies allow their participants to re-live an act of symbolic importance, and by so doing, to re-interpret its personal value in the form of creative dramatics.

The Byzantine pantomimists, the religious theater, and the wandering jongleurs gave rise to a new form of theater, the *Commedia dell' Arte*. Many scholars consider the value of Commedia to the tradition of theater art as its connection to the theater of antiquity. In fact, it is a meeting place of two extremes -- the stiltedness of formal drama, and the unrehearsed antics of childhood that are typified by mime, improvisation, and dance.

Commedia dell' Arte originated in 1550 in Italy, and spread throughout Europe over a span of time lasting nearly 200 years. Although it was comprised of elements that can be traced to Greek and Roman times, as well as to formal drama of its own period, it produced an entirely new arrangement of plots. Together with interludes, music, and dance, it incorporated a vision that left an imprint on succeeding generations.

The action in Commedia was constructed extemporaneously. A *concertatore*, or leading actor, drew out a scenario and outlined main elements of plot or comic business. After the leader finished suggesting a theme with his remarks, individuals would withdraw to plan their dialogue and actions. (Such a practice is often used in modern techniques of creative dramatics and mime). After years of group improvisations, individual actors within a single company often became wedded to their parts and stock speeches and standard routines were used over again. Actors and mimes in other companies occasionally borrowed dialogue or actions from their predecessors.

Acts of the Commedia were frequently divided by *lazzi*, or interludes. Some were a creation of stylized actions based upon foibles so exaggerated that their treatment appeared surrealistic. The interludes were performed throughout the show, silently as mime or during speaking parts of the main action, and connected the whole drama together.

In the same way that Commedia combined two extreme forms of theater, it also drew both attention and opposition from its audience. Members of royalty invited performances, and Paris became a center for the art, even estabishing a theater, the *Theatre Italien*, for its performances. Because of language barriers, machines and scenery became popular, and individual performers emphasized virtuoso techniques to project their roles.

The Commedia travelled to England from Italy and France during the Restoration period. Because satire and ridicule had increased as individual personalities dominated its drama, the Church forced the closing of most continental European showings by 1697. In England, the Commedia found a new audience.

Even before the Restoration, John Rich, who created English pantomime, and John Weaver, a dance-master had selected Commedia characters, and began using them between scenes in major performances. Gradually the activities of these characters became more vulgarized, and their exploits upon stage resulted in acrobatics. Broad humor, chase scenes, and transformation acts were combined to produce an evening of entertainment.

The humor, singing, dancing and theatrical effects found in English pantomime of the period were drawn from the Commedia, which in turn adapted them from early Greek and Roman comedy. However, unlike its predecessors, English pantomime was not concerned with satirizing or imitating life. Instead, it called upon the "universal situation" for its content.

When Grimaldi, the famous English clown, appeared in pantomime, he performed tricks and represented the "little man," who was successively overcome by the smallest tasks. His role was not a particular attitude in relation to society, but instead the tragi-comic character created by Debureau in the French Commedia. After Grimaldi's character had become stable, other actors borrowed from it for their own roles. The clown represents a combination of the wandering jongleur from southeastern Europe, the fool in Shakespeare's plays, and the *zanni* of Commedia. Dubureau and his son were the white-face Pierrots, while the multi-colored costume that later was reduced to rags by Emmett Kelly was first worn by Clown Grimaldi, from whom many modern clowns have borrowed. Grimaldi's gifts of naturalness, constant invention, and the ability to elicit pathos from children as well as adults earned him the honor of being named the clown "Joey." His clown tradition still exists in English pantomime today.

George Fox made pantomime popular in America using the clown of Grimaldi and the bald head and whitened face of Pierrot, the French clown. Pantomime performances had limited success, however.

It was not until the pantomime developed by Charlie Chaplin and Buster Keaton for the early movies of Max Sennett Productions became known that the broad comedy of English pantomime regained its former popularity. Max Sennett's comedies were called the "Commedia dell' Arte gone wild." He encouraged improvisation, and his player's mistakes could be thrown out by editing the film. Slapstick arose in the tradition of the zanni or clown acts of Grimaldi. Beside the use of mechanical tricks, human reactions and pathos were added. Chaplin also borrowed from Grimaldi and Debureau and created the symbol of the tramp as the common man in a hostile world.

The foundation of pure pantomime, or mime as the art is now called, was begun in 1923 by Copeau, a French actor and school-master. He emphasized the extremes of realism and naturalism by introducing exercises that would enable the mime to gain technical precision. Among his many famous pupils are such masters of pantomime as Jean-Louis Barrault and Marcel Marceau.

Copeau believed that the games of childhood could encourage make-believe. His search for authenticity and natural movement led him to an outline of images which could communicate clearly to the emotions of his audience. To this end, he explored the Japanese *No* play, the *Talking Chorus*, and the use of conflict between text and gesture.

The mime troupes of today, together with those companies which feature extemporaneous comedy, are closely related to traditions which arose from Greek and Roman theater, and prevailed through early folk festivals and rituals. It is probable that these activities developed from primitive man's need to integrate the forces which seemed to overwhelm him. Throughout the centuries, man has not only developed aesthetic talents in communication, but has been able to enlighten himself spiritually by reaching beyond his ordinary understanding to a deeper level of thought. He has projected his unconscious drives in new forms through the medium of mime and creative dramatics.

These same techniques have been used recently for children's drama in television and stage, as well as in classical comedies and musical rock operas. The expressions now common are the result of greater exaggeration in the use of body extensions with space, time, and weight.

If creative dramatics is spoken of as a function of everyday life into which people channel their energy rather than as a subject, then many activities of "acting out" can be cited. The arts have become isolated from daily living because of the predominate utilitarian view that time should be spent doing "work." This connotation has promoted a materialistic attitude toward spending time and reinforced the idea that one must earn one's living by doing specific kinds of tasks.

The activities of the artist have never been considered a means for living, but rather a result of living. Therefore, the world of art includes life, but goes beyond it, commenting and satirizing, putting into focus relationships that seem acceptable. Art has required objectivity, use of non-traditional forms, and a viewpoint free from egotistical constraints, leaving the majority baffled and defensive.

Creative dramatics, as it is known today, is a unique combination of historical games, pageants, rituals, improvisations, and mimes. Winifred Ward was the leader who first used the term *Creative Dramatics*, as a title for her book. In the intervening years leading to the present, the term has become scrambled with Children's Theater, a form that uses a script and is comparable to organized theater for adults. Creative drama usually does not use such a script, and has few, if any, accoutrements. Its goals are involvement and process, rather than product. The senses, roles, experiences, practices, and utilitarian goals frequently expounded are basic to its learning potential.

Creative dramatics is frequently used for the understanding of literature. Creative dramatics exercises and structures may be used in a variety of ways. In various forms, they may serve teachers in gaining the trust of students when beginning school, in reducing student stage fright, in aiding involvement and commitment to tasks and ideas, and in taking responsibility for a student's own learning. These uses of creative dramatics suggest subtle ways of changing the curriculum by approaching the learner's attitude.

"I watched in silence, hearing the night."

The theory and practice of creative dramatics are particularly suited for development into an educational program which covers the school years. Creative dramatics, taught through the help of a skilled leader, can be the natural outgrowth of the children's normal play. When children first begin to participate in groups, they frequently engage in what has been termed *dramatic play*, commonly just *play*. Their games evolve spontaneously from the members of the group and use whatever is available in their environment. Often, there is no apparent form to this type of activity except that which a strong member of the group imposes.

A more structured activity, which is called *imaginative play*, can follow from preschool play experience. The structure is generated by the efforts of an adult leader to harness the children's vitality, asking them questions and guiding their answers into a form suitable for group action, and then moving together into the imaginary environment both have created. The best example of what we term imaginative play is an imaginary journey on which the children embark with the help of the leader. Together they determine the necessities for the trip, the destination, and the encounters along the way.

Imaginative play provides a significant transition between children's playing and the next step of creative dramatics, *story dramatization*. Again, the leader uses some stimulus–a story, an object, music, or almost anything–to provide the transition necessary for dramatizing that stimulus. *Creative dramatics* includes all areas from children's daily play to a re-enactment of a story which is not memorized but may be informally written down or scripted. While creative dramatics includes the arts of dance, mime, improvisation, and acting, it can also embrace other school subjects outside the arts.

Application in Curriculum. If a particular period of history is being studied, for example, the class might choose a person who was influential in that period and create situations in which the individual might have been involved. The leader could direct the class to imagine what decisions the person might be making. How might he move as he thought out his problems? Through charades, tableaus, mimes, soliloquys, and short scenes, the class might impersonate the historical figure, absorbing information through use of their subjective, emotional responses. In any event, they would have been active participants in the lesson.

Dramatic activities also can be adapted to lessons in science. Suppose the leader intends a study of symmetrical form and design in nature. The leader could introduce the lesson by asking the class to think of natural objects that may include a center but are surrounded by many parts. The teacher may suggest some things in nature which have symmetry–a flower, spider web, or leaf. The class members might draw one such object. Then the leader could have the class move in symmetrical patterns suggested by the drawings. In a discussion, other suggestions could show how many designs in nature are related, such as the orbit of electrons around a nucleus and the orbit of planets around the sun. Form, pattern, and shape frequently are better understood visually and translated kinesthetically through movement.

The leader might begin a lesson on the principles of automation by asking the students for activities they consider to be mechanical. The concept of a man moving as a robot then could be considered. How would he move and what would be some of his activities? The children could suggest some activities which are easily repeatable because they are habitual. They could mime these activities, and they could mime a machine of their own creation. These activities could lead into discussion of the purpose of machines.

These few lesson suggestions hardly exhaust the possible ways creative dramatics can encompass other subject areas. The leader's and children's imaginations determine which concepts and principles can be incorporated into the creative dramatics program. If the leader is involved, the children can also become involved. When the children become involved, they become open to learning–and remote concepts and principles are immediately experienced.

The leader, then, has special responsibilities. A leader must be flexible and adaptable throughout the total program. The leader must give his students a focus, and guide them to an objective which he states. Yet the leader must not blindly pursue the objective; by listening and observing, he might find it necessary to back up in an excercise, return to planning, extend help to floundering children. The leader also must be receptive and perceptive enough to gauge the tempo and desires of the class. Older children especially, may want to vary an exercise, or may discover new, unanticipated directions the exercise could take. It is the continual job of the leader to take suggestions and reorganize the lesson so that it moves spontaneously. Outright failure often indicates that the class has other needs.

Planning for the Classroom. Lack of a systematic procedure might bring unnecessary problems, especially at the start of a program when children are unfamiliar with creative dramatics. Although methods used may become personal to the leader in time, all lessons should first be organized around a stock lesson plan. Such lesson plans are easily divisible into their major parts:

    the introduction
    motivational activity
    stimulus

release
planning stage
acting or playing
evaluation
replay

Introduction. The first step, the *introduction*, simply consists of making the children comfortable by means of informal conversation. Before each session begins, the teacher should note that the physical environment and the seating arrangements are both safe and conducive to work. Often these preliminary steps are the most important part of the session because they affect the direction the session can take. At this time, the leader should gauge the children's energy level in order to determine the kind of activity that will motivate them.

Motivational Activity. The *motivational activity* prepares the children for the session which follows. The leader can include anything from quiet contemplation to physical exercise. What specific motivational material is to be used must be based on the children's ages, learning needs, and energy level. If the children have their creative dramatics session after school, they may need a physical exercise which will enable them to become energized, focused, and calmed all at once.

The motivational activity is directly related to the stimulus. If the stimulus is a Hans Christian Anderson story in which inanimate objects conspire secretly against their human captors, a perfect motivational activity would be a mime exercise in imitation of an object coming to life. Chapter Three contains many exercises particularly suited to motivational activities.

Whatever the specific motivational activity, the leader uses activity to unite the children in a common cause. The child will feel the release which comes with loss of self, whether in a group or alone. For younger children, activities which encourage this release may be in the form of movement to percussion instruments, singing, or games. Since young children move for the pleasure of moving, almost any signal will motivate them, but they do need the security and unity of direction that a signal provides. The teacher should repeat the beat many times encouraging the children to respond in a number of ways. Clapping, hitting their thighs, and stamping their feet all delight children. Songs and games composed of repetitive, rhythmic material may also work well.

For older children, various physical exercises and movement to music can be used. However, the example should be more complex and applicable to what is to follow. The leader can narrate over instruments or music to induce a calm and receptive mood. Older children can also be motivated by a theme or idea. For example, they might tell of a time when they broke a rule or wanted to break a rule, of a dream, of a favorite holiday, of the occasion when they were most frightened. Or each might perform a simple pantomime in reference to a simple theme. The subject matter should include common activities which are familiar to everyone. The "idea" category for motivational activities can include a suggestion for younger children which asks them to think of a new thing to play with, while one for older children might ask them to think of something they could do to express a memorable experience.

The leader should have definite patterns in mind the children can follow. The leader may direct the children into an activity by using questions directed toward use of a particular stimulus. In contrast, by using a searching question he can call for the expression of their own thoughts from which an activity can develop. Such questions should be either simple or specifically related to the child's own feelings. A real-life approach is especially good for children who are older, yet new to creative dramatics, and are at the age when they feel self-conscious if asked to enact a story. Real-life situations can be used to motivate them to make up their own story which they can re-enact. Many examples of specific motivational activities are included in Chapter Three.

Stimulus. Whatever the motivational activity, the next step is the story, or *stimulus*, an activity which includes the main part of the session. In choosing story material for any group, creative resources, experience, and background are more decisive than age. A child's imagination may have been previously stimulated in many ways. However, the leader must determine the amount of stimulation the child will need. Attention span, the level of emotional excitement, and the balance between passive and energetic activities should be considered when choosing materials.

From about ages *five* to *nine*, children are ready to be involved in improvised or story situations leading to strong conflict. They need the experience that fear and its resolution bring. They will permit themselves to become saturated by the emotion of fear, knowing that a resolution will follow. It seems likely that future frustrations and uncertainities may be easier to tolerate as a result of these creative dramatics experiences. Children enjoy stories in the realm of fantasy. Stories with monsters and giants work well. Sudden transformations occur without reason, inanimate objects become alive and speak as humans, and all is supernatural and dreamlike. From such sources as nonsense poetry, fairy tales, and folk tales, compelling fantasy material can be found. There is always strong conflict and a resolution in such stories.

Making up their own story to act also stimulates language flow and inspires children to act as a group. As the leader asks for characters, place, and plot, the children themselves create the story. The leader may narrate the story as they act it out the first time, so that their movements are directly motivated. Music can be added to the story, and while they are acting, speech and action can come together.

The leader may tell a complete story that is either played or mimed. If the story is so simple that most of the action proceeds from a single protagonist, such as a giant, the conversation will consist of the giant's monologue (given by the teacher) and the children's reaction. One such story, requiring dialogue but simple casting is *The Three Billy Goats Gruff*, because the character of the troll is in clear opposition to those of the goats whose only motivation is to get across the troll's bridge.

Instead of a story, a single idea can be developed. For example, the children can be members of royalty taking on roles of the royal court, when an undesirable character (a beggar or a witch) enters. Given this idea, they could complete the story in their own way. If children's imaginative strength seems highly enough developed, verbal analysis may be omitted by developing a theme and leading the children directly into improvisation. The leader should begin in the early stages of the creative dramatics experience to aid the children in the development of a general plot as a vehicle for their own insights and observations.

From the ages of approximately *eight* to *eleven*, stories about heroes whose assets enable them to reach a pinnacle of power work well. Within the category of folk tales there are many stories in which unassured bumpkins develop into heroes through a combination of their own strengths and a magical destiny.

The intermediate child needs the multiplicity of character development which a simple story dramatization offers. His natural ability to imitate and sympathize is given direction, while releasing inner feelings to provide insights into his problems. The question of the outcome between good and evil remains an individual controversy. As in real life either side seldom wins. The children may not wish to agree, and their evaluation may end with a question, or a many-leveled perspective, rather than a final answer in which right or wrong is resolved. The heros and heroines may undergo unspeakable amounts of suffering which finally contribute to their triumph.

From age eleven on, hero stories still work well, but should be more candid. Biography is valuable. Inspirational and supernatural forces are still acceptable, but on a more tangible level. Joan of Arc might be a good example. The preadolescent sees the world's problems and values as extremely immediate, and the story which provides a resolution to a realistic situation will be important to him. The modern paradox of whether the world can still afford involvement in war is a strong example.

For more sophisticated groups, focal points such as the myths, classics or Shakespeare are all valuable material. There is no better way to teach great literary works than to use stories as a basis for improvisational playing. The whole text first can be read, and then portions may be acted out by smaller groups. Finally, each scene can be played in its order of occurence within the text.

The leader must passively watch the children's reaction to their stimulus. If a lesson is weak or fails, he must figure out why, in order to make necessary changes before the material is used for another session. Chapter Four contains sample lessons which provide many examples of sources for stimulus material.

Release. The leader should follow the stimulus with related activities for *physical release*. If, in the story, a spell has been cast on the prince and changes him into a frog, the children might mime this change. The leader should engage the children in some definite use of those parts of the body which are related to the characters or atmosphere of the story.

Planning. The next step, which is considered the most important for inexperienced groups, is the *planning* stage. The restless energy of young children will be captivated by absorbing material, but during the planning period their concentration will break down unless the leader's questions are very direct. For older children, the planning stage becomes an indirect means of channeling energy and inevitably contributes to their creativity during play. It does not thwart their creativity or force their ideas into tight compartments. The planning stage clarifies the stimulus and provides a definite structure within which their ideas can grow. Children should be allowed to contribute individually to a structure if there is to be meaningful group participation. The social purposes of creative dramatics are as important as those which contribute to individual growth.

Planning is pursued through the leader's questions. First, the stimulus or story to be acted should be chosen by either the leader or the children. Next, they should consider the part of the stimulus which they are going to act. The characters should be discussed What characters are in the scene, their attitudes and feelings, how they talk and walk, and how they would perform a particular action are all important to the characterizations to be developed. This analysis should be carried out quickly, in a matter of seconds, so the enthusiasm does not wane. The setting and the floor plan of the setting can be decided by the group, and they should be asked to show where in the room the scenes of the particular story take place.

It is important here to note that when children reach ages of between *twelve* and *fifteen*, they may need privacy. Allowing them to organize in small groups away from the watchful eyes of the leader is an important aid to their imaginative flow. At this age, their critical faculties become more acute, and they need to be guided toward some ideas for improvement.

Playing. If members of the group have proceeded through the previous steps of creative dramatics, they should be able to develop speed in creating and still retain their absorption. Should acting slow down to a complete stop, with the children not able to carry on gracefully, it is often best to stop and go back to planning rather than to coach from the sides. Coaching sometimes interferes with the children's creativity, and their acting is no longer spontaneous and loses the delight which comes from being actively absorbed. If the leader calls them back to the planning stage again, they will probably know where they need help and will want to offer solutions as quickly as possible. During the playing of their scenes the leader should be actively evaluating the activity in order to guide the student's comments wisely during the evaluation.

Evaluation. For the *evaluation,* all the children should be seated for discussion. The older the child, the more objective he can be about his evaluation. If the group is young or immature, they can be questioned more subjectively. Very often in early exercises, when a specific child is called upon to perform in a group, other children may not watch him or tend to become disinterested. Audience-observers can contribute to self-confidence among the other children or destroy it.

Questions which require positive answers are best asked first. The best type of question is open-ended and does not require a "yes" or "no" answer. For example, "What did you like?," or, "What did you think was good?" The leader can adhere to the same order of parts as he followed during the planning: events, characters, setting. In this way, he may keep a mental checklist so that no large section is left out of the evaluation period. After positive comments, those opinions which consider negative aspects of playing should be even more carefully discussed. For example, the question, "How can this be improved?," should enable those who replay to give advice for improvement.

Between the ages of twelve and fifteen, it is extremely important for the leader to encourage positive comments in order to reinforce the group effort. Public negative criticism focusing on personal mannerisms or other sensitive areas may be emotionally harmful.

The evaluation step can also be a time for the leader to guide the children's thinking toward concepts and values.

Replaying. *Replaying* follows, with new characters for each part; if there are not enough characters for a completely new cast, then those who have performed should play a character different from that played before. The leader should make his own evaluation and consider the following: is their movement clearer? Is there enough interaction between character and dialogue? Is there a generous use of space?

By ten to twelve years, slow motion movements, use of "stills" or freeze positions, and a need for natural pauses become more meaningful if a mood is understood. Examples include changing the timing of the movement, distorting speeches by prolonging vowels, adding a narrator, and using instruments or sounds to accompany mood changes.

It must be noted that the lesson plan form described above offers a wide range of possibilities and should vary with the individual style of the leader. The leader and children will become more confident and comfortable with the form. As they do, they will take off on their own, and their excitement and imaginations will determine the lesson.

Objectives. As one might expect, the objectives of the creative dramatics program are many–long term and short term, measurable and immeasurable, practical and "philosophical". Only a small part of the intent of the program deals directly with drama, but that fraction explores drama in depth. The production of a formal play is only part of a very gradual process for children who have experienced the steps of the creative dramatics program. The last step in the creative dramatics program could be the production of a *creative play*. Unlike a formal play its purpose is not to entertain an audience using props, scenery, and costumes. The purpose of the creative play is the value it has for the players, rather than for an audience. Blocking and lines have become second nature to the players through repetition. The child has had an opportunity to grow into his use of space, and the "stage" has become a natural setting.

The child who has not had creative dramatics, and is on stage for the first time, contrasts vividly with children who have had creative dramatics. If a child is placed prematurely on stage, he might become so overwhelmed and terrified that he becomes either sullen or timid or aggressive and resentful. If the child is outgoing, he might be carried away by his own showmanship. His playing would lack absorbtion and sincerity, the two most valued qualities of children involved in their roles.

The children who have had creative dramatics will move through space as through a familiar medium. They have already extended their bodies imaginatively in exercises and pantomimes with the aid of a story, music, or an instrument. They have developed characters by being guided in the use of their imaginative sympathy, and those characters have become a part of them. As a result, their dialogue is not a superficial layer of character development, but a consistent outgrowth of their emotional involvement with the role. Their accomplishments have been so gradual that by the time they are given a scripted play, at the age of ten or eleven, the identification between them and their role or character seems natural. Indeed, their abilities only seem natural, for they are the result of much experience in creative dramatics training.

The following suggestions may be helpful for the teacher who directs a formal play with children who have had no previous creative dramatics. Before the play is rehearsed on stage, the children can use the preliminaries of creative dramatics for setting the mood of the play, understanding the character, and analyzing the setting. Before formal rehearsals, the players might memorize their lines so that their spontaneity in feeling and movement is not lost by having to stumble over lines. If spontaneity wanes from the efforts of remembering lines and movement, the director can engage the players in pantomimes or improvisations to reestablish their work. In any event the children's "familiarity with creative dramatics techniques" will make them better actors and actresses.

One objective of the program accrues specifically to the subject of drama. The gaining of specific knowledge of other subjects areas could well be further objectives of the program, as stated at the start of this chapter. In many ways, the creative dramatics program can serve as a catalyst through which the entire curriculum is communicated. Creative dramatics is a particularly effective learning tool because it does not encourage the mind-body separation, as conventional school situations do. Except for competitive sports, some experimental programs in dance, and standard physical education classes, there is usually no attempt to include movement work for children, other than inhibiting and preventive measures to avoid chaos.

Few teachers are aware of how to engage movement for a total use of their student's learning capabilities. Yet studies repeatedly show the benefits of such body movement. At the turn of the century, Rudolf Laban, in a study on illness in British factories, discovered that workers whose work demanded consistent repetition of the same physical movement had the most widespread illnesses. One objective of the creative dramatics program is to prevent such atrophy, and to encourage within a structured setting the basic movements of floating, gliding, pressing, dabbing, flicking, wringing, punching and slashing.

Since the philosophy of Rousseau encouraged educators to deal with the whole child, it may seem antiquated to think of each function of learning being equally represented at a given time. The three domains of learning, cognitive, affective, and psycho-motor, overlap and function at different levels within an individual. Within each of these domains, specific measurable objectives can be gained in the creative dramatics program.

The classifications in the cognitive domain most difficult to test are synthesis and evaluation. Yet the creative play, the final step of a creative dramatics lesson, is precisely a synthesis of the various activities, discussion, and planning which have preceded it.

In the appendix, a chart depicts the breakdown of the cognitive and affective classifications. The charts show how each classification can be used in relation to an activity of creative dramatics.

All the categories of the affective domain are difficult to test because the process of growth cannot be determined by the usual testing procedures. Yet these objectives are directly linked to those objectives which movement and drama hold in common, the use of the senses and body awareness. Aspects of the creative dramatics program speak directly to these points. Since learning problems are constantly correlated with motor insufficiencies, the psycho-motor domain needs constant consideration. Obviously, exercises and movements of the creative dramatics program deal with these needs.

After the whole group performs in unison, it can break up into small groups which solve an aspect of the problem the large group just finished. These are the intentions of the initial evaluation step in the creative dramatics program.

Cognitive Evaluation. Evaluation is one of the most sophisticated objectives to be accomplished on the overall scale of learning. It should follow a period of explanation and trial and error work in which first the child evaluates himself in order to discover what to improve upon. The difficulty the individual has seeing himself often helps to develop tolerance when he evaluates others.

Instructional objectives can be firmly stated, consolidated throughout a unit, and tested against definite standards at the end of a study. Unfortunately the student's appreciation for the skills, the depth of his knowledge, and its relationship to his life values cannot be tested in so routine a fashion. If learning is a process of accumulating knowledge over a long period of time, thereby affecting maturity, it should be cumulative and continuous rather than separate, isolated and without application to other areas of life. According to Jerome Bruner, when long range objectives are preferred over short range objectives, information becomes knowledge and transitions between subject and other arbitrarily-drawn categorical divisions are automatically added by the learner.

For long range objectives to become operative, the learning process should adhere to structures integral to the subject itself. If the subject is deeply understood, then a structure becomes apparent; the essence of the subject is discovered, related to life, and transferred to other subjects. Intuition is restored to knowledge, based on activities requiring trial and error, as well as manipulation. When learning takes place on this level, it may become its own reward.

Creative dramatics is a vehicle through which children can be guided to express negative feelings and be in contact with positive resolutions at the same time. Upon entering school, a child's world changes from the microscopic activity of his home life to a more macroscopic environment which becomes successively more and more complex. Such an adjustment requires a way for a child to form a self-concept through an activity which is entirely separate from school work or daily routine. His primitive assertions and adventurous flights need to be accepted by the outside adult world. Creative dramatics offers children the same opportunity for imaginative absorption as did their former play experiences. Unlike their former play, however, it allows more individual scope for the children's activity. The objective of creative dramatics should not be to enable children to satisfy arbitrary requirements within a given time limit, as in the teaching of subject matter courses.

The creative dramatics program gives the learner the ability to seek meaning from life. He must understand himself, realizing values he would naturally share with others. He needs to take responsibility for himself and accept responsibility as a contributor to group efforts. He needs, further, to relate elements common to all subject areas. The creative dramatics program encourages the learner to develop his own inner resources. Through this development, he becomes sensitive to the resources of others, and through interaction of these developing resources, he enriches the environment. The program intends development of the imagination, development of self-concepts, and awareness of internal change and growth. These objectives are certainly less measurable, but without doubt, contribute greatly to maturity.

"But a man does not fight merely to win!"
-Cyrano de Bergerac

3: EXERCISES

The heart of a good creative dramatics program for instruction is a series of lessons suitable for classroom application. This chapter contains essential exercises leading progressively into the creative dramatics process and ultimately toward improvisation. The stated objectives of these exercises are:

> To become involved through the use of senses and the use of space.
> To develop concentration, focus, and imagination.
> To aid plot formation.
> To begin character or role awareness.
> To introduce mime and abstract concepts.
> To move through specifics to begin improvisation.

These objectives represent a flow of knowledge that is depicted graphically in the appendix. Instructors may find this graphic representation suitable for locating and matching the objectives and exercises to their classes.

Some of the exercises are suitable for use as motivational activities for creative dramatics; others suggest possible plot developments that proceed directly from the exercise itself. In many cases, the exercises are designed for use as ends in themselves (especially those in the first section).

Exercises in this chapter are divided into groups, according to the elements of creative dramatics that each contains. These sections are:

> I. Senses
> II. Space
> III. Imagination
> IV. Plot
> V. Character
> VI. Mime and Abstract Mime
> VII. Speech

The exercises within each section are sequential and ideally should be introduced in the order presented. *Variations*, either as presented or as designed by individual teacher-leaders, are optional inclusions for any of the exercises.

It is better to spend five minutes a day on one exercise than to dwell on several exercises for a long time.

Exercises in Chapter Three may be used by teachers of elementary school classes concurrently with the *Lesson Plans* contained in Chapter Four. High School and College instructors should determine which exercises are required by beginning with those involving the students on a more sophisticated level. Examples of such advanced exercises include the following:

Section I, Senses: Beats; Sounds and Listening; Guiding *It*; Rhythmic Movement-Sound; Connect Sight and Sound; Blindwalk, and any of the Blind Journeys.

Section II, Space: Directional Walk; Space and Distance; Space Has Size; and any of the walking exercises with objectives.

Section III, Imagination: Objective *B*; Talking Parts; and Pantomime Passing.

Section IV, Plot: Any of the simple mimes, including the warm-ups for Spontaneous Group Mime; Three Freezes; Move to Narration; and Three Fairy Tales.

Section V, Character: Observation Panel; How Do You Feel When?; Blind Group; Picture Observation; Character Study and variations; Body Language and extension; Occupations; Work Gestures; and Freeze Positions.

Section VI, Mime and Abstract Mime: All exercises are suited to advanced classes.

Section VII, Speech: All exercises are suited to advanced classes.

Because the exercises are very concentrated, they can be extended for use in an almost limitless variety of ways. They may be interpreted by the instructor to become extremely simple or very complex to suit different maturity levels. Even though it is suggested that the exercises within each section be presented to classes in order, they may be repeated later with changes that will enable the students to gain additional depth and knowledge. However, these exercises should not be interpreted as Lesson Plans; that is not their intended use. Rather, they are useful components of a Lesson Plan, and many are suitable for application as motivational or release activities, as described in Chapter Two. A series of Lesson Plans is provided in Chapter Four.

Each exercise consists of several elements. If materials are needed, a listing is given. Introductory material to aid the instructor in preparing the group for the exercise is presented as needed. The body of instructional text is given under the heading, "Instructions." Variations that help the instructor to extend or modify the learning experience are also included. Sample dialogue spoken by the instructor to the class is in bold type, for example: **All of you should sit down.**

The teacher may find a tape recorder useful in some of these exercises for immediate feedback to the children or for review of previous work.

Any trend toward competition between individuals or groups should be de-emphasized by understanding that the whole purpose of creative dramatics is the development of the child within a growth inspiring process. This process is an experience, personal to the child.

It can only be explained tentatively; however, it can be encouraged and captured by the use of proper techniques. One technique for helping children contain their experiences is by understanding how best to physically organize them. If each one has found his own small circle of space, he can move well in a large group. In this way the leader may retain complete control, giving signals and guiding the children on their 'journey.'

Continuing the process, individual children begin to distinguish themselves. In some instances, they require greater stimulation or more challenge; in other cases, they need involvement in another way. Those that require special help may wish to reply as individuals, while those needing unique involvement may wish not to be included in the group. The first instance is more clear-cut; giving them independent responsibility to respond to the group in character usually works. The second situation is more difficult. These children need a character identity given to them by either the leader or the group.

A third step in organization is to divide the group in half, each half waiting its turn and watching while the other half is involved. This step requires greater concentration on the part of the participating half. If the watchers do not disrupt the concentration, growth will be achieved. Both the participators and their watchers develop greater containment.

Next, all should work in small groups, beginning with pairs, threes, etc. If a story keeps moving rapidly from one group to the next, this pattern of organization can be used earlier.

Finally, all of these groupings continue while individuals spontaneously take responsibility and roles within their group. Interwoven within this organization, the instructor gives greater and greater control to the child leaders. Among these group leaders, a give-and-take relationship is carried out so that leader and follower roles are constantly shifting.

". . . conscious use of the senses is fascinating for almost any age child . . . ."

"I listened to the sea in a scalloped shell . . . ."

Sensory Development. The use of sensory awareness encourages use of the imagination and provides an internalized response. Many relaxing exercises also enable children to become more perceptive for continuing drama activities in other school subjects. Although awareness begins taking place in the very earliest years of a child's life, it is frequently not encouraged. Instead, it is soon replaced by other, more competitive, activities. Further development of sensory awareness is neglected. A conscious use of the senses is fascinating for almost any age child. Using the senses enables children to bridge the gap between themselves and their environment through use of their own faculties. Performing the exercises which follow helps children to be alert and responsive. This, in turn, helps them to be more unified when working on a group problem.

Exercise 1 **LISTENING**

Students are allowed to explore and express curiosity about the environment in which they live.

Instructions:
> Close your eyes and listen to the sounds around you. Try to separate those which are near from those which are farther away. Tell each other about those sounds which are near. Tell as much as you can about the far away sounds, or what you imagine the faraway sounds to be.
>
> As a conclusion, the teacher can suggest the children pick out sounds and give as much information as possible about a person or scene suggested by the sound.

Exercise 2 **MAKING SOUNDS AND LISTENING**

Students extend their curiosity by suggesting that people and objects affect their environment.

Materials Needed:
> Percussion instruments or sound makers.

Instructions:
> Make some sounds by using the voice, percussion instruments, or movement of objects. Make these sounds, while the students close their eyes and listen. Student's observations may be used as stimuli for a story that they relate or amplify to their classmates.

Note:

If the teacher is uncertain about achieving workable results, she or he needs to start from a central reference point or framework in which to gather and collect the children's ideas. For example, begin with a commonly accepted place as suggested by the children like a "cave", a "forest", or a "fair". Either the teacher or the children will relate the sounds to activities within a specific environment. In this way a sequence of sounds related to actions can be taped. Environment is the least difficult framework for children to relate to, followed by characters and/or actions. Mood is the most difficult for children to identify with since it is more abstract.

Variations:

Several attempts can be made until the sounds form the sections of a fairly complex plot. Vocal sounds and music can also be used. The listening activity can begin in a large group and be carried out by smaller groups into improvisations suggested by the sounds. For example:

1. A mechanical toy is wound up, then runs down.
2. A cave becomes the setting, with bats, leaks, spiders and unexpected obstacles. The cave comes to life, two trespassers enter for adventure, and a surprise ending occurs.

All groups may be rehearsing at the same time and perform separately before the entire class. Children may become the "cave", bats, other obstacles, as well as journeyers.

Exercise 3 **COLLAGE OF SOUNDS**

Students learn the necessity of listening to each other's viewpoints.

Materials Needed:

Sound producing equipment.

Instructions:

Compose an arrangement of sounds using any of several sound cues, including reading, voice, instruments (noise-makers), or music. Play these cues for the students, instructing them to listen to the composition and allow it to suggest ideas about movement related to their plot, theme, historical period or special environment. Ask them to describe their feelings. Theme, characters, or place may be suggested first. Again, a tape can be made either by the instructor or children.

Exercise 4 **BEATS**

Students learn that it is necessary to listen in order to hear who you are.

Materials Needed:
Drum (or any percussion instrument).

Instructions:
Use a drum to beat out the syllables of your name. Beat out your mood or feelings as a way of communicating to those in the group. Beat the syllables of your partner's name. Beat out the mood or quality of someone next to you or someone you've gotten to know. Different word categories may be written on the board. The children use the beats to interpret items within the category. Some sample categories include; colors, feelings, weather, lines, shapes, etc.

Exercise 5 **SOUNDS AND LISTENING**

Students must listen to hear sounds change.

Materials Needed:
Simple sound makers.

Instructions:
Have the children form a circle. A child who is IT stands in the center of the group and must keep turning slowly and keep his eyes closed. To begin, the leader who is standing outside the circle points to one of the players and has him make a sound. The sound may be made on any object or instrument that is passed around the circle in back of the players, while IT keeps turning. If IT closes his eyes or is blindfolded, the source of the sound need not be passed in back. Whether standing in back or included in the circle the leader may reroute the object. The objective is similar to the game *Beckon*. IT has to guess where the sound is coming from by pointing. He may remain inside the circle until he succeeds, or each child may have one turn.

Variation:
1) A simple variation is to have a different noise-maker for each child in the circle around IT. IT must then identify both the source and identity of the sound or the kind of sound made. 2) In a second variation, IT must identify a vocal

sound passed from player to player around the circle. The player who passes the sound first makes a "face" at the person to whom he passed it on. After the vocal sound has been passed to several different students, IT must trace its path.

Exercise 6 GUIDING *IT*

Students are responsible for guiding IT's course.

Materials Needed:
Simple sound makers.

Instructions:
The group is spread out providing enough room for IT to move through. Sounds are made by players to attract IT. IT must try to approach the noises while blindfolded, but avoid touching those he hears. Greater control is needed by the players, who should only make sounds when IT approaches and yield to other players after he passes. The game also requires greater sensitivity from the student playing IT. There is no winner, for an equal amount of competition is needed by each participant.

Exercise 7 RHYTHMIC MOVEMENT-SOUND

Students listen and see a beat or pattern of sound and follow it with movement.

Instructions:
Start a basic beat by clapping your hands, stamping your feet, or snapping your fingers. Now, a second person should pick up the beat. Now, another. Continue adding students until many are involved. After the beat has been sustained, diagram a new rhythm on the blackboard, and have students experiment until they state the new beat either taking turns or joining in unison. Another form is then taken up, and so on. Encourage the students to change their method of response and beat, using the visual pattern as a control for loudness and competition. In very young groups, a follow-the-leader approach may be successful, by having a leader physically produce the beat. Suggestions of visual representations of beats need not follow a theory, but can be invented and referred to spontaneously. In this way, the symbol becomes secondary to movement and sound.

Exercise 8 **FOLLOW THE LINE**

With sound and a floor pattern students are conducted through space, eventually making different shapes with their bodies.

Materials Needed:
A yarn, line or tape; percussion instruments.

Instructions:
Either of the preceding two exercises may be combined with Exercise Eight. Students try to balance on a yarn or tape line on the floor as if it were a tightrope. A second group of students provides accompaniment on percussion instruments. The rope-walkers first take their cues from the beat of the instruments, but with practice become conductors for their sound orchestra. After a short time, exchange walkers and orchestra groups. Younger children proceed on the line as a group, with follow-the-leader type movement. Older children are more able to wait their turn, instead of traveling in small groups.

Exercise 9 **FILL IN THE LINE**

Challenges students to fill an incompleted pattern, while introducing movement and dance.

Materials Needed:
Pieces of yarn, or tape.

Instructions:
Drop a line on the floor in a spontaneous manner. The line should be incomplete, and made of many different pieces. Students can fill in the spaces left vacant in the line, creating or completing the design. Teacher and students may alternate in creating new designs of yarn and spaces, and one group of students can challenge another to repeat their line.

Exercise 10 **CONNECT FEELING AND SOUND**

Students concentrate on the sense of hearing. (Exercise Ten may be combined with Exercise Four).

Instructions:
The students close their eyes. The teacher starts a beat alone by clapping, stamping, or snapping fingers. The teacher should

then tap an individual student at random to change the leadership. The tapped students modify the beat, then yield to other students. After all have participated, members of the group should pick up the beat for a few seconds in unison.

Exercise 11 CONNECT SIGHT AND SOUND

Students watch a group move to a musical beat, then reproduce the beat after the sound has been turned off.

Instructions:
Members of the class should watch a volunteer group move to the beat of a piece of music while covering their ears. The music is then turned off, and individuals from the audience try to reproduce the beat either through movement or clapping. After all volunteers have tried to match the sound, the music is replayed.

Variations:
1) First allow movement without students covering their ears; the reproduction can take place after sound has been stopped. 2) If having students cover their ears proves impractical, the moving group can first listen to the sound, then reproduce the beat with the help of a strong leader.

Exercise 12 SEE WITH YOUR HANDS

Students pass common objects from person to person while blindfolded, concentrating on each object's features.

Materials Needed:
Unique, passable objects that are texturally interesting or squiggly.

Introduction:
Let's everyone sit in a circle. Your hands are uniquely your own, and this is an important part of identifying you through fingerprints. Look at your own hands and those of your neighbors. Discover which part of your hand is most sensitive, the fingertips, palm or back. The object is not the study of palmistry, merely the uniqueness of each individual hand. By placing attention on the hand, students are made to feel very important.

Instructions:

The instructor should put some bland music on as background. It will help fill the silences that might prompt embarrassment or giggling. **Close your eyes. I am going to pass some objects around for you to feel.** While passing the objects, the leader should keep up a steady stream of soft-voiced comments, never allowing the student's attention to wane. Ask questions, such as, **What shape is it? How does it feel? Is it furry? Does it feel like it might squirm? Now pass the object to your neighbor so he can feel it too!** After all of the objects have been passed, and each student has held one, collect the objects and put them away. Ask them to describe the objects, while leading them with guiding questions. **What did you feel that was different and that you can still remember with your hand? What else did you feel? Do your hands feel more alive now than they did before?** The instructor may wish to pass the objects out again with the student's eyes open, so that they may compare the object with what they thought they had felt.

Variation:

Familiar objects, not specifically chosen for their unique qualities, are passed in the same way as before, then listed on the board before they are brought out to see. The leader sets up categories according to the variety of different textures (smooth, bumpy, prickly, or silky) or shapes (round, square, or pointy), and has the students try to recall the objects according to questions asked. **What object did you think was oval, smooth, and cold?**

Exercise 13 **BLINDWALK**

Students find that ears and hands can be used like eyes.

Instructions:

In older groups, the blind partner follows a sighted leader. Younger groups, however, require close supervision and preparation, for children are sometimes sadistically cruel to playmates. To prevent this, the experience must be talked up as one in which the seer must help his "blind" partner develop trust because he has complete responsibility to guide the hands of his helpless companion. If such trust is developed, the "blind" player can trust his leader while climbing up a precipice (not more than chair height), then jumping off.

Variations:

In a simple variation suitable for students who are not shy and are more daring, the blind player (remaining blind) becomes a leader for his sighted partner. This will help develop the senses of touch and hearing. More challenging is another version, where half the class or group watches while the seeing players lead "blind" partners on a walk through the classroom.

Exercise 14 **BLIND JOURNEY**

Students develop the courage to walk through an obstacle course without sight.

Instructions:

Students and leader set up many obstacles, but include a pathway through them. A student is first allowed to look at the obstacle course. Next he is blindfolded and spun before starting off in a direction that leads through the obstacles. When the player encounters an obstacle, he tries to reconstruct its position in relation to the safe path and other obstacles, then charts his course to arrive "home" safely. The object is to go through the obstacle course and return.

Variations:

More than one player in the obstacle course serves to complicate the action. Eventually, a whole team of students can move through the obstacles, after first studying the course. They lead and follow each other through the difficulties, while developing responsibilities to other classmates. All could hold on to a single rope. If eidetic memory has been developed, a person may become very skilled in the Blind Journey by carrying a mental picture of the field. Such students should be challenged by having them repeat a verbal rhyme or passage from memory as they cross the field. Eventually, such students will carry a mental chart of the obstacles, and can adapt this chart to verbal instructions.

Exercise 15 **LISTENING TO MUSIC**

Students find that a high level of concentration is necessary if they are to absorb nuances of sound and recreate them in form.

Materials Needed:
    Phonograph or tape player; electronic, classical, and story music.

Instructions:
    Talk to the students about the possibilities of three different kinds of music, i.e. electronic, classical and "story" (ballet or opera). Think about the music and try to see the images, the action involved, and the theme that might have caused these images and actions. Students may then describe their experiences in a general discussion that provides the basis for a dance, mime, or improvisational scene. If this is to serve as an introduction various possibilities exist for continuing: 1) the class may work as a whole group, some moving, while others watch, and reverse; 2) small groups may work in separate parts of the room, using sound equipment, or remembering their music by segments and moods.

Exercise 16 MOVEMENT AND RHYTHMIC CONTROL

Intense concentration is needed to reproduce a kinesthetic form.

Instructions:
    Play the game of *Simon Says.* The leader should emphasize the follow-the-leader actions while leading the children through a series of in-place, body-movement exercises. Depending on the age of the children, the exercise will vary in difficulty. Such exercises may either be done to musical accompaniment or silently following the leader's rhythm. A volunteer can provide a steady drum beat for the exercises.

Variations:
    A simple variation is for the leader to instruct the class to follow his movements one beat behind. Such instructions should be followed by movements that are clearly punctuated. The whole group may alternately be broken into smaller groups performing to the same beat or music with separate leaders. Still another possibility is to mix the class so that different actions are being followed throughout the room. Student leaders are appointed and groups spread out in the room. Within the different movements, each group must still follow its student leader. Instructors should explore still further movement possibilities as well as themes.

Exercise 17 **OPEN-LIGHT, CLOSED-HEAVY**

Students become acquainted with the space which surrounds them.

Instructions:
With as much space around your body as you need for stretching, imagine that you are resting on the space and that your body feels very light. With the lightness you become larger and larger, as if you were a balloon being blown up. You sail away, walking through the clouds. A bird flies up, pecks at you and you begin to fall. All the air in the balloon gradually escapes and you fall to the ground. If the instructor is dealing with an older group, less literal terms than "bird" and "balloon" may be suitable. The instructor may then wish to ask how it would be to float and sink in air and water. Questions asked might be: **Why do balloons rise sometimes? Can you show what happens in a drawing? Can you draw a picture of the air inside the balloon before it rose, and after it rose?** A similar line of questions dealing with floating objects can be explored. **Let's make a big circle and be like the light object that floats. What would we do to be like the heavy object that sinks?**

"We were together as one."

Familiarity with Space. The concept of space can be handled by students more easily if they have already cooperated in some group situations, such as those suggested by the previous exercises, or if the exercises are used to relate to an activity, giving emphasis to particular parts of the body during character development.

English authors, in books dealing with creative dramatics, have placed much attention on the use of space as a concrete medium. Two outstanding authors who have expressed this concept are Brian Way and Peter Slade. Both agree that the child's inner resources are affected in direct proportion to the way in which he uses his personal space and progresses to work with larger groups. Children should begin moving at the same time but within their individual space. Each time a movement lesson begins, warm-up and relaxation exercises should be reviewed, adding a few warm-ups each time and slightly changing the nature of the relaxation exercises. The warm-up period ideally lasts about five to ten minutes.

Stimulating a child to expand his vision to include imaginary objects in space, as suggested by the first few exercises in this section, gives a more concrete, three-dimensional quality to this space. If the concept of each child taking responsibility for filling his own space is built from the first creative dramatics session, and is consistently repeated by the leader in the suggestion, **Find your space,** aggressive behavior will be greatly curtailed. Instructors should remember, however, that *creative dramatics is not an outlet for aggressive behavior; it is a channel for personality growth.* The leader can redirect the child's energy by suggesting different weights and rhythms, by helping the child take on a variety of living and non-living forms and, within these forms, promoting interaction with the environment. Not only is aggression limited, but shyness is forgotten because the ego is not under scrutiny. Instead, objectives absorb the attention. In addition to general loosening and focusing of attention, the exercise can lead into the lesson.

The development of psychic distance for the very young child has a special meaning whenever spacial concepts have been emphasized. In their first attempts at creative dramatics, children form a small circle in much the same way that the primitives did during early rituals. This shape is protective–it includes them all. From this point, they are encouraged to move about, yet remain in their circles of space. At first, little conscious exchange takes place between these individual spaces, and yet these circles become diffused and overlap. More opportunity for movement activities are required for equidistance to be established. The more opportunity a child is given to move freely in his own space, the less need he will have to take space from someone else.

These exercises continue the development that began in the previous exercises and should also be continued in order.

Exercise 18 **DIRECTIONAL WALK**

Children begin to know and trust the environment, while finding enjoyment and motivation to move.

Instructions:
Find a spot at the opposite end of the room. Try to walk straight toward it without bumping into anyone. Walk back across the room but this time keep as much distance around your body, between yourself and others as you can reach with your arms and legs stretched. When you walk back across the room, walk naturally while keeping that distance. After trying the above, the leader then instructs the children. Pick out another spot on the wall to walk toward. Keep staring at it as though it is taking your picture. Turn around in front of it as if it were a large eye looking at you. Let yourself be seen by it. Go back to the opposite side of the room, but walk back using a half circle floor pattern rather than a straight line. Try other geometric patterns.

Variations:
A simpler variation of Exercise Eighteen would be to have the students walk from one end of the room to the other as fast as possible without touching another student. Next, have them walk slowly, keeping varying amounts of space between them and the other children.

Exercise 19 **SPACE AND DISTANCE**

Students become involved in order to concentrate on images.

Instructions:
Across the room from where you are standing there is a small door. Since it is all you can see you move toward it. Now a magnet is pulling you toward the door from where you are standing. The space around you is filled with green growing foliage and while you are pulled toward the wall you want to stop and pick fruit and candy off the trees. As you reach out you again notice the small door. It is opening so you continue toward it. When you get to the door, you can see inside and the trees and bushes are filled with candied fruit. The door begins to close, so you quickly get through. You've made it through the door and keep trying to taste the candied fruit. Or whatever else the leader prefers to describe. The fruit becomes like stone, but you continue to reach out hoping to find something that is real and soft. Continue the narration if children are able to react to the images. Each time you put

your hand out, the things you reach for become little animals which snap at you, but you keep reaching because there is a magnet drawing you to follow these animals. They turn and run away and you follow. The animals disappear into a hole.

From here an underground environment could be suggested and a story which leads to discovery may be discussed and played. The use of sound either in the form of music—electronic, orchestrated, or percussion or sound effects would help concentration during movement.

Exercise 20 SPACE AND EQUIDISTANCE

Students become involved in follow-the-leader movement in order to establish equidistance.

Materials Needed:
Recording of marching music.

Instructions:
One line of several children follows a leader as he makes a floor pattern. A second line follows a leader as he covers a different portion of the floor. Still a third line may join these two. Continue adding groups until every member is involved. The same floor plan can be followed by each group, until all are involved and equidistance between children is achieved. After the children have become comfortable in using the space allotted them, the leader can change the floor patterns, add arm movements, and make other changes in force, time, and use of space. The leader may also number the groups, calling upon them alternately to freeze their motions, then move.

Exercise 21 SPACE HAS SIZE

Students cooperate in pairs or small groups.

Instructions:
Show that you are inside a space that becomes smaller. It is closing in upon you. You are inside such a small space that you cannot move. How do you feel? How do you react? The teacher should explain that having too little space can be frightening because one's self-expression and freedom for discovering are limited. The teacher then may guide them into pairs or small groups by asking them to find a partner. **Find someone in the room who seems to act like you when they are**

in a small space. In young groups, allow the children time for discussion among their partners. **Can you show any of your feelings about space in a mime? Let's organize some of these ideas under headings which have resulted from our discussion.** Examples of headings and related topics may be:

Ideas	Feelings
Overpopulation	Fear
Imprisonment	Anger
Disease	Hope
Pioneering	Freedom
Exploration	Wonder
Friendship	Loneliness

If a common idea such as, "How the relation to space affects people's lives" is explored subjectively and objectively, themes related to life may emerge.

Variation:
All of you are surrounded by iron wires which keep you inside a very small space. Continue if the group can identify and utilize the images. **You've been enclosed and can't get out. You try. There is an opening which you squirm through. Finally you have all the space you need and you are a creature which flies.** Music may enhance movement. It should neither suggest soft delicate movements, nor build erratically. Rather, the music should be steady, yet strong. *La Mer* by Debussy is a good example. After the narration a discussion of feelings in relation to the obstacles and space described should follow, providing meaning to the student's experience. Questions allow the students to compare their reactions. **How did you feel? Why did you feel that way?**

Imagination. One of the aims of the creative dramatics program is the development of the imagination, in the belief that knowledge acquires depth and perception when the imagination is active. This goal will become the most difficult part of the program, particularly in upper grades, with children who have had no previous training. We carry hidden within us rich resources which have not been developed, because no rewards are given for development of the imagination. The only value of that inner growth is the awareness of the creative process; an awareness that often brings pain with its growth.

Keeping or holding an image in the mind enhances and develops the imagination. Concentration and absorption are particularly essential. Absorption furnishes the condition in which imagination can travel, spiral, and leap. It requires a maximum of energy, yet furnishes energy. Absorption also provides shelter, and with this comes trust and a condition of safety and peace in which the imagination can grow. The potential to gain this depth is much greater among youth to whom the opportunity is rarely offered. Paradoxically, the duration through which the imagination of a child is affected is much shorter. A child's need for physical release often blocks his receptivity, unless his energy can be utilized so that both imaginative and physical outlets occur simultaneously.

Several of the preceding exercises overlap with the portion of this chapter dealing with movement and mime. Children need much direction when they are moving their bodies, because they cannot be left to move imaginatively if their imaginations haven't been developed. Such students frequently will move erratically and without form, will feel embarrassed and inhibited and may lose much of the confidence that has been built up. Giving them an image to adhere to helps their body to think. Such techniques as freezing, using music, slow motion, or mirrors will not only guide, but will place controls on the movement. Their energy will not be dissipated into embarrassed giggling or talking. Sudden transitions also help to take them by surprise, and their quick energy can be absorbed when the instructions keep coming. Lack of a transition does not bother children. Lack of movement does.

There are two objectives to movement exercises: to enhance physical motion so that the imagination can be extended through movement; and to give as wide a variety of movement alternatives as possible, not only those stereotypes which have been fostered by society. For example, common stereotypes for girls tend toward the delicate, soft, or non-descript; for boys, harsh, aggressive, violent, and defensive movement. If these stereotypes were obviously switched, the girl or boy in question would not be accepted by his own peers. Using images that require reaction and the spurring on of otherwise objectionable movement takes the child by surprise and he develops his body in a new way.

Older children, age eleven and up, can start creative drama participation at this point. The preceding exercises can then be brought in at intervals.

Exercise 22 **HAVING AN OBJECTIVE** *A*

This exercise can be done on increasing levels of sophistication, as described in the variations. Variations 1 and 2 should be performed in order.

Materials Needed:
A small object (to be hidden).

Instructions:
You are searching for a white poker chip which is hidden in this room. When you see where it is, leave it there, don't tell anyone where it is, and go sit down. All members of the group complete the search. How did you feel while you were looking? Did you feel self-conscious? Why not? This is the way an actor feels when he's on stage. His only thought is his objective. Can you imagine your objective and act as if you're looking for the poker chip? When the music starts, act as though you are looking. When the music fades, find it. Were you able to concentrate so that you did not feel self-conscious? What did you do? Did you keep the image of the object in your mind? Or did you have to think about it? Keeping or holding an image enhances and develops the imagination.

Variations:
1) Think of something which holds great value for you. When the music starts, begin to look for it. When the music fades, find it and carry it back with you. What were you looking for? Why were you able to look for it? Can you think of another object that you could concentrate on more easily? Perhaps change to something which is lost that has to be found quickly.

2) Listen to the music and use your imagination to visualize a place. You don't have to look for anything or have an objective unless something pops into your head. Now, just move to the music and try to visualize what kind of space it is you're moving in, and what you might be looking for. If the imaginations of the students are tapped so that their inner resources are brought forth, many interesting variations on the

general "search" theme will occur spontaneously. In older groups, the need to communicate their experiences verbally should be encouraged.

Exercise 23 HAVING AN OBJECTIVE *B*

Students will generate many variations from this basic structure. They are introduced to character development and *through line of action.*

Materials Needed:
Wadded piece of paper.

Instructions:
Close your eyes and walk toward a wad of paper that I have placed about 12 feet in front of you on the floor. Most children will hesitate and be short of their goal; a few will overreach; fewer still will be off to the side; and only a tiny number will find the paper. **The trip needs to be taken quickly, before your image of the paper fades away upon closing your eyes. Try again.** The process can be made more complex by providing peripheral instructions. Discuss with the students the similarity between concentration necessary to successfully locate the paper and the actor's concentration in developing a character and subsequent character's through line of action in a play or scene. **Did you feel self-conscious in this exercise? Can you tell me why not? Having an object to walk towards and concentrate on absorbs your attention and makes outside conditions not so distracting. Have you ever been able to find your way in a dark room? How did you do that? Sensing the objects in space in relation to other objects while blind depends on the more proficient use of the senses which haven't been relied on by a sighted person.**

Exercise 24 TALKING PARTS

Re-emphasizes observation and stimulates imagination by using parts of the body to communicate.

Materials:
A mattress box (or other very large cardboard box), divided into four sections. Each section may be removed separately, and is held in place by wire fasteners. The sections allow

students to show head and hands, shoulders, waist, pelvis and torso, and feet.

Instructions:

A small group stands behind a wall or box stage, saying something simple, reading, or talking to each other as if involved in a phone conversation. The remainder of the class attempts to identify them from their voices.

Continuing the development, several pairs should stand in front of the class, allowing it to examine their hands and feet. The new group then replaces the previous children behind the box stage. Have couples display their hands or feet behind the appropriate divisions of the box. These body parts may be used to mime actions, particularly if the children can relate to a character role or conflict situation. Add other portions of the body by removing sections of the box.

As a final step, all sections of the box stage should be removed, revealing all of the children's bodies. The exercise should proceed over a long period of time, giving the child time to explore the part of his body emphasized and visible. The gradual revelation of the entire body also provides the child time to become accustomed to his stage presence, reducing traumatic feelings.

Exercise 25 WHAT'S AROUND?

Students develop imagination by observation and retention of images.

Instructions:

Take a good look at this room (or a picture provided by the leader). **Now close your eyes and recall as many of the objects or people in the room as possible.** The leader should then divide the children into small groups and appoint a leader for each. Have the students walk around the room, looking at specific items of furniture arrangements of objects, colors, and outstanding details. The leader should have prepared a list of questions regarding the room's contents. **Everyone take your seats, and close your eyes. Here is an answer sheet.** Give a sheet to the leader of each group of students. Then ask the class questions from the prepared list. **How many doors are there in the room?** The leader of each group should not give the correct answer until after all group members have been given a chance to answer the question. Try the exercise again, this time adding music and having the students return to their seats when the music stops.

Variation:
Walk around the room to the music, noticing those people in your own group. Look at their clothing, hair, attitude, and other characteristics. Question as before. Have the children respond to questions about themselves. Those answering questions should keep their eyes closed. Another simple variation is to change the placement of large or small items in the room. One or more children can close their eyes or remove themselves from the room, returning after the change has been made. After careful observation, they tell their group what was altered.

Exercise 26 IMAGES TO MUSIC

Listening is accomplished by degrees, gradually allowing the environment to become integrated into the personality.

Materials Needed:
Taped music or record player. Music should be varied in pace, volume, etc.

Instructions:
Close your eyes and listen to the music. How does it make you feel? What do you think is happening? Children need listening practice before they can develop situations fully enough to build a plot around them. Instructor questions may aid this development. What happened first? What might have been the cause of that? What was the difference between the first and the second part? Let's listen to it again. As the piece plays, the instructor points out significant changes in the music, suggesting different actions. What part could we act? Where would that take place? Would we run or move very slowly? Kinesthetic reactions and visual images are more intense, and the environment, movement, and character development are more powerful, while the eyes are closed.
If the leader feels capable of putting the children's suggestions together, a simple journey with obstacles and actions may be narrated while the children move to both spoken directions and inner images sustained by the music.

Exercise 27 **PANTOMIME PASSING**

Students explore a charade-like game that introduces dramatic movement and action, while discovering numerous variations which assist the memory.

Instructions:

There are many relay games using pantomime. A series of games progressing into greater use of the imagination include the following:

1. Each person in the circle forms an object in pantomime and uses the item.
2. The first person in the group forms an object and uses it. The second person forms the first person's object, then his own. The third person has three objects to form, his own and the two before him. Continue the series as long as the items can be recalled in order. Many variations are possible. It may be decided that the single item preceding is the only one that need be repeated; or two items before; or three; etc.
3. Several categories common to the students are written on the blackboard. (For example: food; clothing; work; emotion; and age). Only two or three categories are chosen for use. Each child chooses to pantomime the use of an item from one of the categories. The first person chosen establishes the category to be used. All those who have chosen items from this category form their own object as well as those of the children who go before. If the number of children participating in this category is too large, a variation such as contained above might be considered. After completing the first category, continue to another.
4. The first person called upon forms his item and establishes a category. The leader continues calling on children individually, and they form items included in the same category. This continues until the leader calls, **Repeat!** At this point, the next person repeats an item used before, but going into greater detail. The repeat command assures complete attention by other students.

Exercise 28 **WHAT SHALL I BE?**

An ideal intermediate exercise suited to many classes, this exercise provides experience in using space, movement and gestures.

Instructions:

Find your space, and think of yourself as (for example) a piece of spaghetti which stands up and collapses at certain places in its length. What would you do? Move your head, shoulders, chest, hips, legs, knees, ankles, and hands. Now freeze! Imagine that you are fire. How would you act? Move! Freeze! Think of yourself as a plant which is all closed up for the night. Listen to the music. As you hear the music, you begin to open up. The wind comes up, and starts to blow until you fall over. Many extended story lines are possible and may be suggested by certain types of music or individual pieces. Opening and closing, growing and shrinking, rising and sleeping are all universal forms common to nature and man's daily pattern in life. Each child should be able to use and identify with these forms.

Exercise 29 **A JOURNEY**

Young children should be able to accomplish this exercise after only a few preliminary exercises in listening and forming visual images to music.

Introduction:

In preparation for a journey, the instructor should learn from the students what kind of a journey they wish to take. Oceans, outer space, the moon, ghost towns, the jungle, the woods, and many other settings are ideal for imaginative journeys. After selecting the place, the conditions can be established. What is it like? What will we find there? What will we take with us? Why are we going? What will happen? Who will be the first to see it? How will it end?

Instructions:

By having the imaginary environment set up, creative energy is channeled so that the children can work together for a spontaneous situation. The instructor controls the movement by establishing as many obstacles as possible: volcanoes, quicksand, man-eating fish, sharp rocks, thin bridges, steep cliffs, and deep grass. Have them get ready for the trip, pack their supplies, dress for the expedition and have them move to the narration or music. One problem with the journey framework is that it allows a free and spontaneous atmosphere between the children and must be carefully led, controlled and set-up to avoid loss of focus and direction. Other examples of journeys are provided in the lesson plans contained in Chapter Four.

". . . It had been a long long time since we had seen the sky . . . ."

Simple Movement Plots. As this brief explanation on the use of the exercises as motivational activities overlaps information contained in more detail in Chapter Four, the creative dramatics instructors planning the use of these exercises should refer to that material.

The motivational activity is directly related to the stimulus stage of most lesson plans. These simple plots are inspired by narratives, questions, or suggested themes. As such, the exercises presented do not exhaust the possibilities. When emotional themes are considered, the rhythm of motivation, stimulus, involvement, rising action, and crisis can be considered on deeper levels involving catharsis.

The simple plot form is also discussed in Chapter Five, Improvisation. If ideas from the participants adhere to a structure, this structure becomes the "plot." If they are the creators of their own "plot," they will instinctively create a series of actions which seem to flow from one incident to another. Action motivates character; from the stimulus of character a plot form may be developed. Most children are not concerned with plot, tend to become lost in numerous sequential happenings and get bogged down by it.

The more story material to which they have been exposed, the more natural will be their imaginative flow. It must be remembered that ancient storytellers never really ended their sagas. Rather, a complete historic era might become a series of episodes or a journey. Many lesson stories contained in Chapter Four will provide aid in helping to train young characters to consider a plot sequence when they create their own scenarios or plot outlines. It is nevertheless possible and satisfying for young players to continue a series of fictional strands which branch out in all directions, beginning and ending anywhere.

Such questions as, "What makes a story exciting, meaningful or important?" can prompt a discussion into the components of a plot. A plot must contain a problem, an adversary, a conflict, a complication and a resolution. These concepts aid an investigation into plot construction.

Other important elements of plot construction are tension, prolonging suspense, and crisis. These elements are also discussed in Chapter Five.

Exercise 30 **SPONTANEOUS GROUP MIME**

It may be useful to review WHAT SHALL I BE?, Exercise 28, and IMAGES TO MUSIC, Exercise 26.

Instructions:
> Divide the class into groups no larger than six students and give each group a number. Each group shall choose a sport like those used during recess or P.E. Now begin to play that game,

making your movements large, so that the mime is easy to see. After you begin, I'll call out one of the group numbers, which means that the other groups freeze. Now, everyone begin in slow motion. You play the sport, but feel very heavy. You are stuck in molasses and can hardly get loose. There are weights on your hands and feet. You relax and feel very light, but you are still moving slowly. All groups freeze. Group One, the surface of your playground is so hot that you have to keep moving quickly to keep from burning, and have to jump in the air. Group Two, the ball you are carrying is made of green slime, and is hard to hold. The instructor keeps adding complications to the game, changing its speed, use of weight, space, etc. Ultimately, the instructor turns over the responsibility for freezing and moving to the groups. Guidelines may serve to help the groups. No group moves while another is moving. When one group stops, another starts. In this way, space is shared and focus is achieved.

The leader may have to call the numbers of the group for several sessions before they can be left to share the space on their own.

Variations:

This exercise can also be performed using other group activities, including entertainment, fairs, sightseeing, or a party. Briefly plan problem situations beforehand.

Exercise 31 **EATING**

Students are presented a clear, simple introduction to mime gestures and actions.

Instructions:

The instructor suggests a food item to be eaten by the students. In front of you is a banana. Pick it up, hold it, show how large it is, peel it, break off the top, and stick it into your mouth. Take your time with every gesture, especially the chewing. Take another bite and chew some more. Really show that you have something in your mouth. Peel some more and break off the last part. Pop it into your mouth and chew it up. Wipe your hands. After this introductory mime, the instructor then reverses roles with the class. See if you can tell what I am eating! Don't say anything until I'm through. In each case the food is distinctive, such as grapes, hot dogs, or ice cream cones. What were the things? How did you know? What was the difference between the apple and the orange? Seeds? How about the way it was held? Now, let's each choose a food that is different due to the way you need to handle it when eating it. Think about it. I'll give you a minute and a half to mime it. Go! While they are working, the teacher should watch for those mimes which are most clear, calling on these first to show their mime to the group.

Variation:

A simple variation of the basic eating mime is to have everyone choose a food and begin to eat it. Halfway through the food, they must pass it to a neighbor, who continues eating it. Another possibility is to have the members of each group choose something to eat, then brush their teeth. Suggest that all members in the group eat the same thing, but choosing something that is messy or hard to remove, such as taffy, peanut butter or watermelon.

Exercise 32 **SIMPLE SCENARIO**

Prior to introducing scenarios to a group, a review of exercises using narration to conduct movement may be advantageous.

Instructions:

Listen to the music and think of a conflict between a group and one person. One such story line might be that all the students are being put in jail by a cruel tyrant, and as he turns to leave the cell, they jump him, get the keys, and escape. Take suggestions from the students to provide a starting point. **We want an antagonist who is after the group. Who shall he be? If we can catch him off guard, how can we get even?** It is usually easier at first if the protagonist is the group, and the antagonist provides the conflict to which the group reacts. Other arrangements include: one person leading the group in a positive relationship; one group against another group in a negative relationship; one group leading another group in a positive relationship; individuals from two groups meeting antagonistically after stepping out from the group; and many other variations. **Now we should begin to act out the story. What should be the most exciting moment? Why? Let's see if we can make it work that way!** After playing the scene, the leader may ask questions which help to make the scene more significant, such as: **How does this scene relate to life? Is there really any resolution or conclusion?** Allow the students to embellish the plot, if appropriate action develops. The instructor might wish to introduce technical terms from playwriting, such as introduction, rising action, crisis, climax, falling action, and conclusion. Such terms usually require a diagram and examples in a story structure.

Exercise 33 THREE FREEZES

Students create tableaus from action moments in a story.

Instructions:
Choose any story to tell, and select three freeze positions that tell the story. Some easy examples for one actor are: 1.Grab something that looks good; 2.Drink it; 3.Hold his stomach. 1.Tie one shoe; 2.Tie the other; 3.Try to move and realize that both laces are tied together. If students have difficulty isolating an action and communicating it in a short scene, the instructor might show them a section of motion picture film, freezing moments of its action.

Exercise 34 MOVE TO NARRATION

Students and instructor should review those exercises dealing with narration prior to attempting Exercise 34.

Instructions:
The instructor should narrate a simple story, such as *The Three Bears*, which everyone knows. With the children moving around the classroom, perhaps to music, the instructor asks them to **Freeze!** This assures their attention while frozen, and prepares them to act out the dialogue while giving the leader control.

Variations:
Three main variations are suitable for use with this exercise. The simple story may be told by a large group, each student taking his turn until the story is completed. If this is a new approach, it should be done several times prior to use as a scenario. The children can act out the action described before a new storyteller begins. An alternative way of proceeding is to have several students retell the story as they remember it, pausing at intervals for the players to act it out. A final variation is to have one group perform the first part of the story, with other groups to perform the parts of the story that follow. This method works well in large, older groups and provides an attentive audience.

Exercise 35 **THREE FAIRY TALES**

This exercise works particularly well if children will volunteer to be the leader's "puppets." The freeze positions described in Exercise 33 provide an alternative method of presentation.

Instructions:

The instructor tells a story composed of three common fairy tales. The students discover those fairy tales which they think make up the story. She had a good time in the forest that day collecting flowers and butterflies for her grandmother, but by the time she arrived, it was nearly dark. She could hear a voice laugh and cackle saying, "You better watch out as you use that needle, or you might get stuck!" She found herself sewing, and suddenly she did stick herself with the needle and everything changed. She saw a large palace and many people who were becoming frozen. All except for her grandmother, who continued to cackle as she and everyone in the castle fell asleep and slumped to the ground. Then she had a dream about a rabbit who hopped around the rows of cucumbers with a farmer chasing him. The rabbit would get stuck, but always seemed to be released by his helpers. Once, he got stuck in some gooseberry bushes and then ran all the way home. When the little girl woke up, she was in her own bed with a handsome prince standing beside her. Everyone started to move again. And she could hear her grandmother screaming, "Let me out of here!" The handsome prince went right to the closet door and saved the grandmother. The instructor may choose any fairy tale for the composite story. A good way to proceed is to ask the class which fairy tales they wish to use. Which incident will be taken from each? What shall we use first, second and third? After their story is told in stop-start fashion, the instructor can help them recall the action, by asking simple questions. What happened at the beginning? What followed? What part was not exciting? Why? How did it end? Shall we act each part?

At this time the teacher should pick people to replay the scene or scenes. Finally, replay without narration while sharing the space between the groups.

Exercise 36 **EPISODES**

Children listen to hear the separate parts of the story.

Instructions:
   A simple story, broken into continuing episodes, is told. Each group listens to the whole story concentrating on the separations between episodes. The leader should then number the class into groups. Each group acts out one of the episodes in numerical order. For clarity, the single episodes may be listed both in order and according to the number of groups.
   Each group may expand and add more detail to a single episode, but should not carry its action over into the next segment. In this manner each group must remember the entire story. An outline may be given by the children after the story is told by all the groups.

"Why, who makes much of a miracle?"
-Whitman

Character Development. The objective of this section is to initiate the understanding of character development in movement through an identification with common experiences (*emotional memory* and *given circumstances*), and environments.

When forming characters, children create character types or roles, rather than the subtleties or nuances of an individual personality. Complex character development is not commonly a part of creative drama because the eccentricities and individual traits of a distinct character, when incorporated into the realm of creative play, often seems labored and lacking in spontaneity. Instead, children imitate those things and persons they have experienced. Whether they will find an outlet for their emotional understanding and empathy depends on their feeling of involvement and trust within the group. The preceding exercises have helped to channel energy and remove inhibitions. The leader may narrate the story to stimulate the children's imaginations before movement. The leader alternately may also engage children directly in a conflict situation, projecting them into a role so they are both surprised and delighted. When the children are surprised, the spirit of play frequently overcomes the fear of appearing foolish in front of one's peers.

The following exercises may be developed in more depth if the exercises such as those in the preceding sections are first covered. They are simple enough, however, to require no introductory preparation.

Exercise 37 **OBSERVATION PANEL**

Students use dialogue in a natural situation, reporting on their immediate environment. It also provides an introduction to Exercise 39, Blind Group.

Instructions:
> Study the room, noticing the design, major pieces of furniture, details, everything that you can take in. Close your eyes, and try to reconstruct the room. Work with small objects first, but move on to larger objects if this is difficult. Try to see as many visual details as possible, including color, design, shape and the relationship between objects in the room. After this static observation, ask the class to move about the room, noticing each item separately, going up to it to see all its detail, and then backing off to find its relation to other objects. The technique is sometimes referred to as "living cameras." Invite those on the reporting panel to go up to the front of the room. The panel members close their eyes, while the audience asks them questions about the room.

Exericse 38 **HOW DO YOU FEEL WHEN?**

The student is asked to recall an emotional experience.

Instructions:
Ask the children to describe their feelings verbally or physically about the following experiences and those they might make up to ask each other.

1. Have you ever had dreams of flying? Describe what it felt like.
2. What is it like to walk on stage for the first time?
3. How do you feel as you are swimming below the surface of the water and looking at ocean life?
4. How would you react to walking in the dark with the feeling that someone is following you?
5. Does going very quickly through space, on a bike or roller coaster make you feel differently?
6. How about getting caught doing something you're not supposed to be doing?
7. How did you feel diving off a high diving board for the first time?

Exercise 39 **BLIND GROUP**

Exercise 37 should be fully explored before beginning this exercise. Promotes trust among class members and openness to environment.

Instructions:
Think of yourself as being a certain type of person by answering some of these questions. What age are you? What type of clothes do you wear? Now stand up and form a circle in the room. Close your eyes, and move clockwise around the circle. The instructor should allow the students to walk with their eyes closed nearly one half of a revolution of the circle. Then stop them, or have them walk backward a few steps, then forward a few, and turn to their left or right. With their eyes still closed, begin a music background, and tell them a story-line. You are in a hurry, but can't walk fast because of the slippery ice. The sun comes out and it is very warm and you open your eyes. You begin to look around at all the people. What type of character is your neighbor? Sit down where you are. Let's have about six of you stand up and walk as your characters. Where are you going? Do those of you in the audience think you know who some of them are? Allow the class to examine each student's character in detail.

Variations:

The group can decide to go as individuals to a common destination. Each may decide to go to a separate place and on the way meet in one location (for example, a store to buy something.) Instead of an external orientation from the leader, try a blind walk. **Close your eyes and walk carefully touching the people around you. Reach out to be sure that someone is there. If someone is there, take hold of his shoulder, because you are all blind and uncertain of your way.** The instructor should then begin a story line, carefully prepared by the choice of previous exercise. **You are taking a walk in the woods and the person who is leading knows the way. But something strange happens. For some reason, the line stops. It is very cold and it's snowing heavily. You find out that the leader has run away. What would you do? How would you finish this?** Several solutions are possible. Take suggestions from the class, and repeat the exercise with different endings.

The exercise can also re-enforce a commonly-shared feeling such as fear of loss or being lost, helplessness, joy in belonging, and unity. These feelings can be discussed and a common theme and actions representing that theme may be selected by the leader and group. **What feelings, for example, would be experienced in the theme "freedom" versus "imprisonment?" What action would be chosen to show the transition from imprisonment to freedom? Would it be crossing over a border between two countries? How can we set that up? What is our situation? Waiting for inspection? Escaping through a tunnel?**

Exercise 40 PICTURE OBSERVATION

Provides an easy way of obtaining scenarios for other exercises, while developing memory.

Materials Needed:

Pictures of people.

Instructions:

Hold up pictures from magazines or paintings, as many as the children can absorb. Have one group of children ask the other group about the pictures. The group questioned should make up about one fourth of the class. The instructor should guide the questioning to character traits of the people pictured. These traits can then be adapted to later characterizations. Change the pictures as each group changes places.

Variations:

A simple variation is to time the observation period for each picture, allowing one minute of study. Then have the leader of the small group write down the details remembered by the whole group.

After a single picture or a connected series of pictures have been presented, allow about three minutes of discussion before asking for suggestions from the whole group. **Who are some of the characters? What is their relationship? What was happening? Where did this happen? Let's see if we can make up a story about this!**

Another approach is to direct their observation, asking, **Can you find everything that is blue in these pictures? What items start with an "S"?**

Exercise 41 CHARACTER STUDY

The need for subjective identification with a character, through which the students can empathize, is important to accepting a role.

Materials Needed:

Pictures of people in various situations.

Instructions:

The instructor holds up a series of illustrations, asking questions about each. **Choose any of the people in these pictures as a character. Does this person like sports? Does he have a car? Begin to think about some possible questions you would ask of the character.** The leader should use close-ended questions to stimulate discussion. Close-ended questions are good leading questions because they are not difficult to answer, especially when dealing with an unformed character. **What do you do in your spare time? What is your favorite food?** After the students have developed a short biography of the person that they are investigating, an interview by the class can take place using their biography for responses. This introduces the character to other members of the group. Members of the class take turns in the hot seat, answering questions until the class can identify the picture from which the chosen character was drawn.

Variations:

One variation is to have the newly-developed character, played by his biographer, walk into the class, pose, and walk out. If the group is unable to identify him because of too brief an exposure, he must return and answer questions. A second variation is to subject several of the characters to a situation, perhaps a fire or eating in a restaurant. The situations, in this case, must be quickly established. Allow several groups of new characters to deal with the same scenario.

Exercise 42 **COLORS**

Interpretation of color aids in expression of emotions.

Instructions:
The instructor passes out duplicate pieces of colored paper to students in the group, making two reds, two blues, and so on. Each person in the circle then mimes or acts his color. After the members of the class have guessed the colors, students with the same color become partners. One student from each pair becomes an inanimate object, with the other student using that object according to the color. For example, if the color was red, and the object was a toaster, the student might become angry because the toaster is stuck and burning a piece of bread.

Variation:
Have each color find its complement. Together they create a scene. The instructor can aid this approach by hanging a color chart on the classroom board. This complementary color variation is a fine way of introducing conflict and can facilitate character development.

Exercise 43 **BODY LANGUAGE**

Instructions:
Let's find out how our bodies work when we become other things! A background of music may aid the children in moving to the spoken scenario. You are very heavy. Your body is being pulled to the ground, and you lie there all bunched up like a sponge full of water. Gradually the tide goes out and you are exposed to the sun. The water evaporates and your body becomes warm and dry. Show what happens to your body. You expand and open until your arms and legs can be seen. Following this introductory exercise, the instructor should add complications. One part of your body becomes heavy. You are like a puppet operated by strings. You can drop and raise your head. Your hands. Arms. Elbow. What's the difference between being open and walking along, and being closed as if someone just dropped your strings? Let's try being open. Closed. Can you show, just by standing in one

place with one simple movement how you would look if you're being forced to go someplace that you don't want to go? (Closed). Show how you would look if you were going somewhere exciting! (Open).

Extension:

Now let's make a list on the board of places and feelings we have about these places. From their suggestions, the leader forms a list on the blackboard. An example might be:

Places	Feelings
beach	happy
graveyard	scared
school	awful
circus	excited

Now divide the class into three groups. Each group choose one of the places and one of the feelings. Decide what you will see and what you will feel about going to these places. You have only 30 seconds to decide. When we start, each of you move as an individual, with everyone moving at the same time. Walk around the room as if you are walking to the place on the board that you have chosen. Remember how you feel about going there. What do you see? Walk and sit down as though you are there by yourself. Group one, Ready! Begin. Stop.

Could the rest of you tell how they felt? Why? Where were they? What were they looking at? What about their use of space? Next group? Begin!

Continue using the groups. Finally, simple walks and freeze positions may be assigned to the whole class. They will soon understand that body language may be conveyed by their stance and walk.

Exercise 44 MOVEMENT TO VOCAL SOUND

Many of the exercises in the Senses section which coordinate movement and sound would be useful for review. Each student becomes a member of an orchestra, using either sound or movement, or both.

Instructions:

The instructor should choose a simple and intriguing story. Pick a narrator from the class to tell the story, cueing one group for movement, and a second for sound. An illustrative discussion by the leader, using several students from the class, may prove helpful. Place the script, scene, outline, or scenario on the board, with directions for movement and sound. If a fairy tale is chosen, such action and sound will be self-explanatory. Examine with the students the elements of the story: its characters, props, setting, and background.

Variation:

Students could also work together in small groups, planning independently their actions and sounds, based on one story. This enables the instructor to give each group individual attention. A good example of such a sound story is given in Lesson 9, A Trip to Earth.

Exercise 45 OCCUPATIONS

A list of occupations and daily actions can be placed on the board as motivation and review for character development.

Instructions:

Think of any activity people do for a living. Choose a job with physical action, so that it will be easy to communicate. Keep in mind the weight and resistance of objects, for example a traveler and his suitcase. Work in groups or pairs.

Variations:

To vary the exercise, complicate it with situations that require more action, such as being very tiny in comparison to the object handled. Alternately, the freeze technique developed in Exercise 47 can allow each person to reposition when the leader stops the action. At the command **Go!**, anyone in the performing group can lead the group into a new occupation.

Exercise 46 WORK GESTURES

This exercise should not be attempted before other exercises in this section that deal with movement and direction.

Introduction:

Begin by doing warm-up exercises. As part of the motivation, ask individual students to show the difference in motion between several occupations, such as a taxi driver and an airplane pilot.

Instructions:

Choose a simple work gesture that tells us what you are doing! Many possible examples of professional movements are suitable, including such examples as a balloon salesman, dentist, painter, or fortune teller. Students try out their characters before the class. The instructor should complicate the action by providing a setting and scenario or simple plot. **You are in a restaurant. You enter one at a time and sit down to be served. The waitress will come to take your order.** It is important that the players think in terms of their role wherever they are. Their dialogue and mannerisms will be guided by those qualities they instinctively choose to represent in their roles.

Exercise 47 FREEZE POSITIONS

Exercises which instill internal involvement and trust or help to deepen the value of this exercise will provide a useful review.

Instructions:
Have the students walk around, then freeze into any position. Start the children again, and ask them to freeze into the same position as before. Describe different situations for them to freeze into, for example a position they would take if they were posing for a newspaper picture. Have them freeze into characters that would be the opposite of the one just performed. After acquainting them with the freeze technique, suggest group patterns where the group freeze will take place. **Watch a spider web being made. Begin. . Freeze! Now hear a siren and go to the point where the fire has occurred. Begin. . .Freeze!** Discuss what they saw and what would be the circumstances. Next, single students should be encouraged to step out of the freeze, and relate to the group while remaining within their individual space. The student either begins a monologue or shapes the other children into a new arrangement. They respond as objects or characters as he encourages them to react.

Mime. Elementary school classes which haven't begun the lessons in Chapter Four should skip the remainder of Chapter Three. The following sections are intended for use in those classes already familiar with sustained exercises. However, students who have developed self-discipline and have become involved in their drama activities may also be ready to begin mime. Specific exercises should be practiced to create the illusion necessary to express ideas in mime.

A high level of concentration needs to be developed to give the participants the satisfaction of working. Once they are given an idea of the many possibilities that exist, some of the shyest and least verbal individuals will work long hours to perfect their ideas in mime form. Often, a small group can be left to work on their own. *Occupational mime*, better known as *pantomime*, may be introduced along with most of the previous exercises. Alternately, mime may be introduced separately by including exercises from this section.

If only a few find the mime form fascinating, allow them to continue, in depth, by themselves. The remaining exercises may be covered according to the interest level of the rest of the class. The mime group may then give performances based on their own unique ideas and contribute to most class projects.

Warm-up Exercises. Warm-up exercises are especially important in mime training. The instructor should explain that some motions used are very difficult and, in order to do them, some training must take place. To communicate without words, the body must be very versatile in its movement and be able to move in ways that might not seem natural for daily movement activities. The basis of mime exercise is first to be able to separate the body into the following sections: head; trunk, hands, and arms; base, or lower body. The following exercises emphasize these separations. **Roll the head; move the hands in a circle from the wrists; the arms in a circle from the shoulders; move the trunk or top of the body from side to side in relation to the hips without moving the hips; then move the hips from side to side without moving the torso.**

A more complicated warm-up exercise emphasizing body sections is the following: **Stand with feet slightly spread, toes out. Place the toe, then heel of one foot down while bringing the weight of the hips over the foot with exaggeration. Now shift to the toe of the other foot, bringing the heel down and the weight of the hips over the new foot. Repeat as though walking in place.**

Exercise 48 **THE SNAKE**

A good general exercise for warming-up. The Snake helps loosen the entire body while preparing it to lift a bundle.

Instructions:
Keep your feet flat on the floor and bend over with your head at the level of your knees. Bend your knees and push up with the balls of your feet, bend backward, arching your back with your arms spread open as if to lie on the air. Bend over again and keep the whole exercise flowing as one continuous movement. The body will resemble a snake when viewed from the side.

Exercise 49 THE BUNDLE

Strong feet and legs are needed to create the illusion of lifting a heavy object.

Instructions:
1. Bend the whole body over to lift the object. 2. Bend the knees into a squat position. Place the arms under the bundle. 3. Raise the object up by getting the feet and legs to take the weight of the whole object. 4. Shift weight under it still more when the object is at waist level.

Exercise 50 THE ROPE

A mime exercise which emphasizes the torso and hip motion.

Instructions:
Place both hands to your right side on an imaginary rope, the right hand in front of the left, and pulling the whole body away from the hands so that the elbows straighten. The torso should move away from the hands first and then the hips should follow underneath. Reverse this movement bringing the hips and arms, then torso, together. Continue to first pull away, then bring together, on a 1, 2 count. Repeat this action several times. The arms should straighten as the trunk moves away, and bend as the arms and trunk are brought together.
The exercise may be extended by adding the following: 1)With both hands to the right side at the pelvis, move the hands and pelvis together. 2)The left hand moves in front of the right to grasp the rope. 3)Next, the right hand moves in front of the left to grasp the rope and, while reaching with the right hand, pull the whole body away from the hands so that the elbows straighten. 4)Now pull both the trunk and hands together so that the illusion of pulling the rope is created. Do exercises on a 1, 2, 3, 4 count as written. Combine the rope and baggage into a complete mime — a hitchhiker has been

waiting for a long time and is getting disgusted. Suddenly a car stops and he is so excited that he almost forgets his pack. He signals for the car to wait for him while he gets his pack. He begins to lift his pack, but can only get it half way, then drops it. He tries pulling it with the rope, but the rope breaks. Then he tries pulling it by the top, but falls over it. Finally, he decides to leave it altogether and take the ride.

Exercise 51 IT IS GUARANTEED

Students will enjoy greater physical freedom.

Instructions:
> One of you is a salesman. The other is a buyer. The coat or article of clothing which you are trying on begins to do strange things to you. Be specific about the changes the coat is making. Decide on an ending. The scenes can be done separately, at the same time, alternating back and forth between groups, and speaking during the pauses.

Exercise 52 OBSTACLES

In this exercise any obstacle which is understood by the children may be used. The leader should define the obstacle's space, helping the students to visualize it.

Instructions:
> You enter a tunnel, the sides of which you have to show with your hands. It's very dark inside the tunnel. You have to feel your way at first. You are looking for a treasure. You come upon a large box but cannot figure out how to open it so you go on until you bump into a barbed-wire fence. You decide the treasure must be on the other side, so you crawl through the fence. The tunnel becomes very narrow and you can't go any farther. You turn around and go back through the barbed-wire fence, find the box, and find your own way of opening it. Eerie music can be used which keeps the pace steady, or the students can keep the pace according to the leader's drum. The instructor may wish to simplify the scenario for younger groups, or complicate it for older ones.

Exercise 53 MACHINES

Students mime the actions of pieces of machinery, developing timing and coordination.

Instructions:

The instructor sets a large machine into motion, using students for the working parts. A demonstration can take place at first by having two children perform in a mirror relationship. One begins a simple, slow movement while the other follows closely behind. Then have one move from side to side like a pendulum, while the other moves up and down. Add a third person who moves in and out. A fourth might keep the same beat but move in still a different manner. Continue until the entire group is involved. After the large machine is moving, the instructor may wish to halt its progress, dividing the members into smaller groups that invent their own machines. Some examples are: a hairwashing machine, banana-peeling machine, or a smog-reducing machine. At first, music or a drumbeat may help to keep the action moving, but the instructor should encourage the children to provide their own sounds controlled by their movement.

Exercise 54 BALANCING

Students gain confidence in movement and concentration in preparation for mime.

Instructions:

Walk around the room keeping your regular speed. Turn and go the opposite direction. Freeze! Make a square on the floor by walking in a square pattern. Do not overlap into your neighbor's space. When you have completed the square, walk on a diagonal through its center. Now, begin again. Walk slowly. Stand on one foot, keeping your balance. Put your foot down and pick up the other foot and feel your balance. Take a step forward and then backward, feeling the change in balance. The slower you go, the easier it is. Continue balance exercises until some proficiency is demonstrated by each member of the class. Then, have them stand against the wall, placing the body from the back of the heels to the head against the wall. **Pretend that a string is attached to your head, and is being pulled so that your body is perfectly straight from heels to head.** No emphasis is given to raising the chin, shoulders, or chest. The necessity of posturing to provide proper gait and breathing can be emphasized. Repeat the walking portion to create other floor patterns.

Exercise 55 **LINES MAKE SPACE**

Students explore shapes with movement.

Instructions:

Look around the room, noticing all the different shapes, including lines, circles, rectangles, and patterns. Now, choose one of these shapes, and find a way to make it with your body. In young groups, the children can make the shape with their bodies, or mime the object and use it. Between the handling of the object and making its shape with their body, the instructor can emphasize the transition between involvement *as*, and involvement *with*, the object.

The children can differentiate between using and being the object by quickly rotating to connote change. After you have formed the object or pattern, walk inside the space that was formed. Fill that space with your body. Now it is moving in upon you. Step outside and walk around it, showing all the edges, points and parts. Lift it up and carry it. Now, notice your partner's shape. Look around the class at everyone's shape. Explain it to the class by showing the shape in movement. Call upon your partner so that you can handle the shape together.

The leader may use this exercise to follow up the main elements of line and shape in their artwork, in sculptures, line drawings, or designs.

Variations:

Letters and numbers may be traced by the body, while being accompanied vocally. Alternately, a leader can be chosen from the group to select a form. The leader may then move in front of the form as the group follows him. A third variation allows individuals or groups to explain visually their form to the other students, detailing how it works.

Exercise 56 **CONTACT GYMNASTICS**

Instructions:

Leaders or instructors who wish to expose their class to movements that require much space may enjoy the following exercises:

Back to Back. Two students link arms in a standing position, back to back, and slowly squat until they are seated with their knees bent. Then, they slowly rise until standing and repeat, this time extending the legs as they move, ending in a fully-seated position.

Side to Side. Two students link arms, side by side with their feet touching. As the pair descend, all the pressure should be on the inside leg, which remains bent as the buttocks are lowered, and the outside leg is stretched out. Then, as in Back to Back, the inside leg can be stretched out if the pressure between the students is maintained against the legs. When three or more students are involved, this exercise may be done in a circle with students facing each other, or with their backs to each other.

Up and Down. Both students link arms, as in Back to Back. Because one student's buttocks must fit in the small of the back of his partner, it is best to pair students of similar sizes. One student then bends forward, with his partner raised into the air facing the ceiling. When proper balance is obtained, the partner's arms can be held out, extended from the elbows by the bottom person, so that they are stretched above both heads. The top person may also be left suspended without any holds.

Exercise 57 THE WALL

With one gesture the student can show that space is three dimensional.

Introduction:

A series of simple exercises will aid the students beginning this exercise. **Hold your arms straight out to the sides, lifting the palms so that they are at right angles to the arms.** The stretching of the arm muscles will make application of the palm to an imaginary wall more agile. **Now place the hands in front of the body at head level so the palms are flat as though on a wall. The arms pull away from the wall quickly, with the wrist leading. Now bend the hand at the wrist so the fingers and palm then curve over the wrist and are slapped on the "flat surface" with the lower palm leading to show the "wall."** This exercise is done with the hands, and emphasizes the movement of the palm in a wave motion. Once the entire hand becomes limber, there is more of a contrast when the flat surface of the wall is shown. The exercise is known as *l'appelle* (the call).

Instructions:

Repeat l'appelle exercise with both hands, trying it at several different heights from the floor, but keeping the space about one foot from your body. Have the entire class set up an imaginary wall running the length of the room. In the center, have half of the group on one side of the wall, half on the other. **Now shake out your arms to relieve tension.** Have each student move across the room. **Think of yourself as suddenly being pushed on stage. Can you show the wall enough to establish its presence, but not "follow" it?** The point is to get across the "stage" without being self-conscious. The instructor should remind the students that having an objective helps. Discuss self-consciousness versus attention.

Exercise 58 **THE LABYRINTH**

Introduction:
The Greek myth about Theseus can be casually told to help the students understand the nature of a labyrinth.

Instructions:
Have you ever seen a labyrinth? Could you describe one? What do you think the purpose of this labyrinth would be? Have you ever seen a house of mirrors? Since a labyrinth has many corners, how would these be shown? The instructor can begin demonstrating the mime gestures, followed by the class. The hand should be cornered and each hand should be slapped on a plane which is at right angles to the previous one as the turn is made. **Let's design a Labyrinth. Let's draw it on the board.** The labyrinth design can be as complicated as necessary so more designs can be made. **If one of you is leading, can the rest of you follow him to form the labyrinth?** The instructor can alter the story to be acted out by following the suggestions of the students. Since a labyrinth is a sequestered trap, the principle problem can be considered to be the bull who is being misled while the others escape. The bull is at one end. The scouts have been sent to trap him. **Those of you who are scouts can befriend the bull, who starts to follow you. In the meantime, the youths are waiting at another section for the signal to escape. Finally they are signaled by the scouts. Since it is dark, each tries to find his way by staying in back of someone else and feeling along the wall until he arrives at the entrance in time to be lifted out. The scouts leave the bull, and they are pursued through the darkness arriving just in time to be saved.**

The plot can be conceived through combination of the teacher's questions, the student's responses, and their comments. Following the basic exercise, the students can walk through the labyrinth to music, while being pursued by the bull.

Exercise 59 **THE KITE**

Several techniques are combined. The Rope should be reviewed.

Instructions:

Blow up an imaginary balloon. It grows in size, and you can show this by the distance the fingers are from each other near the mouth, and by the distance the other hand must reach out to hold the balloon as it grows. The knotting can be shown by turning the fingers toward each other and circling the wrists away from each other. Since the balloon is lighter than air, it should be mimed as rising in the air. The string can be shown by alternating raising one hand, then the other, over the head, grasping the string with thumb and forefingers a few inches above the head as the eyes follow first one hand then the other. This gives the illusion that the balloon is rising. If the balloon is quite large, the illusion of being pulled off the ground can be created. Since the same pecking motion and "walk" can be used later with a kite, the walk will also be explained. It could be called a space walk, because the body acts as if it is lighter than the atmosphere. In this sense, the body moves against the air in slow motion as if the air were an impediment and heavy enough to hold the body.

Thinking of the air as if it were water helps create the same illusion. It would be simple to say it is a slow motion walk, but space walking is more complex. Besides walking slowly, as force of gravity becomes lighter, the gravitational pull is redirected, to come from the kite or balloon. The whole body is being lifted into the air, as well as impeded or slowed down. This part of the exercise is difficult, for it requires patience and control. The ankles must be flexed and strengthened, putting the toe down ahead of the heel in a very exaggerated way, first one, then the other, until the legs are slowly lifted and lowered. When this becomes more comfortable it will be possible to lower the whole leg slowly, circling it or just allowing it to move in circular fashion at the side of the body. When the walk is combined with the originating "lift" from the kite, the whole body seems to rise, giving the illusion that a draft of air has been caught by the kite.

Variations:

With the idea of the kite technique, students could develop several themes. One is "The Broken Kite", letting the kite rise while using the walk to show contentment. This is done so that when the kite becomes caught there is a contrast and the problem is dramatized — freedom versus captivity. The concept can be used in any plot where escape is necessary. Several attempts are made to lower the kite: throwing rocks to dislodge it, pulling the string until it breaks. Finally it is loosened. The child bends down to pick it up and discovers a hole in it through which he can place his feet. He throws it down and walks off.

Exercise 60 **COUPLES MIME**

Placement, form, and shape are emphasized by sharing objects in space.

Instructions:
Count off the students and organize them into couples. **Show that you have a pole between you which is about six feet long. See if you can keep the length of the pole the same, while moving backward and forward, and to both sides. Don't lose the pole. Keep it in the middle of your body. Stretch your whole body, raise your arms above your head, your feet out to the side while keeping the pole between you.**

Variations:
You have a table between you. Show how long it is, how high. Step over it, slide under it. Both of you lift it up, carrying a glass vase on top of it. Put it down carefully. Take the vase off and turn the table on its top, then over again so that it is right side up. Now push the table together as if it were putty, and make a large ball of gum out of it. Now, pull and stretch it as though it were taffy. The next time you stretch it, it will become a sheet. Stretch the sheet between you and fold it up.

Carry or push something that is heavy and that takes several of you. After you've delivered it, show what it is by how you use it. Push a car that finally starts. Everyone get in. A tire goes flat. Get out and fix the tire, then everyone gets back in. All four tires go flat.

Carry a piece of glass that is about 6 feet by 8 feet. Since it is glass, it can't be found until it is stepped on or walked through. The problem is how to show that it is glass.

Several persons can be carrying a coffin. They get tired and put it down. One gets curious to see if anyone is inside. He opens the lid and the body waves, so he waves back. He nods with approval to the others, as if to say that it was all right: There is a body inside. They shrug, close it, and carry it off.

Exercise 61 BOX PASSING

Size, detail, and function are observed and imitated.

Introduction:
A general mime exercise warm-up should precede this exercise.

Instructions:
Sit in several circles. Each of you show that you have a box in front of you. Show its size, shape, and how heavy it is. Now, open it up and show what is inside. Close your box, and pass it on to the next person. Remember its size and shape. Open the new box and take out whatever the first person took out of it. Didn't you see it? Well, pass it back and watch what he takes out. Now pass it back again. A possible organization is to have all the even numbers perform while the odd numbers watch, then reverse. Have the students pass the boxes until they have their own box back. How do you know it is yours? By the contents? Then throw all that stuff in the center of the circle. After all the items are in the center, use it as a grab bag, and see how many items can be pulled back out from memory. Each person may alternately pull out the second item they mimed.

"The fish told him to go back, all was as before . . . ."

Abstract Mime. Following these simple mimes, students may wish to expand their understanding of mime movements to include the expression of abstract concepts. When three gestures are used to represent life, death, and immortality, images are concentrated as in a poem. A statement about life is captured by a mime who uses his arms as eagle's wings, wafting and gliding until shot; then becoming limp, he instantly appears to descend. Another statement about life is made when the mime carries a large bundle which constantly reappears no matter how many times she leaves it or tries to elude it.

The exercises which follow are for students who become involved in mime techniques because of their power to represent ideas in a nonliteral form. One's own commitment to practice and to be continually inspired is not contained within the intended scope of this book. These exercises and a few ideas are included for those who wish to create from their own resources.

Exercise 62 **MOVEMENT IN SPACE**

Unusual character qualities are assimilated by changing ones relation to the environment.

Instructions:
> The instructor should provide a musical background. **Stand up with your arms out from your sides. Turn your whole body, making a circle with your arms that is parallel to the floor. Move your arms all around your body and think of that space as far as you reach as your own private space. Remember to keep enough distance when you move so you can balance yourself with your arms without touching anyone else, and look as though you're flying through the air. You are light, and the air is light. Nothing is holding you down. Now, think about moving in water. There is more to hold you down. It is more difficult to move, but the water can also hold you. Your body feels large, and your arms and legs feel small. Your body begins to float like a bubble. Now you can go anywhere.**
>
> The leader can continue the narration by changing weight, (heavy-light); time, (fast-slow); space, (straight-twisted), and direction. The basic efforts of movement are ideal for use as changes: dabbing, flicking, floating, gliding, punching, pressing, slashing, wringing. **Walk straight ahead, gliding. You are very heavy but move quickly, writhing, lashing out, and twisting. You are a dragon slapping at space and searching.**

Exercise 63 **FILL YOUR SPACE** *A*

The relationship between space and the body is changed.

Instructions:
Close your eyes and imagine, really *see*, a scene. You are on stage in that scene, using the space which surrounds your body as far as you can reach. Next, you are in a living room, and you allow your own personal space to join that of the living room. Now you are in an auditorium. Imagine your space joining with the large space and uniting with it, and becoming one.

Variation:
Another possibility is to use the senses to reach outside the body, so that sounds in the immediate environment disappear. Lift your hand as if to touch an object which is very far away. Now, visually bring it nearby. You can make it seem near, turning distance inside out.

Exercise 64 **FILL YOUR SPACE** *B*

Energy is released into space.

Instructions:
This exercise should be undertaken after reaching a point in the relaxation exercises when the body is calm. **Concentrate on your chest area. Let your energy move from a point in your chest out through your arms, head, abdomen, pelvis and legs. Send the energy out through those extremities, up through the head, out through the fingers and toes. Send it as far as you can from your chest. Keep sending it out and imagine the rush of energy being emitted from your chest. Now, bring all that energy back and store it in its source within your chest.**

Variations:
As the students progress, this exercise can concentrate the energy of the legs, arms or other parts of the body. For example, the stomach or diaphragm is a center often used for obtaining balance. The abdomen may be used as a center if a character with a heavy walk is developed. These exercises should all begin from a central energy source in the body and end by redirecting it back to that same source. After concentrating the energy, large muscle activities (such as chopping wood, molding clay, or hitting a ball) channel the energy flow from the center of the body into the activity.

Exercise 65 **MIME PLAYS**

Introduction:
   After the students are comfortable with mime exercises 48-64, they should be reviewed. Include slow motion and freeze, as well as other ways of changing speed using different rhythms.

Instructions:
   Ask for student volunteers. Explain what is expected of them. I've got several mime plays that are simple to do, and I'll help you through them. Maybe there will be some suggestions from the other members of the class as well. Form the class into groups of five or less. Each group is given a play. After you get your play, work on it by going through it several times. The first time, try it in slow motion. The second time, your director should call freeze four times, during the rehearsal, allowing individuals to step outside and look at it. The third time, exaggerate the movements in slow motion. Lastly, do it at normal pace. When you're finished, watch the other players. I'll put these steps on the board for you. The following mimes can be used, or the instructor may wish to make up plots for class use.

   Each person blows up the same balloon and passes it along. It get larger and larger, so large that everyone holds on to it and floats off.

   You are looking at a late, scary television program. You think that you hear noises outside. It is your cat.

   Everyone looks up into the sky. A flying object comes closer and closer. It lands, and each person goes near it to catch it. All pounce on it at once and tear it to pieces through excitement and frenzy. No one allows room for a new experience.

   Each person finds that he is in a box which gets smaller and smaller. The box gets so small that each person becomes afraid and tries to get out. Each reaches out in the dark, and finds another hand. This gives them hope. Together they help each other walk through the darkness, feeling their way, only to find a wall which encloses them all.

   Artists start painting a large mural with small brushes and tiny delicate strokes. The enthusiasm mounts and they change to larger brushes making firmer and more aggressive strokes. They begin to use their hands, throwing paint and turning their bodies around to imprint the canvas. They then lower the canvas to the floor and pour paint on it while sliding and roll upon it. Finally, they realize that they have become the work of art and all pose proudly in a tableau.

Exercise 66 OPEN-CLOSE, LARGE-SMALL

A mental attitude can shape the body.

Introduction:

Warm-up the students with the following exercise: Let the wrists, elbows and arms fall. The shoulders fall as the waist bends, then the knees bend. Stretch up slowly, as you rise. The head moves last and the jaw is left open. It is as if one vertebrae at a time were being lifted. There should be the smoothness of a flower opening and closing. The knees and head are bent at the same time.

Instructions:

The only way to provide an environment in mime is by the reaction of the character. Some children have no eidetic memory and need to relate by changing their size. The environment is felt kinesthetically instead of visually. Sit still for a moment and watch your body dematerialize. You are becoming smaller, so that by comparison, everything around you is large. You get up to move, and discover that your pace is accelerated, and you are more anxious. Your legs are shorter. You cannot reach as far. You change from a person into an animal squiggling under a rock, hiding, ready to crawl out again cautiously, and find food. Now, you are an inanimate object, a ball, mechanical toy, or whatever. You are moving according to the force of whoever manipulates you. The leader can make these outside influences more real by describing some of their effects. Then have the children rest for a moment, and help them grow. When they get up, they should portray the difficulty of being large, uncoordinated, and massive.

Variation:

Have the members of the class react to a story, such as being 'little people' in a science fiction story, both when small and after growing large. Alternately, an evolutionary theme may be narrated by the leader while the students move as individuals. Finally, name large objects for them to handle in twos or threes as in Exercise 60, Couples Mime.

Exercise 67 **SHARING SPACE**

A greater interaction between people physically and emotionally.

Instructions:
> Imagine your body contained in a bubble. Feel the texture of the spaces around your body with your hands, knuckles, elbows, feet, knees and hips. Explore the space at all levels. Now, work with a partner, and consider the space around each other's body. Watch only your partner's eyes. Trace each other's bodies, and work in small configurations starting with one finger. Now give and take, moving in relation to your partner. As he provides a stimulus, you begin to respond to it. Have another person join in the movement. Keep adding persons until many are involved. Rhythms can be changed by altering the movement with a metronome or drum. Try different levels of movement. **Now, move through Jello. Use all the surfaces of your body.**

Exercise 68 **GEOMETRIC SHAPES**

Encourages concentration for promoting spontaneous group shapes and movement.

Instructions:
> About 15-20 students stand side by side waiting for a cue to begin movement. Various patterns to be formed can be discussed, according to how many are chosen.

    3   4   5   6

> If three are tapped, a line is formed; if eight are chosen, two squares are formed, etc. Other patterns to be chosen can include triangles, circles, and various geometric shapes. The groups may refer to board drawings later while making the shapes.
>
> After the shapes have been discussed and decided upon by the group, all should stand with their hands cupped in front of their bodies so the leader may select participants by dropping a coin into their hands. Those chosen move to form the pattern corresponding to the number of participants.

Variations:
> To extend the exercise, ask for categories of movement possibilities such as: games, entertainment, work, art, ritual,

defense, health, or other areas included in basic human activities. After the category is chosen or called out, one person within the geometric shape can lead the others in performing actions related to the category, as the rest of the group responds.

Exercise 69 MASKS

The body is freed from identity.

Introduction:
There are definite reasons for wearing masks. During the interlude between being oneself and becoming a character, there is the experience of effacement—when the performer becomes nothing or neutral. He divests himself of his own traits and does not take on new ones; he stands naked and free, relaxed and without tension. He is both everyman and no man. He must be no one in particular so he can become universal. This *neutral mask* serves to blot out the feeling of the individual and the restrictions which often come with self-consciousness. When the face is covered, the body is often freer to expand emotionally. See picture on page 96.

Instructions:
The idea for a short and simple mime can be given to a group of about eight. Events may include a ship embarking or departing; a friend approaching or leaving; watching someone on a merry-go-round; an airplane landing or taking off; or using binoculars to watch various happenings. The same mime (or another) can be performed by other groups. Individuals in the performing group pair themselves with those in the audience group. The members of the audience answer questions about their counterparts. Questions which the audience answers, might include: Where are they? What (or who) are they watching?; What emotional response do they have to those they are watching?; Is the person going or coming?

Speech. It has been taken for granted that dialogue or monologue is motivated through action or stimuli. However, some very simple speech exercises can be used to enhance verbal flow. These exercises may be introduced whenever the students are motivated to use speech. They should be first used in small groups, with the whole class involved at once. The leader can encourage groups to volunteer, or may call on separate groups until they are comfortable enough to complete the exercise before the class.

The early exercises in this section may also serve to lead students into speech situations.

Exercise 70 **SHOWING WHERE**

Through a scenario of action, students are introduced to speech and situations.

Instructions:

Student A shows by mime where he is. As soon as Student B guesses the setting, he joins in. If student B is wrong, student A can speak to him, but doesn't reveal the place directly. (If B is correct, A may show his acceptance of B, but not reveal the setting.) Several other students may join in, one at a time. The instructor may help students in choosing a setting by listing some common ones on the class board. For it is important that the settings be real places, rather than imaginary. The drama in real life is frequently overlooked, and ordinary situations are passed over or ignored for their commonplace aspects. For clarity it may be important to allow two students to interact at a time, in rotating order.

Exercise 71 **SHOWING WHAT**

Students introduce their awareness of "What" actions.

Instructions:

Follow the same format as Exercise 70, substituting gestures demonstrating "what" for "where." Only in mime scenes or plays, where action adds to the plot, can repetition remain valuable. Here, however, action should not be repeated but re-enforced or complimented. The instructor may wish to clarify the actions by asking questions, such as, **What were you doing? How could it have been made more clear?** Explain weight, size, shape, and motions. If the first student's actions are unclear, no progress is gained by allowing the second student to guess at length.

Exercise 72 **SHOWING WHO**

Moving from where and what, students explore characterization.

Instructions:

Development of characters is more complicated to communicate than a simple setting. The best way to avoid a bedlam of confusing clues is to have student A enter, accompanying his mime with a monologue until student B enters and a dialogue begins. To avoid any direct naming by student B, or other characters, dialogue should conform to general statements relating to student A's identity. Student A may wish to play a specific character, rather than profession. For example, he might choose to be Dr. Schweitzer rather than a general physician. After student B guesses the profession or character, he may join in the action, and a third student can enter and question their identities.

Exercise 73 **BEGIN A STORY**

Instructions:

The instructor should make a list of the class's suggestions for the categories of Place, Person and Action. Divide the class into groups and have the students from each group decide upon one item under Place. Each student may decide upon the same or different characters and actions. As each group takes its turn in front of the class, each student enters singly into the unplanned situation. Usually, it is best for no more than five students to comprise a group. The rest of the class forms an audience for the smaller group, trying to guess the actions, characters, and places portrayed. Each person has a chance to talk when he enters. After entering, each student must listen for opportunities to speak. Whatever is said or mimed must be accepted by the other players and not changed. In this manner, no character can dominate the scene.

Exercise 74 **GIVE AND TAKE**

Materials Needed:

A ball.

Instructions:

Form a circle about 12-14 feet wide, and one of you stand in the middle. The center person throws the ball to anyone in the circle; they throw it back to the center. Play the game in slow motion, expanding each movement, but keep it a surprise when you throw the ball to someone. The ball should be taken in when catching so that the whole body begins to grow around it, moving back and forward. **Keep the rhythm of passing the ball going. Make your movements smooth.** There should not be any jerkiness to the motion. As soon as a rhythm is established, and each member of the class can anticipate the movement of the ball, more players can enter the center.

Variations:

Leave just one player in the center, but add several balls to the game. Emphasize the give and take of the balls. The players around the circle and in the center should be able to anticipate and plan their timing so that not all of the balls reach the center at the same time. Alternately, use one ball but no center person. The person throwing the ball makes vocal sounds while the ball is in his possession, then stops when the ball leaves his hands. At first, have the sounds follow feeling words, then try color words. Develop a rhythm to match the movement and sounds.

Exercise 75 **TENSE AND RELAX**

Materials Needed:

Music optional.

Instructions:

Tense and relax your face, neck, top arm, bottom arm, hands, chest, thighs, calves, ankles and feet. Shake them out. Sit quietly or lie down. Clear your mind of thoughts and images, and check your body to be sure it isn't tense. Listen to the music, and imagine something that takes thousands of years to grow, but when it reaches its full height, slowly collapses. As soon as you hear the music, begin to grow into whatever object or thing you can think of. Go with the music until the climax is reached, then begin to relax in the character of your object. Relax. Repeat, and this time think of the main parts of your body that are being used as if they were isolated.

Variations:

There are many variations possible for this exercise: flowers that grow and wither; candles which stand upright, are lit, and melt; a coat placed on a hanger that falls off. Other tense and relax exercises may include opening a door which is tight, then free; or preparing to throw a spear, and letting go. The instructor may even want to introduce comic mimes, such as making a speech to a very large audience in a dignified manner, then waving to someone in the front row.

Relax and tense situations can also be used. Introduce them by single sentences or quick changes in body positions. For example, suggest to the group the following: **The phone rings late at night. Someone informs you that your cat (or dog) is in their house.**

Exercise 76 ACTION-RESPONSE

Enables group interaction.

Instructions:

The leader moves and the group reacts or responds to the movement. The initial movement by the leader is like a question, and their reaction or response is an answer. The answer may be a duplicated movement, such as a mirror image, or it may be an individual response by each member of the group. Other possible responses are: echoing (Each student duplicates the first answer given following one beat behind.) And opposition. (Individually or as a group, each responds using a reverse image.).

This structure can be used with small gestures, single words, or in the form of dialogue.

Variation:

Groups may be dispersed on the floor the leader and members separated by members of other groups. The leaders guide their group members in the sharing of space, either in a stationary position or constantly moving.

Exercise 77 REPORTING

Cooperation in groups or pairs. One person must be comfortable in verbal expression.

Instructions:

While you are working, your partner comments on what you are doing as though you were on television. Some suggestions are: painting an abstract design, making a sculpture out of empty coke bottles, digging a canal through the earth, climbing. You may be doing either the possible or impossible. Your partner does not need to know exactly what you are doing unless you tell him or want him to know. He may just be using his imagination along with you.

Exercise 78 SEE IT

Provides cooperation in a group and verbal involvement.

Instructions:

Everyone in your group is looking at or for the same thing.

Decide what the object is so you can talk about it as though it were really there in front of you. Some suggestions are: a ship in the distance which has just set sail; something valuable that has been lost and for which there is a large reward; a plane with someone you know on it about to land without landing gear; or waiting for survivors in a mine disaster.

Exercise 79 WHICH IS STRONGER?

Verbal ability motivated by argument, general character identification, and cooperation in pairs are explained.

Instructions:

Ask the class for suggestions of opposite pairs, such as: love-hate, find-lose, hope-despair, black-white, and sun-moon. **Choose a partner. Each of you take a character which is the opposite of your partner. Have a conversation to prove which is stronger. One way to prove this is by what you can do. Fill in the statement "I am strongest because I can. . ."** Number the couples. When the leader beats a drum, these numbers can be called, and the couple chosen begins their discussion. They are quickly cut off by the drum as another couple is called upon to replace them.

Exercise 80 STAY WARM

Explores verbal spontaneity.

Instructions:

Divide into threes. One of you choose any task to do. After you have been doing it for a while a second person from the group comes to tell you how poorly you're doing it. You continue the task. Finally defend yourself or give in. A third person from your group comes to tell you how well you're doing, and gives helpful suggestions. Discussion can follow about how feelings were affected during the two incidents.

Exercise 81 MOTIVATION

Commitment will produce verbal spontaneity.

Instructions:

Divide into couples. You are going to be given a special job or special privilege which you want very much. You must convince the person you are talking to that you can take this extra responsibility. Think of something you want or wish to do very much. People can change roles and perform alternately.

Exercise 82 **THE QUACK**

One person in the group should be verbal and imaginative enough to keep the others going.

Instructions:
>One of your group is an inventor. The others are part of your invention. Your invention may be logical, or absurd and nonsensical. Arrange the parts so that each will be comfortable during the time it takes you to explain your invention to the larger group. Suggestions include: a machine for all occasions, a meat maker, a food taster, or a mistake finder. The machine may speak for itself if asked by the inventor. The machine may move as the inventor indicates.

Exercise 83 **HELP**

The player requires the ability to abandon oneself before the group.

Instructions:
>You have a problem. Show us what it is. Urge someone from your group to help you, or someone from the class. Several may have the same problem and each may entice the other to be of help. Perhaps you can share each other's help. Some suggestions might include: you can't stop sneezing; you keep stepping into uncovered manholes; or wherever you step, you're walking on marbles.

Exercise 84 **THE IMPOSTER**

Explores verbal abandonment and cooperation in small groups.

Instructions:
>Divide into groups of three. You are trying to explain something strange, unusual or terrifying to someone who hasn't had a similar experience. Decide what you are going to talk about and then make it as vivid as possible. Bring the others into the conversation by asking them questions. If you wish to change the conversation, bring up a new topic. If you are not convincing, the others can stop you and ask if you are making all this up. You must even attempt to convince yourself.

Exercise 85 **BE READY**

Aids the students in developing verbal cooperation.

Instructions:

Your group is performing on a television show. Decide upon the kind of show and the topic of discussion. One person stands behind each member of the group. They take their cues from the leader, who indicates which panel member is to speak next. As soon as the leader points to a panel member, the person standing behind him presses his shoulders as a cue to speak. When signaled a second time, he presses the shoulders again and the speaker stops. In this manner, the speakers need not think about their turns, but instead become involved in the topic. Possible topics for discussion include: famous people remembering their childhood, secret wishes, and favorite hobbies.

Exercise 86 MY PLACE

Explores verbal cooperation and character identification.

Instructions:

Each person in your group has received a large amount of money and is planning a city or a recreational center. Each of you has definite ideas as to what must be included. One person may take charge and locate these ideas on a wall map, and either play yourself or play someone else. Try to resolve your differences. It would help if you had a definite character in mind. Some suggestions the instructor might offer to make the characters interesting include: having gold hidden in the basement and thinking of oneself as the wealthiest and most powerful person in town; wishing to be president of everything; always playing a musical instrument in the imagination—a guitar, piano, drums; or being always concerned about one's appearance.

Exercise 87 MARKET PLACE

Aids vocal projection and character identification.

Instructions:

You are a group of people who for many years, have devoted your lives to the making and selling of crafts and products. Since this is one of the oldest markets still running, you are being interviewed by a television reporter. Each of you has an individual stall but your excitement in being interviewed causes you to speak out of turn and interrupt each other. Decide what kind of people you are; what you sell; what kind of street calls you use; what unexpected situation could take place.

4: LESSON PLANS

In this chapter many lesson plans or formats are organized according to the guide given in Chapter Two. Each contain a Motivation, Stimulus, Release, Planning, Playing, Evaluation, Replaying, and Conclusion. The leader's initial responsibility lies in guiding the first four steps, since remaining steps cannot be thoroughly planned in advance. As the leader becomes more confident these steps will become less distinct. A form will emerge that is a combination of the group's dynamics and the leader's own style and intuition, based on knowledge of the group.

The amount of guidance a group needs should be quickly determined; as a result the leader should organize them as described in Chapter Three. Another decision will be the position the leader plays, ranging from teacher-leader-director to actor-guide and finally into character protagonist or antagonist as the group moves from less to more experienced.

CHILDREN		Smaller and smaller groups
Whole group at once	Half of a group at a time sometimes acting as audience	work separately and occasionally become an audience for each other

less —— *more*

Involved in character and as director	Leader is in and out of action	Leader occasionally suggesting instructions

LEADER

The lessons which follow are only suggested formats or plans for organization. Some are followed with themes for possible extensions using similar formats.

Ages Five to Seven. In the elementary years, children of specific ages seem to have specific needs. For example, between the ages of five to seven, children begin to establish a self-concept which can be gauged by having them answer "Who am I?" in movement. The movement may follow recorded music, piano music, percussion instruments, or the children's own sounds. A suggestion can be made that the children become mechanical objects or animals, acting to the rhythm of the sounds. The leader should encourage them in the nonsense sounds and *gibberish* which accompanies their play.

Rhythmic movement is essential for beginning creative dramatics with young children because it channels their free-flowing energies. Sources with built-in rhythm are nursery rhymes like *London Bridge* and games like *Here We Go Round the Mulberry Bush*. These rhymes not only contain the children's energy; they unify it and guide them individually to improvise in pantomime, so that even though they are all performing at once, they may all have an opportunity to express themselves.

During these formative years, it is not important what the children say, but that they have an opportunity to say it. The purpose is to begin language flow. It is wise to keep any pantomine, bodily movement, or word emphasis to these rhymes the same each time, so that the children may build a repertoire. They will become familiar with the rhyme and know it well enough to use it in its variations.

At early ages, the journey format enables children to both explore and occupy space imaginatively. When taking a journey, the group should begin to plan through the leader's questions: **Where shall we go? What will we find there? What do we need to take with us?** For example, they might begin a journey guided by narration of going to bed early and getting up in the middle of the night. This allows an atmosphere of spontaneity and absorption—the two most necessary qualities for the development of imagination. In this beginning journey, the leader might guide them to look for a treasure. He builds towards this climax by choosing objects for them to focus upon and increases the tension until the object is found.

Both music and lights can be used to motivate children to explore space in an unstructured and deeply personal way. Encouraging them to explore space will enhance their creative imaginations later when developing plots from themes and writing scenes. At this age, their entrance into a room is called "the happy entry." They enter, forming a spiral pattern that, over a period of years, becomes first a shaggy circle, then develops into smaller circles. These spacial concepts will begin to appear in the pictorial compositions of their artwork and their movement as they establish equidistance.

The less mature the child, the less able he is to be guided by music alone without the aid of a story structure. If a class is very advanced at this age, it may be possible to provide them with a plot from which they can compose either a mime or play. Their ability to carry out this task will be evidence of their maturing spacial concepts.

The most workable simple incidents or stories are those with one antagonist and crisis point, in which the teacher has the advantage of leading action indirectly. The same story later can be added to, making the crisis the result. As the idea of form develops, students can be led by questions to create their own stories from sounds. A planning period, in which students develop the plot, can be initiated and carried to conclusion. After the story has been told or set up, the leader may request individual comments in the planning period. By asking questions, character development can take place. At first, everybody can be everything: half mime Snow White, and half mime the Witch and then exchange. Casts may be changed several times, but the more outstanding players should comprise the first cast chosen.

In addition to those exercises which encourage language flow, the leader of early age groups should begin work on pantomiming. Many mime exercises lend themselves to this young age. To begin a session, the leader directs all the children in an exercise which will pacify them physically and prepare them for the *stimulus* to follow. The exercise should be selected not only according to levels of difficulty, but also should be related to the area of bodily control in the stimulus the leader intends to carry out. For example, if the story to be told is "The Sorcerer's Apprentice," in which inanimate objects are constantly changing shape by means of hand and finger motions, then the leader should conduct exercises using the hands and fingers. Next, ask the children to imagine that they are mimetically changing the shapes of objects while they use the same motions. By disguising the exercises and using them imaginatively, the leader is directly teaching control; this results in confidence later. Children are easily stimulated if they can be appealed to imaginatively, particularly if they can extend their inner reality into outer form.

Simple exercises which direct the whole body in one large movement begin preparation for those mime exercises which are taught in the motivation and release phases that precede story dramatization. For example, students' bodies can be directed to form single letters of the alphabet, numbers, or simple actions such as playing an instrument, eating a bowl of something hot, and other mimes suggested by the leader.

When children enter school they begin to be keenly self-critical and competitive. Performing individually satisfies not only their competitive spirit and need for self-esteem, but can provide for small muscle exercise as well.

Mimed actions which suggest a specific task are referred to as *occupational mime.* Occupational mimes concern all mime movements that include work activities, such as threading a needle, chopping wood, or scrubbing the floor. The performance of the single mime can lead into a group mime, bringing relief to the timid, and offering the overly active a channel for concentration.

The exercise of rowing a boat provides an example of an occupational mime. It engages the children's large muscles and enables them to escape from an imaginary storm. Those who survive the storm are washed up on the desert island to the accompaniment of wave sounds made by the other members of the class. The wave sounds become sprites who beckon them into a circle and show them how to weave a "magic" cloth, using small muscles. They are returned by riding back on the magic cloth.

Besides simple gestures, occupational mimes can utilize actions using both small muscles and large muscles in connection with the student's emotions. The leader may suggest that they are "little people" pulling together on a single, but very heavy, large rope. When, at last, they find what is at the end of the rope, they realize they have pulled up something which is very terrifying, and run and hide. One member, however, is brave, and anchors the rope to examine the "thing." An exercise such as this leaves room for their own imaginative extension. The students may change their occupation before they return from hiding, adding noises that would scare the "thing." The same exercise can be carried through with a good character, such as Santa Claus. Undergoing an abrupt change of attitude in reaction to a stimulus can absorb this age group imaginatively.

Ages Seven to Nine. During the ages of seven and eight, children can be guided to move to music without self-consciousness. Their use of the floor space can progress from one large circle to many smaller circles, eventually relating to the stage in a tongue-shaped pattern. These patterns demonstrate their physical and emotional growth. It is also evident, however, they would not feel comfortable performing in front of a group or audience. When they improvise to music, they should have the chance to listen to the music once. The music should be used as a stimulus, not as an absolute framework to which their ideas must conform. If the music is carefully selected and contains no strong climaxes it can be used as a guide for their story journey without preparatory listening.

During the ages of eight and nine, large muscle development should continue along with small muscle use. Both are stressed in exercises taught for their own sake. Longer periods of activity must be broken by sessions in which relaxation and rhythmic movement can be alternated.

Children in this age group work together, but care should be taken that they follow regulations such as using slow-motion movement when fighting. Competitive activities should be avoided because development among individuals is uneven. Mimes can be made in pairs to develop particular muscles, explore movement, and develop quality in gesture.

Exploring their own inner resources through *sense memory* allows these faculties to become fascinating tools at their disposal. Response to a leading question on objects in their environment, pictures, or their own sense impressions provides sufficient motivation from which to build a story. The students will respond in action to longer stories, provided the stories include many different kinds of activities. Instructors may wish to provide *locomotor movements*, use of small muscles used in mime, and rhythmic movement that is controlled.

By age nine, children should have been involved in a wide spectrum of movement activities to prevent them from becoming only spectators later. Everyone can move for a few minutes to a mood the music suggests, and a simple plot can be added. Feeling should be stressed over character's actions, so that concentration and movement are united as the teacher narrates and the children move.

Ages Ten and Eleven. By the age of ten and eleven, other demands may have crowded out a creative dramatics period. Many rationalizations are common, but most frequently this occurs because of the teacher's lack of knowledge of how to proceed. The need for creative drama at this age, however, remains vital, because sex antagonisms are strong and tend to obtrude. If a consistent program has been carried out through the grades, and individual showing off has struck a balance between skill and enthusiasm, the students will be encouraged to risk embarassment for the sake of enjoyment.

Every aspect of creative dramatics can be used. Particularly useful are movement games in which attention is called to the extension of particular parts of the body. The older the child, the more conscientious he is about the possibility of being able to directly apply what he learns. If the teacher says that a mime, activity, or story utilizes a certain gesture, he can fully appreciate this learning experience by instantly seeing its usefulness. In this way techniques can be stressed over stories or improvisations.

Both extremes of movement should be given emphasis. Very large muscle movement can be carried out as a sports game is mimed. Slow motion activity can be added and a suggestion given that the students synchronize their movement to a metronome or background music. If they are reminded to keep the memory of this slow movement in their muscles while responding to a story, graceful movement will become pleasurable. Specific situations should be given that matches their understanding of the environment, such as a playground activity.

The sexes can be divided and a plan of action suggested to which they can add. Longer discussions with realistic purposes are more easily begun. For example, a proposed story of having a space war between Mars and the Earth may be added by the students. Mars men, earth men, earth women, and Mars women become possible groups.

The leader and the group need to plan both a crisis and a general action, around which four smaller groups can improvise. For example, the earth men are blasted off by the earth women. The former arrive on Mars' surface and make a discovery. The Mars men are alerted and engage them in battle. Realizing they are trapped, the earthmen offer to use their discovery as a basis of an invention that will be beneficial to both planets. A few earthmen return and a few remain as hostages. Communication is set up between the two spheres, and whatever are the results of the discovery, its benefits are useful to both.

Experiments using the student's sense memories and *emotional memories* can provide motivation for improvisations. For example, a student might eat while talking on the phone. He must then decide what he is eating and a topic of conversation. Both must continue at the same time. Another example might be the recollection of an embarrassing situation that the students were once involved in.

Remind them how they felt. Help them name the symptoms of embarrassment, and ask for a volunteer to mime the situation.

Improvisations could be worked out in small groups after a number of embarrassing situations have been cited. This approach may alleviate tensions that begin building up as a result of social situations. If emotional feelings are expressed outwardly during improvisations or discussions, a bridge may be built between inner and outer development. A channel for deeply felt and often hidden emotions will be forged and assimilated by the individual process of growth.

Areas of specialization can and should be acknowledged if a performance is to be put on for a domestic audience. In such performances the children's independence becomes more pronounced. Often the teacher is unable to cope with legitimate individual demands in creative dramatics unless the group develops the attitude that a "production" is the result of many talents. (In this light, tryouts can be held and though everyone is chosen, the members of the group can identify with their individual "stature of greatness.")

A single story situation from either chapters Four or Five may take from three minutes to three weeks to perform or produce depending upon additions and alterations. The performers will wax or wane in spontaneous fashion depending upon the children's enthusiasm for the story. If the leader wishes, he can have much influence in directing their creation. The leader's fortitude is most often the foundation upon which the school play is produced. Children tire of repetition, unless it is repetition with variety.

If children wish to expand upon a creative dramatics project and present it to a group, the leader should guide them through their scenario so that it becomes spontaneous, not stilted. To retain vitality, the drama should be made more effective in terms of timing, use of space, and sound. As the children see and feel the need to make their drama more meaningful, the leader should help them make changes. If slight alterations are made each time the drama is repeated, one complete run-through is usually all that is needed before making a presentation. In this way the most important elements of creative drama, vitality and involvement, are retained, and the drama doesn't become a monotonous repetition of lines.

From age 11, children will begin working inexhaustibly on their own projects, and the drama period can be an occasion when all subjects can be brought together. A theme may be discussed and carried out into a plot. After the problem has been tentatively chosen by the class, writers can combine their ideas. Accompaniment by percussion instruments can be added by those who do the music.

By this time, if the drama program has been continuous, the students should be able to work independently or in small groups, and content and movement should be continued naturally. Difficulty may arise with large groups. *Stills* (freeze positions) can be called for to achieve balance and focus.

Small groups can work on their own variation to the general theme by following the objective that there be a wholesome interchange of contributions by individuals. Individuals in the group can provide inspiration to each other, and bring a focus to interdependence. One group can begin an action, with the next group to begin where that group left off, or stopped with a "freeze." The entire scenario can be developed continuously, as groups attach their ideas to each other's "freeze" position or scene.

Exercises for Mime and Movement. There are also specific mime exercises that are adaptable for children over age eight. For ages eight to eleven, the exercises which make up either the motivation or release phases can be repeated with variations. Alphabet mimes that were used with younger children can become slightly more complex. For example, an activity which begins with the same letter is added after the letter is mimed, in mime form. If the letter "A" is mimed, the word "aim" might imply a weapon set into position.

Instead of a mimed action, a relaxing activity also can be led. The leader can narrate the circumstances of the children becoming balloons. At first, the balloons can all be crumpled up on the ground until they are inflated and allowed to blow away. Slowly they descend back to earth. If the goal of the exercise is to lead students into a story as well as envelop them in a calm mood, it should follow the same rhythm as the story.

Between ages eight and eleven, specific techniques which lead to control and expression can be taught in the form of exercises, without being included in a story situation. Separate parts of the body can be explored and related to different emotions. For example, the problem of how the hands would variously appear if greed or kindness were shown, would be considered. The feet, the head, and the torso are encouraged to react to a single character trait or an emotion, while styles of walking, as well as other indications of character, are analyzed. After a detailed observation has been made to select particular traits, there should be little conflict or superficiality when a character is established.

Following this analysis of character, the children may choose from a story a character whom they wish to play, and give the reasons for their choice.

When children are nine and older, it is possible to teach techniques before proceeding to impromptu scenes. If technical skills and basic exercises are taught, they should be intermittently reviewed, to ensure the children's progression. Basic mime exercises consider the body in three divisions: those exercises for the head; those for the torso; and those for the base of the body. These basics include exercises for all parts of the body and can be taught at any age level.

Leading a group in relaxation exercises is beneficial, particularly if the creative dramatics session takes place at a time in the afternoon after the children have been involved in many other activities. One such exercise begins by having them rotate their feet and toes in each direction. Following this, each joint in the body, including the knee, hip, shoulder, and neck is rotated. The waist can be shifted in a circular motion from side to side as well as rotated, and the shoulder blades can be moved toward and away from the spine.

A second exercise which promotes relaxation is to have the children lie on their backs, suggesting that their limbs become heavy as lead. The leader can lift and let go of their limbs to test their looseness. They should then stretch in every direction and let go. A particular set of muscles can be tensed and slackened as the period of muscular release is enjoyed. After a few slow breaths, the tension can be transferred to other parts of the body.

By comparison with relaxation exercises, reaction exercises should be presented to develop technical skills and economy of movement. A word, a color, or music can be used as a stimulus prompting the reaction. The class may be arranged in a circle with partners diametrically opposite. Each couple reacts to a phrase while the rest of the class observes. The class may be divided into couples who start to walk toward each other from as far away as possible, then meet and react. Individual couples may take turns or one line may partially walk together, with the next line then taking its turn. The reaction can be either in terms of a character or situation. The leader can call phrases to be mimed, beginning with, "I think. . ." "I hear. . . . " "I know. . ." "I feel. . ." Or the leader can offer a choice of objects or moods to be filled in by the most meaningful reaction.

Each of the above exercises may be a suitable stimulus for preparing a group mime. The success of a group effort depends both upon the development of individual members and the unity of purpose established by the leader who sets them up. At first, only a few members should be chosen to begin a scene which can be enlarged to include a crowd. Within the crowd scene, individual characters can create a center of interest or a "focus" by reacting. This reaction can lead them to another, larger, focal point. A "still" can be called, which will reveal whether the scene has intention.

If a group is large, it should be divided into several smaller groups. The smaller groups can each work out their own mimes, and each mime can be shown separately to the whole class or in sequence, as part of a longer story. The leader may place all the younger children in one group, so that he can give them special attention. However, before the leader can give his undivided attention to any one group, he should be sure that the other groups have in them children with ability and talent.

If children are called upon to interpret each other's mimes, they will be encouraged to work for clarity and simplicity. Depth of character is also necessary, but depends upon the level of identification a child is able to reach.

Children between ages 10 and 11 are much more responsible and sensitive to other members their age than at any other time. There should be no criticism until it is set by the teacher and it is clear what is being criticized. There is no need for negative criticism. A critical attitude can be developed on the basis of group cooperation and individual personality clashes can and should be avoided.

Character Development. The movements and mimes discussed above should develop small and large muscle coordination. Just as essential for effective creative dramas is character development. Convincing character development in later years stems from the leader's early demand for a high level of concentration as he introduces a character with whom the children can empathize. It was mentioned previously that a suggestion such as **"Be a giant. . ."** is not sufficient to insure that children will draw upon their resources of ingenuity. A mood should be established as the leader describes a character and scts a feeling through which their emotions may become captivated.

At any age, the leader should guide the children in character portrayal by first describing an animal. They should close their eyes during the description and not open them until the character has been fully developed and they are ready to move. After developing an animal's character, they might work on a human character and weave it together with their interpretation of inanimate objects. The imaginative concentration required for making inanimate objects believable is very demanding. When it is combined with the task of developing a human character, the maximum amount of imaginative energy is required.

Children may develop characterizations naturally, by means of their imaginative sympathy. Either they need to work with characters which are understood because they are part of their experience, or the leader's description must be so lucid that they can identify completely.

Techniques for character development among older children can be taught directly, and through questions, basic knowledge about their environment can be applied. How does an old man walk? A middle-aged man? The beast in *Beauty and the Beast?* More detail from the standpoint of selection can be considered. People can be compared to objects in nature. For example, a character might be described as tall and straight, a redwood tree type.

Emotional memory should be developed for use within character development. It is, at last, realized that a character can determine plot, theme, and the action of a story. From this step the child should freely choose his own character. On that basis, the question can be answered, "What would you do as that character if you were at a certain place?" "...with a certain person?" "...doing a particular thing?" Character development can also be explored in pairs, perhaps from a suggestion that one say something rude to the other, as might take place in a simple domestic scene between a mother and father, or neighbors. The opposite approach of complimenting the other player also can be used.

Specific questions on character development include a wide range of possibilities: How do you think the character would walk, talk?; Why would the character walk or talk that way?; What unusual quality does the character possess?; What kind of activities would the character be doing during the first part of the story?...the other parts?; Are you like the character in any way?; Is that character like anyone you know?; Are you afraid of this character in any way?; Do you admire this character? Why?; How do people show their feelings?; How would this character show his feelings?; How would the character act before showing this feeling?; How do you think the audience will feel about this character?; How do you want them to feel about this character?

As the children empathize with universal traits of character, musical works can be re-introduced to inspire movement to universal themes. For example, the leader may narrate a story involving change, destruction, and reconstruction. She might tell of peasants working under the afternoon sun. As they work, they hear the sounds of guns and bombs in the distance. The peasants may collect their wheat and store it; they may burn it; they may leave the crops and begin to evacuate their village. These scenes can be planned after the children have heard a piece of music, according to the mood and movement that the music suggests to them.

Because children in the intermediate age group have a natural affinity for the strong outward qualities and romantic aspirations of heroes, a leader may be tempted to inspire their imaginations no further. His own knowledge enables him to realize the discrepancy between the pure ideal and the human ideal so that he can guide them toward a fuller interpretation.

It is wise to help the students attain a fuller depth of character analysis through the use of questioning, analogy, writing assignments, and improvisations. It is important to explore the outstanding accomplishments of character development before the adolescent has become internally involved in his own personal problems. If the adolescent has never exhibited or identified his emotions with feats of success, however, he may feel the embarrassment which comes with self-consciousness when called upon to make this identification for the first time.

For the convenience of the instructor using this handbook, the lessons are divided into the main steps of the lesson plan. These steps are: motivational activity, stimulus, release, planning, playing, evaluation and replay. While the divisions seem quite distinct, it is not intended that they be so to the students; all transitions should be smooth and natural. No introduction has been provided for the sample lesson, because that step is highly dependent on the individual class's needs. However, a general goal of introductory material should be to make the students comfortable. If the condition or layout of the classroom presents difficulties, the introduction might provide for the leader and students to rearrange the furnishings.

In all the lessons that follow, bold type (**All of you take your seats.**) indicates comments by the instructor to the students; italic type *(He went into the woods.)* signifies the student's response; and medium, or normal, type (The class should dance in a circle.) indicates general instructions to the teachers.

"... one of the giants started to drown.
He yelled for help, but the fairies just
looked at him ...."

Lesson 1 **THE DROWNING GIANT**

Motivation:

If my puppet wanted to know how many times he hit his drum or clapped, could you tell me by doing the very same thing in movement? *Response.* The leader makes his puppet clap four, uniform times. **Again.** *Response.* Now I want to change it a little. The leader's puppet makes two soft taps and two loud taps. How many taps did he make? *Response.* How are the taps different? If necessary, repeat the taps. How many taps did he make? *Four.* See if you can clap the same number the same way the puppet did. The puppet makes two taps slowly and the second two rapidly. In younger groups, the instructor might wish to ask the students how the taps differed from those of before. Let's put both taps together. Two which together are soft and fast, and two which together are loud and slow. He'll do that again. Now can you stand up and do that with your whole body? Ready? *Response.* Some of you clapped, some stamped, most of you moved your whole body. Now can you walk and move the way the sound makes your body feel? Play intervals of fast-soft taps and slow-heavy taps. Let the children know that two sharp taps indicate they should freeze and give the leader their attention. The same signal can consistently indicate the same direction. Now since your bodies are listening so well, fill the space in the room and just follow the sound. *Response.* Two taps. Come to this corner of the room and rest. What did the sound make you feel like? What kind of creature? *Response.* Can you listen again and see if your faces and arms are listening to the sound while you're sitting here. *The fast-soft sound was like a fairy moving or a nice bug like a butterfly. The slow-heavy sound was like a big animal who would hurt you, or a giant.* Half of us are going to watch the other half move to these beats. We want to see if there are lots of "fairies" and "giants" out there. Move from that far wall all the way over to that wall as soon as you hear the beat. This half move first. *Response.* (to other half) Did they talk with their bodies the way the sound talked to them? *Response.* Now the next group has a chance to do some different things. Over to the wall. Ready? Change the beat so that it isn't as even. *Response.* Come on back. How did they walk? *Response.* Two taps. Let's rest.

Now we're going to play a game. This is our game. The fairies are on one side and the giants on the other. They will walk toward each other, shake hands, and see if they can turn around, while facing each other, and walk backwards. If necessary demonstrate for clarity. There are a variety of activities which can take place: pulling on an imaginary rope so that they get closer together, walking toward each other in mirror, walking toward each other bounding or throwing an imaginary ball back and forth. For some of these activities they need to be in pairs. The object is for the group to move together, into a relationship, after which they simply meet by turning around each other, and try walking backwards. Two taps. Sit down and rest. What was most difficult about that? *Going backwards.* I don't think you'll be doing that often. But the fairies and giants do meet. What do you think happens? *Response.* Where do you think they meet? *Response.* Select the answer that is related as closely as possible to a forest where the following takes place:

Stimulus:

There was a forest in which some very light and tiny creatures lived. They called themselves fairies. They loved to swim and splash in the pond. Sometimes the giants would come, and then there wasn't as much room for the fairies so they left. One day the fairies were there and started to leave because the giants had come. As they started to leave, one of the giants started to drown. He yelled for help, but the fairies just looked at him because they were so small. The other giants just looked at him and said if they came in to save him they might drown also. The drowning giant said, "If I sink here I will pollute the water and then you can never swim in it again. If you'll help me out I'll never scare you away again for I cannot swim here anymore." So the fairies tried once more working fast to raise his weight with their wings. A spider came towards them and the giant said he would save them from the spider if they'd save him. The spider started spinning a rope which the fairies pulled out and carried to the giant and all together they pulled and pulled, even the giants pulled, and out he came.

Release:

Do you think we could all get together and pull on an imaginary rope so that it looks real? If we're all together then we can really have a lot of weight. Here's the rope. Let's pull. *Response.* Now let's use the same rope in a tug of war. We need two judges to decide which way the rope is going according to the weight. Remember to keep the rope in your hands. Go. *Response.*

Planning:

Rest and let's plan the story. What kinds of activities will the fairies and giants be doing? *Splashing, throwing frizbees, swimming.* Which group comes to the forest to do this first? *The fairies.* Then what happens? *The giants come so the fairies have to leave.* Next? *One of the giants starts to sink so the other giants leave.* Why? *Because they might sink.* What does the sinking giant say? *He wants the fairies to help him.* What do they say? *They say they're too light.* Then who does he want help from? *The giants, but they're too heavy.* What does the giant promise the fairies? *He says he'll let them swim and play there anytime, if they'll help.* Why does he say they must help him? *Because he'll pollute the water.* Then what happens? *A spider comes.* And is the spider friendly? *Well, . . .yes.* How do you know? *He starts spinning.* What do the fairies do with what he spins? *They take it to the giant and begin to pull and then the other giants pull also until he's out.*

All the giants stay here and all the fairies go into the pond. Who will be the spider. *Response.* Who will be the drowning giant? *Response.* Where's the pond? *In the center.* All right, fairies in the pond. The giants start all the way from there as soon as I start tapping and giants come towards the pond. If this is the first lesson then the leader should serve as narrator to keep the action going.

Playing:
One day in the forest, a group of fairies was playing in a pond. They were having a glorious time swimming, splashing, throwing frizbees. Start tapping. Suddenly some giants approached. The pond wasn't big enough for both fairies and giants, so of course, the fairies, being the smallest, had to leave. The giants got into the pond. They too were having a glorious time until one giant began to drown. He splashed and thrashed, and all the other giants became so frightened that they ran away. The fairies, hearing the commotion, returned. The drowning giant asked for their help, but they said they were too light. The drowning giant called to the other giants, but they said they were too heavy and might drown too. The drowning giant called to the fairies again. He said: *If I drown I'll pollute the water so you can't ever swim here again. Please help me. I'll let you swim here all the time.* The fairies tried once more. A spider appeared and started spinning a web. The fairies took the rope she spun to the giant and threw him one end. They pulled and pulled; even the other giants pulled. And finally out came the drowning giant.

Evaluation:
What did you think was good? How will the fairies know when to return? When will the spider appear? When will the giants reappear to help the fairies pull on the rope? What would a spider

spinning a rope look like? These and similar questions might be asked to help the children evaluate the performance.

Replay:

They should decide how they want to replay the scene. Will they change roles, add dialogue, try it without the narrator? After those points have been established, continue with replaying the scene. A transition from a game into movements which are reinforced by percussion instruments inspires character development. The difference which the beat established between the characters creates a conflict which should be resolved. Such a resolution of conflict is all that is required to establish a simple plot.

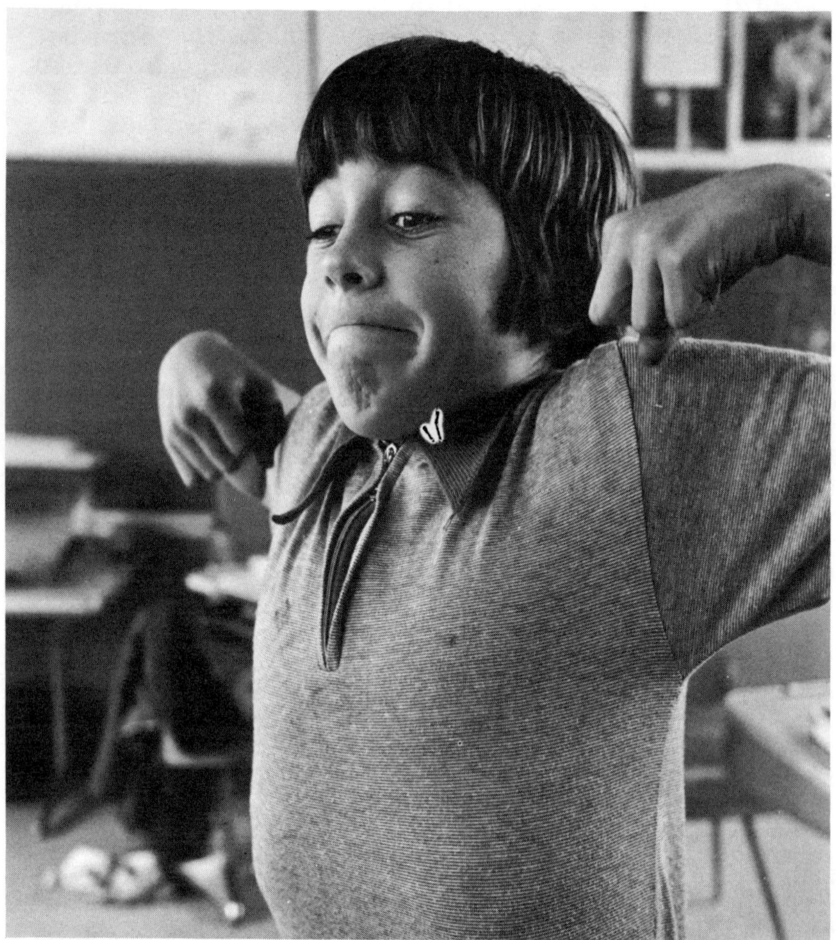

"He realizes that each thing he does they copy . . . ."

Lesson 2 **THE PEDDLER AND THE MONKEYS**

Motivation:
I want you to find your own space in the room. Make a circle around your body with your arms spread out as far as they will go. Turn around in your space. Reach over your head and bring your arms down to your sides. Reach forward from a standing position and bend at your waist, forward and then back. Think of all this space as a farmer would think of land he has cleared for his crops. . .this is space for you to exist in. Let's see all the different kinds of movement you can do. . .reach above your head. . .touch your toes. . .are there any other movements you can do in your space? While I beat the drum like this, one tap at a time, just continue to make different shapes in your own space. I saw so many different shapes. . .no two alike!

Now think of yourself in this space as being enclosed in a box, or bottle, or a bubble, and wherever you walk, keep the bubble intact so it won't break. Can you show me your bubble? Try to see it for yourself. . .all the colors of the rainbow are in it. Begin to walk very carefully inside of it. Now can you move from side to side as though you were a very tall tree with tall branches that are being blown about in the wind?

When I begin to play the music or to beat the drum, I want you to become very small and then grow. When the music tells you that you are as large as you can be, stop and turn toward each other to make a forest. The children move as the leader narrates. He can go through the forest also. Each person is a separate tree in the forest. Now everyone I touch on my way back tries to get through the forest also. The leader can touch half the children and in this way divide the group into two large "group characters." See if you can go through without touching the trees or letting the branches touch you. Note the reaction.

This time all the trees in the forest are to become plants. As soon as I begin to play the music, the rest of us who just moved so carefully out of the forest will be animals, missionaries, or pirates. When all the plants in the forest have grown to full height we will walk through the forest again. Is everyone able to move through the forest without touching any of the plants? The leader can put on the music, begin to lead the group, and narrate as the group moves through the "forest". It is difficult isn't it? Everyone must take a lot of different shapes in order to get through without any of the plants touching you. Some of the plants might be poisonous so we have to be careful. There were a lot of different plants in the forest, weren't there?

Now let's change groups. All of us who were "people" before become the new forest. All those who were the forest can be whatever kinds of people they can think of. As soon as you hear the music, the new forest grows with the music into the strongest shapes you can imagine, but this time keep moving very slowly so that we can't even see you move when you grow. Can you do that? Put Beethoven's *Pastoral* on. Can the rest of us still get through without being touched? Become whatever kind of person you think the drumbeat suggests to you and move in an imaginary forest. Narrate over sound as the children move, helping them to avoid contact and retain concentration. As soon as you hear two taps with the drum come over here and sit down. Continue to narrate and then beat out the taps. If they don't respond with conviction, have them repeat their movements up to that point and then give them the signal again, complimenting them upon improvement.

Stimulus:

Let's all sit down here. I want you to close your eyes. Try to see a forest. . .feel yourself going through it. . .hear the noises in the forest. . . Elicit responses from them according to their characters and feelings about either being the forest or being in it. At this time the story which was previously mentioned can be told. The story could be briefly summarized and told in the following fashion by the leader.

A peddler and his wife live on the edge of a forest. Every morning when the peddler gets up, he thinks of all the beautiful hats he could make. His imagination flies away with every passing object. One morning he sees a beautiful bird with purple, white, and blue feathers, and he tells his wife that he can just imagine the hat he could make out of these colors. His wife reminds him that he will never get to the market place to sell those hats that he has been working on for the past months if he keeps dreaming about all the hats he could make. However, he promises her that he will plunge ahead so that he can be off soon. She reminds him again that he said the same thing yesterday and by the time he got ready to go, it was too late in the afternoon and the sun was beginning to set. If he doesn't go today, they will surely starve because they have no money and no bread. He rushes through the hats he is now making, packs his bag with those hats he intends to sell, and sets off, assuring his wife that he will return before nightfall. . .for it gets dark in the forest early. When in the forest he is so happy to be on his way that he makes up a song. . .Hats for sale, hats for sale, yellow, white, green; some for you, some for me, the finest you have ever seen.

There are some monkeys in the forest who hear him, but keep hidden. He becomes a little tired and so loosens his bag and sits down beside a tree and takes a nap. The grandfather monkey travels down to get the peddler's hat and puts it upon his own head. All the monkeys follow the grandfather and each one picks a hat out of the open sack and places it on his head just as the grandfather does. The peddler is, of course, awakened by all the commotion and when he sees what has happened be becomes very angry. He shakes his fist at the monkeys who only respond by shaking their fists back at him, a monkey's favorite action being to copy whatever he sees. Then he stamps his foot which they also do. He realizes that each thing he does they copy so this time he slowly takes off his hat and throws it on the ground. They all take off their hats and throw them on the ground. All colors of hats can be seen floating down to the ground until there is a bright spotted sea of color which the peddler very quickly gathers up, laughing and laughing as he does so. The monkeys laugh and laugh also. And off he goes singing, "I'm on my way with hats to suit each kind of day." He is so happy now with the joke he has played on the monkeys that he sells all his hats and is back by sunset to tell his wife all the news.

Release:

After this story is told, the children will be eager to release some of their energy and act the story out or move about. The most economical movement would be for the leader to incorporate some of the actions of the story into this release. **If I were the peddler and you were the monkeys, what would you do if I did this?** The leader could shake his fist, stamp his foot, and throw off his imaginary hat to which the children will respond.

Planning and Playing:

Where would the forest be? *Response.* **Over here? Who are the trees?** *Response.* **Get over there to get ready for the monkeys. The rest of you are monkeys. Who's the grandfather monkey? I'll be the peddler coming through the forest with my bag of hats. When do the monkeys get into the bag?** *Response.* **After he's gone to sleep. That's right. Let's begin.** This much needs to be established upon the first playing.

Evaluation:

After it is acted once with the leader promoting the action as the peddler and speaking as the narrator and as the peddler, then a child could be invited to be the peddler. The one problem would be that the child would copy the leader's peddler. In any case the child will be copying something, if not the character, then the story, so the teacher should just encourage more additions to the drama. The scene with the wife could be added. Music could be added or the sounds the monkeys make, if the children haven't already added these. New songs could be made up to accompany the story which all could sing. This would be an exercise using rhyming words and phonics. The plot could be changed slightly so that all occurred at night and the mood would become more eerie (music: *Danse Macabre*). The leader would have to be sensitive to the enthusiasm of the children in order to add interesting variations, and yet not carry on to a point beyond their enthusiasm.

At first the story will be acted out very quickly and not very clearly. To add more dimension, the leader needs to remind the children how they moved as the forest and that she will beat a rhythm on the drum for the trees to begin to grow for the second acting out while narrating to accompany the reactions.

Replaying:
Now the trees begin to grow slowly and when they've reached their full height, the peddler walks through and sings. He's very happy, but he becomes sleepy and so he decides to take a nap. Just then the grandfather monkey. . .who's the grandfather monkey going to be this time?. . .creeps down and grabs the peddler's hat. . ." The story is retold as the children act it out. This is usually a better way to have young children review a story. . .keeping all of them actively involved rather than having them sit and talk about it. Use a drum for a control, tapping the beats in the story according to the movement of the peddler and then the monkeys, and then have them sit down as soon as they are tired, or at the end of a segment. For example, **Nightfall came and the monkeys went to sleep. Lie on your backs. Keep your own space around yourself. Be very still and see if you can hear your own heartbeat.** Give, them something definite to do. **Hear the peddler singing; imagine what the monkeys might have dreamed that night.** Sometimes a story can be acted over as much as ten times. Each time any portion can be added onto. . .action, dialogue, emotion, mood. If children are older, and particularly if their experience is limited another method of preparing to act out a story is to have the leader remind them of the action by the use of questions.

Replanning:
After the peddler sits down and goes to sleep what is the first thing the monkey does? What do the rest of the monkeys do?

When the peddler wakes up, what does he do? What do the monkeys do? Continue until the whole story is reviewed. As soon as it is cast and the places of action are pointed out it is ready to be acted out again.

Beckon

"Let's go play in the giant's garden."

Lesson 3 **THE SELFISH GIANT**
(adapted from the children's story by Oscar Wilde)

Motivation:
Could we make a great big circle and lift a basketball to throw
back and forth. *Response.* Now will someone volunteer to be in
the center and we'll try to hit you below the waist. *Response.*
How about playing *Beckon?* (explained in the glossary section).
A variety of games, such as jump rope, blind man's bluff, and
Beckon can be played as part of the motivation for the story.
After playing they should be calmed and yet exhilarated. Let's
sit over here. Have you ever had a favorite place to play, a
place you wanted to play but weren't allowed to? A place
where you could climb trees? *A secret place in the trees, a
place where an old man lived and he always let us in.* What
were some of the things you would do there? *Hide, have
picnics, climb trees.* We're going to do that in the garden where
we're going.

Stimulus:
It is such a beautiful garden because every spring all the trees
flower and the children want to go in to play after they come
home from school. One spring the giant was not there. In fact he
hadn't been there for several years so the children decided to go
in and play. They knew they were happy there.

Soon he returned from his trip and when he saw all the
children playing there, he yelled out, "My garden is for me to
play in." He had already built a high wall around the outside but
the children had entered anyway so he placed a sign on it which
said "Trespassers will be prosecuted." He was a very selfish giant.

He went to bed and when he woke he could hear the wind
blow and the hail and rain strike the roof. The giant wondered
why spring hadn't come. After many weeks had gone by he was in
his bed and heard the most heavenly music. He thought the King's
musicians must be passing by. The hail stopped and the North
Wind ceased. A delicious perfumed fragrance spread from his
garden to his bedroom. He realized that spring had come at last.
He jumped out of bed to see.

The children were creeping through a hole they had made in
the wall. Wherever they had placed themselves on the branches,
the trees began to flower.

In one corner it was still winter. A little boy held his arms up
trying to reach a branch. The giant's heart melted when he saw
this, and he decided to go downstairs and place the little boy in
the tree. "How selfish I have been," he thought. "Now I know
why spring didn't come." He very softly opened his door to the

garden, but when the children saw him, they all started through the hole except for the little boy who by this time had tears in his eyes and did not see the giant coming. The giant lifted him up into the tree, and the little boy threw his arms around the giant's neck. It was not winter anymore. "I've been very selfish," said the giant. He knocked some of the bricks out and said that the children could come play every afternoon. And every afternoon the giant would play with the children. But one day he remembered that he had not seen the little boy whom he had helped into the tree. He asked the children where their friend was. They said he had gone away. So the giant played with the children less and less often, and he became old and sick.

One day he looked down into the garden and he saw the most marvelous sight. All the trees had white and pink blossoms on them, except the tree where the little boy had been. It had silvery white blossoms with golden fruit. He could see that the boy was very weak and blood was rushing from his hands and sides. He ran downstairs and across the lawn and saw the boy and yelled, "Who has dared to hurt and wound you? Tell me who it is and I will kill them." The boy replied, "These are not wounds of hate, but wounds of love. Once you helped me and let me play in your garden. Now I'm going to take you to play in my garden, in paradise." The giant had knelt before the boy. And when the children came to play that afternoon, they found the giant lying dead under the tree, white blossoms falling on him. They covered him with the remaining blossoms. The story can be changed so that the biblical references are left out. The boy's dialogue at the end could be changed to, "I have been ill and now I must go away. I wanted to thank you for letting me play in your garden." Many variations are possible. The story is so strong that it will stand.

Release:
Have you ever seen a garden like that? *Sometimes in the Spring.* Can you close your eyes and see the garden? Pause. Let's go to the garden in this room. Will you take turns leading us in follow-the-leader all around the garden? Use a tambourine or tambour. The children can gain a sense of the whole room as the garden. The leader can stop them anytime with the two taps on the tambour and add comments. Change leaders. Remember the trees, don't bump into them. All right, come on back.

Planning:
Do you remember how the children got into the garden? *Through the hole in the wall.* What were they doing when the giant saw

them? *Climbing trees.* What else? *Playing tag. Throwing a ball.* And then the giant became very angry. *He yelled at them and said it was his garden. He put up a sign that said you'd go to jail if you played there.* What did the children do? *They ran away.* Then the giant went to sleep. What was happening outside? *It was winter.* What else? *There was a lot of noise of hail and rain outside.* Can we make that noise and sound like winter all together? *Response.* That sounded very frightening. Then what did he hear? *It was spring and he heard some music.* What else was happening? *The children were coming in to play.* What could they be singing? *Response.* What does he see? *Everyone climbing a tree, except the littlest boy who can't get up into one.* Why can't he? *He can't reach.* What does the giant do? *He runs right out and lifts him up.* What do the other children do? *They begin to run and are almost outside the wall.* What does the giant say when he lifts the boy up? *He says what a selfish giant he has been.* And what else? *That the children can come back and play here.* If the children are nearby then they could hear and come back. What does the giant do? *He plays with them.*

Release:

Could he play Beckon with them? Let's see. I'll be the giant. Everyone in a circle. Why don't you be the leader who chooses the person to step into the middle? *Response.* Let's sit down. Something changes in the story. Do you remember what it is? *The little boy is gone.* How does the giant find out? *He asks them and they tell the giant that the boy has gone away.* What does the giant do then? *He doesn't play with them anymore and he gets old and sick.* When does the boy leave? When they play Beckon? Then the giant could leave and all of the other children could play. Does the little boy come back? How do we know? *All the trees change and become so beautiful that the giant goes down to look at them.* What does he find out? *The little boy has been hurt.* What does the giant say and how does he feel? *He's mad, and he says I'll kill them! But the little boy says it's all right because the giant let him play in this garden. And now he had to go.* What happened to the giant? *He started to die and the white blossoms covered him. And the children poured more blossoms on him.* Who's the little boy? How do the children get through the wall at first? *By taking the bricks out.* Show me?

Playing:

Can each one of you find your tree to climb and then imagine that you're up in the top of it? Stretch and reach up. Find an apple or some fruit to eat. Let's get down and begin by taking out

the bricks and coming through the wall. Remind them about handling each brick separately. After they're inside the garden and playing, the leader enters as the giant and guides the action for this first run through. In the character of the giant, the leader can yell at them so that they go back through the wall. The leader then goes back to the castle to sleep and while sleeping gives them the cue for winter noises and the spring noises which follow by means of a monologue.

The children should be coming in to play so that the trees will be transformed. If they're not making the move, then a gentle overt signal from the gaint would help. The narration of the leader in the character of the giant should guide them also. **The trees are all blooming except for one. That's because there's no child in it. I'll go down to the garden to help him.** If they have forgotten to run away remind them in the form of dialogue. **The children are still here. They have made the trees blossom. Why isn't this one tree blooming? Can I help you? Tell your friends that they can come back anytime to play in the garden.**

The children can stay and if they do the giant can address them directly. The playing can be directed by the leader as the giant. In dialogue, the giant can ask about the little boy and return to his castle giving the excuse that he is old and tired. He can also usher the other children out saying he is sick or to come back when they have found their friend. He can moan in his castle about the boy and then give the cue for the boy's appearance by saying that he sees one tree which looks so beautiful that he wants to hurry down to see it up close. A motion for the boy's entrance might be necessary. The leader as giant must engage the boy in dialogue. At first there may be little dialogue.

Evaluation:

Cues should be discussed, how the children feel, how angry the giant is, and what is important in the dialogue so that it can be heard by the other children using their own words. This story has been told to children in grades one through seven and acted out in groups where the ages were mixed. The older children then became narrator and/or giant. Children will redo a story if they like it and other additions can be made. The space concept needs to be reinforced here, particularly when they are in the garden playing and finding their own tree. The concept of leading and following which was introduced during the first part of the lesson follows a principle of giving and receiving which is necessary to creative drama.

Extension:
Since the giant's house can be easily imagined by the children it might be selected by the leader as a possible living quarters for many orphaned children. Working in drama with young children should be based on a project in which they are aware that their assistance is needed. When the importance and seriousness of the task is understood, their self-image gains stature.

Motivation:
Do you remember the giant's garden that we just played in? I received a letter from him and I want to read it to you.

Dear Class:
I am getting old and I can't take care of this large house any more. I remember that you children liked to play in the garden. So you may continue to play there whenever you wish.

There are many things I have had to leave behind in the basement and in some of the upstairs rooms. I hope you and your teacher can make use of these things.

The house is for sale, but whoever buys it will need to do a bit of fixing.

Say hello to everyone for me.

Sincerely,

Andrew Moss
Giant

I wonder where the giant has gone? I wonder what a large man like him who lives so far away from town would have stored in his basement? If people were going to live there what would they need to store? If the children seem concerned about the giant, and in a state of wonderment about his house, then the prospect of exploring it could be included. However if they seem disrespectful and ready to take over, another facet might be introduced:

Are there people who don't have homes of any kind? If answers are either evasive or unclear, bring the discussion to a personal and more immediate level. Where I work there are some children who don't have parents. Do you think having a permanent place to live where the children could all be together would help them to be happier? What do people need in order to live? Do you think we'll find those kinds of things in the giant's house?

Planning:

Mr. Moss said there were a lot of supplies stored away in some of the rooms and in the basement. What do you think an old person living out in the country would need to store? Let's write these things down. This probably should be done on the board by the teacher as dictated by the children. Now can you copy them on your piece of paper to be sure that we have a good account of what we might find? Whenever you come to any of these items be sure you check them off or remember what there is. Where are we going first? I think we'd better all stay together until we draw a map and are more familiar with the place. Do we know the way?

Playing:

After the journey is taken, the area explored, all can return to talk about the items found. Further exploration can result in a map being drawn of the house.

Replanning:

If a number of children are going to live there what do you think they will need? How much space do you think each one will require? What would you want to place in this space? *A bed, box for toys, some drawers, closet space.* What else?

Replaying:

Now find a space on the floor and walk around in it. See if you can find a place for all the items you've mentioned. Measure the items with your body. Drawings may be made on shelf paper by each child. Measuring devices using the body lengths to equal precise dimension might be used.

Replanning:

Do you think the children would be able to live in this house? If not, can you think of any way we could change it so they could? How would we be able to buy it? Would we be able to sell any of the things that we found? Do you think Mr. Moss would have some ideas? Do you think he would come back if we asked him? What do you think he might need? There are many answers to these questions, and scenarios would develop accordingly. If the children said that Mr. Moss should return, and they would help to care for him, then the scenario can develop in such a way as to find him. The house might be shared to accomodate the orphans with Mr. Moss's help.

The leader may direct the questions so that the children help make decisions about whether or not to buy the house, how to raise money to buy the house and what kinds of living agreements it would be wise to keep. Essentially the children would be making decisions, later applying these decisions to group activities and individual concerns that affect daily living. Action should follow each decision so that children practice and test their choices.

After children feel comfortable in an imaginary place, the same area can be called forth in the classroom as needed by the children. Using this private space as solace the theme of running away from home could be played.

Have you ever thought of running away from home? Would you go to a place where you felt wanted? Where would you go? *To the Giant's house.* Would you stay there long? What would you be thinking about on the way? How would you feel? Do you think anyone would miss you? Whom would you meet? Well, let's get ready! The action may include the children packing their bags, going on a journey, perhaps spending the night, meeting each other, and talking to each other about their common experiences.

As a conclusion and way for the group to alleviate its member's private experiences so that they represent a commonly shared experience, ask questions such as the following: What was it like? How did it feel? Why do you think you did it?

In both the orphan children and the experiences of leaving home themes, there is a common motivation of rejection. This motivation stems from many private experiences which, when shared, provide a strength through relationship and indentification.

"*The animals slept and were warm under the snow.*"

Lesson 4 A SACRIFICE

A story which requires an attitude of calm from the children follows. This story combines the quality of Indian life and its closeness to nature with that of Western Christmas, and may be used to explore trade and sacrifice.

Motivation:

The instructor can begin by asking questions basic to developing a drama. **What kind of animal character would you like to become? Where do you want to be?** It is then possible to blend the dramatic elements of time, place and characterization into any scenario. Within large groups, many characters can be included, while time and place are both necessary requirements to provide conflict. The attention of young children frequently requires continual re-focusing upon an object or action, in order to guide their thinking and imagination. **Close your eyes and see if you can hear where I walk. Don't open your eyes until I ask you.** The leader should make several patterns around the children before asking them to point to where he walked. **How would you walk on snow in order not to leave tracks?** *Response.* **Think of something you want for Christmas, and draw it in the snow.** *Response.*

Stimulus:

All of you are animals and it is winter. You have found your own place to be warm. But you also smell a hunter who is stalking you for prey. After a time, the hunter finally goes away without finding anything to shoot. The leader may wish to become the antagonist. As soon as the hunter leaves, all of you wait until night, then come out of your hiding places very quietly and take all your belongings with you. Because it is night, you have to keep your eyes on a tiny bird that is leading you through the gloom. You also have to watch for danger.

During these actions, the leader should play music to accompany the children's journey and intensify their search. Moussorgsky's *Pictures at an Exhibition* is one piece of music that may be used. It is cold and dark, but you must follow the little bird. After traveling through the night, the bird alights on the outside of a cave. There is a voice inside which calls all of you. Inside the cave, there is a warm fire. Everyone sit down and warm yourself, then all become hungry. A voice is heard, speaking to you. "There is enough food buried below you to satisfy your hunger. Take and eat what you need, and gather all the rest to last you through the winter." After the children have acted out the digging and eating, the leader should again narrate the mysterious voice:

"Are you willing to sacrifice your most treasured possession or Christmas presents for the food? If not, you may have to remain hungry." *Response.* "Now that you have eaten and are warm, I will tell you why the bird led you here. I am old, and will soon die. When this happens, you are to spread my ashes through the forest so that a new forest will grow in the spring that will protect you. Now, you must be tired and need to sleep." With this announcement, the voice fades away and the animals lay down and go to sleep.

In the morning when they awake, all the animals notice that the voice is gone, but in its place the bird stands over a pile of ashes. They all take the ashes, and place them carefully into their pockets. Then the bird leads them through the forest back to their homes. Each has plenty to eat for the winter, and soon the sounds of spring can be heard. When this happens, the animals remember the ashes, and spread them throughout the forest. In every place that they scatter the ashes, trees begin to grow. Soon, the forest is a thicket of trees and bushes, and the animals easily hide from the hunters. They also follow the little bird back to the cave for protection whenever they need its safety.

"Only my potion has power to cure you."

Lesson 5 THE FUZZIES

Young children need preparation to participate in the free-flowing processes of thought and action necessary to become fully involved in creative dramatics. Exercises contained early in Chapter Three provide many vehicles for obtaining this involvement.

Motivation:

One method of rechanneling and focusing attention is to directly involve the children in building a story. The leader can again begin by asking those questions used in *Lesson 4, A Sacrifice.* **What kind of characters would you like to become? What time of year is it? Where do you want to be?** By obtaining answers to these questions, the basic setting of a scenario may be easily obtained. The leader may then match the situation to a story, experience, or anecdote. From their answers, the leader decides whatever aspect of the scenario matches the children's level of excitement.

Stimulus:

While telling the story the leader can move, helping the children to acquire a kinesthetic response to its events. **There was once a town full of happy people. They were happy because everyone had these wonderful, delightful creatures called fuzzies. The fuzzies were soft, warm, and cuddly. Each fuzzy could give a family as much food as they needed, delicious food like ice cream and watermelons and chocolate cake. They would clean their houses and help with whatever work needed to be done. Because there were plenty of fuzzies, the people freely gave them to their neighbors, and received them as gifts.**

Now in the town there was also a magician, who used to sell magic potions to make them happy. But since the fuzzies arrived in town, he had nothing to sell. He thought long and hard, and finally decided that he should tell the people that the fuzzies would run out if people kept giving them away.

The townspeople had never considered the possibility that the fuzzies might run out! There were always more than enough fuzzies to go around. But as they looked around, the magician's words and spells made them think that there were fewer fuzzies than there had been before. There really weren't, of course. It was just their imagination and fear clouding their reason and thoughts.

The people began to spread the word that the magician had said the fuzzies would run out, and began to hoard them. Some people even began to steal the creatures. In a short time, all the fuzzies were kept in cages with big locks, and were very unhappy. Because they were unhappy, the delicious food and work that the

fuzzies gave gladly, soon ran out, and the people were reduced to poverty and unhappiness. The magician could sell his potions again and he was the only happy person in the entire town.

One day a person was revisiting the town and noticed the difference. He had brought a fuzzy back with him and showed the people that a fuzzy could do anything if they were given away. This made the magician so angry, he protested. Someone gave him a fuzzy, and he became happy for the first time in his life. Now he knew what the people had felt. He, too, began giving fuzzies away.

Release:

Can you tell me what a fuzzy is like? Show me a fuzzy! Hold one and throw it up and down. Can you do different things with it? What are some of the things you can do with it? Why didn't the magician like the fuzzies if they could do anything?

Playing:

All of you are in the town giving and receiving fuzzies until the magician comes. Acting the role of the magician, the leader goes through the story responding to the children's reactions. In this way the leader can give the children cues for involvement. **Look at all those people down there, they're happy and I'm not. They won't buy any of my potions. I know what I'll do!** The leader will soon be able to recognize children who wish to play a particular character by their reaction to the story questions, becoming more vocally or physically involved than their classmates. Each time it is replayed the leader can ask the children for more of the story, adding to their involvement. Action and dialogue is narrated by the leader until the children begin adding their own.

Many of the scenario outlines contained in Chapter Five lend themselves to the lesson plan described above. Although intended primarily for improvisation, teachers may wish to explore other possibilities earlier in the creative dramatics progression.

Lesson 6 THE CAVE - A JOURNEY

Motivation:
Think of the space in front of you as being like clay or a substance you can mold easily. See if you can make an actual form with it. The shape you make doesn't have to be a definite thing like a horse or a castle or a statue. Just feel the air as a substance. Begin. *Response.* Use other parts of your body besides your hands. Use your back, your elbows. Get underneath your object and all around it. Begin to move the object toward the center of the room. Give it a push. Put a rope around it. Pull it in. Attempt to divide the room of children in half: Those on this side of the room take the shape of the object you've made or something non-human. Both directions might be needed to supply the child with an image. Those on this side move close enough together so you can make one shape. Get as close together as possible without touching. Now see if the rest of you can get through this jungle of bodies without touching them by trying to move your body into as many shapes as you need.

Begin with the music *Hall Of The Mountain King*, by Grieg. Some positive comments should be made about the difficulty which helped them to create so many unusual shapes with their bodies. This time those who are moving through the bodies are going to be surrounded on both sides by trolls. You will be moving down a pathway inside a cave through the middle of the trolls. Those who didn't move last time will be weaving in and out, but not touching the visitors as they come through the cave. Also, the visitors to the cave really can't see the trolls. The trolls don't want them to know they're there. They want to get the visitors into their secret room at the back of the cave. As soon as I put the music on, those who moved last time, become the two lines of trolls facing each other. Those who formed the shapes last time become the visitors that move through the trolls. Continue with music. Comments should always be accepted briefly and questions asked in relation to what was set up. Let's sit **down.**

Stimulus and Planning:
We're going to take a walk through a cave, but what kind of a cave is it going to be? *A mountain cave, an undersea cave.* What grows in an undersea cave? What would the sides of the walls feel like? Can you feel it in your hand? Let's see. Demonstrate by moving together the fingers and the palm of one hand. **How many things can we name that we could find in an undersea cave?** *Cobwebs, moss, insects, spiders, bats, slime, rocks, branches, pools of sea water, lichens, fungi, fossils, a skeleton, treasure.*

What if we wanted to collect some of these things? What would we need to carry? *A bag, a flashlight.* But even with a flashlight it's still very dark. Besides a flashlight what else would we need to be sure of finding our way? *A rope, or feel along the wall, or hang onto someone's sweater.* Look around in here. There's nothing in the way, nothing to trip over or fall over. We're going on a blind walk.

Release:
You're going to be led around as freely as you trust your partner. On the way, I want your partner to give you the chance of touching those things in this room which would give you some of the experiences of touching unusual things like those in the cave that we mentioned. I'm placing you in the trust of your partner. Decide which of you will be led this time and which will lead. Pause. **Begin.** Same music. We'll do it again only with a few changes. Change some of the directions for those who are being led. Invent objects that your blind partner must step over. At this point take a child and ask him to close his eyes. Tell him to walk along until you tell him to step up. Step down. What other objects can you think of? *Branches, water.* Here are some real chairs they can sit in. Here's a box they can step over or jump from. Invent turns they need to take and have them touch objects that will be newly scattered around as soon as the new "blind" person closes his eyes. Two different boxes of unique objects can be provided that have unusual textures. **Begin.** Music.

Planning:
Let's sit down. Did you think of any new objects that could be found in the cave? *Response.* What are we trying to find in this cave? *Treasure, monsters.* If you find anything that you want to bring home with you, what do you need to carry? *A bag.* Who's going to lead the way? Where's the entrance to the cave? Remember it's very dark and you need to lead yourself by one hand along the sides of the cave and hold your flashlight with the other hand or hold onto someone in front of you if you don't have a flashlight.

Playing:
Ready. When I begin the music start through the cave. Play music to end. Stop the music. The cave is filling up with water. The tide is moving in because the tide is rising. Should we get out now? Our chances are good. Or should we continue toward the treasure and have to hurry? *We can come back.* Even if a few want to stay inside, most of them will want to be safe and it is the leader's

place to lead and channel their replies into a single structure at first. **All right, let's leave and we can come back.**

Replanning:
Let's rest and plan our return trip to find the treasure. Let's have some trolls. Volunteers? Who will find the treasure? Who will help carry it? What kind of movements would the trolls make toward the visitors? Remember the trolls don't want to touch them or let them know they're there. Why? *Response.* **Let's listen to the end of the music and see if you can visualize what's happening. Play the music to the end. It should last anywhere from one to two minutes.**

What did you see? *The trolls don't want to frighten them away because they want the visitors to get back to the secret room. They've created a monster back there because they've taken out his heart. When the door opens, the light from the room with the monster inside is so bright that the trolls disappear. The monster gives them the box and follows them out because inside the box is his heart.*

The leader can organize his thoughts in any way that allows the children to go and return as a group with some purpose and escape from some antagonistic force which the music suggests. **Where do you find the treasure? Who will carry it? Why don't the trolls want to be seen? What happens to the trolls? When do they disappear?** *When the music is strongest and the monster comes.* **How could we end it?** *Taking out the monster's heart from the box.* **Who will do the ending?** *Response.* Since the music only runs about three and a half minutes they might want to repeat it until they perform their actions in coordination with the music, changing parts each time.

". . .step in the middle of the cake and become the electric beater."

Lesson 7 **THE PARTY**

The following outline extracts the two main parts of the longer lesson plan explained in the first part of this chapter. The most important sections of the lesson plan are those included below: the motivation, or warm-up, and the main body of the lesson, produced by the stimulus. Under each heading are steps which should be clear in the leader's mind if he is to proceed without a paper in his hand.

LESSON PLAN OUTLINE FOR YOUNGER CHILDREN

I.   Motivation or warm-up: Getting ready for school or getting up in the morning.

A.   Brushing your teeth

B.   Getting dressed

C.   Eating breakfast

II.   Stimulus (e.g., a leading question): What would be some of the things you would do if you were getting ready for a party?

A.   Buying things in the store

B.   Making a cake

C.   Decorating the room

When beginning creative dramatics, it's easier to offer simple structures that the children can develop; in this way the leader's control and their involvement is insured. To channel their ideas a leading question should be asked.

Motivation:
   What are some of the things you have to do to get ready for school in the morning? *Get dressed, brush my teeth, decide what to wear, put on my shoes and socks.* **Each one find his space and choose one of those things to do? Do it slowly. Take your time and as soon as you hear the two taps, freeze.** *Response.* **Two taps. I saw so many different things. I wish you would share them with us. Maybe we could do that by getting into groups.**
   All of you be in the first group. Designate those and physically have them move into a separate group. **Same for groups two and three. Would you all move as slowly as you can. As if you just**

woke up. Like this. Tap on the drum to provide a gauge for tempo. See if those of you in the other two groups who are watching can find out how many ways there are to get ready for school. Do just what you were doing before. Ready? *Response.* Always, after children have performed, make some comment that is pertinent and that will help the understanding of those watching. The second group begin but would you use a speed like this? Produce taps that are faster. Ready? *Response.* Now the third group, speed up because you're going to be late for school. Ready? *Response.* Several variations can continue for future lessons using the same material which young children will not tire of. The above could be used as a warm-up either for the following two variations, or for the next lesson. 1) Now this is group one, this is group two, and this, three. Remember your group number. I'm going to call your group's number and only your group can move. The other groups partly freeze but be ready to move as soon as I call your number. Move in the same way you've been moving — waking up, getting dressed, and so on. Ready. 1.....2.....3..... I'm going to count again and mix up your numbers, but this time I'm going to call them a little faster. Listen for the drum beat because you've been doing it at a regular pace, and I'm going to change the speed. Ready. 2--slow; 1--fast; 3--regular speed. This can be continued many times around changing speeds after which some rest should be taken. If they are resting by sitting on the floor, the next part can be explained and tried first in this sitting position and then done in a standing position.

The second variation: 2) Let's have all teeth brushers in the first group, all the dressers in the second group, and all the breakfast eaters in the third group. Remember last time when we changed the numbers and the speeds? Let's see if we can do that again.

Stimulus and Playing:
The second or main part of the lesson could be approached by asking for their answers to a leading question. What would be some of the things we would need to do first if we were getting ready for the party? Now as soon as I put the music on, find your own space, and a magic rope. Follow the rope until the music stops. *Response.* Now this is group one, this two, and this is three. Groups have been reshuffled by the movement. Let's begin at the beginning by waking up. Today is Saturday, the day of the party, and you're excited. Down on the floor. As the music and my voice tell you, begin to wake up. Music should be lyrical at first and move into an energetic tempo. Speak over the music. **You**

wake up and you get dressed—don't forget shoes and socks—eat your breakfast; it's your favorite. Feel how heavy the spoon is, and show where the bowl is. You want to taste each bite. Finish up and carry your dishes to the sink. Now go to brush your teeth. Let's see how many different ways there are of brushing teeth. If they are familiar with having groups called individually while the other groups stop to watch, then the numbers of the groups can be called so that each group can watch the other. **Let's see how many different ways there are of eating breakfast? Can you show what you are eating and if you like it or not?** They need to be reminded of physical properties so that they can respond through action. Kinesthetic memory of daily activities can be restored by the dual challenge of being prompted by the leader's direction and being witnessed by an audience.

Evaluation and Planning:

At this time lead a discussion based on their observations. **Did anyone see an unusual way in which someone brushed his teeth?** *Response.* **What did he do?** *Response.* **Who gargled or brushed his tongue?** *Response.* **Did anyone get the mirror spotted or spill water on the floor?** Two drum beats.

Today is the day of the party! Let's have group one go shopping. **What will you get?** *Response.* **Where is the store entrance?** *Response.* **Show us the stalls.** *Response* **Who will be the cashier?** *Response.* **Who is the clerk?** *Response.* **Where will he be? Between the aisles? You might need to ask for help. In group one, each person enter and get your supplies. Are we ready? Do you know what you are going to get?** Those of you who are sitting watch one or two people and try to see what they are buying. **Talk if you want to. Begin.** *Response.* Two taps. **Come on back and sit down. What did Fred buy?** *Response.* **Was it clear? Why, why not?**

Which group will make the cake? *Group two.* **Who bought the cake decorations in group one? And the cake ingredients from the store? Is the cake a box cake or made from scratch? Who knows how to make a cake from scratch? Let's see everyone make a cake and Claudia will tell us what to do. Anyone else who knows?**

Playing:

They could pantomime the cake making from a sitting position making small gestures or use the *lilliputian exercises* which could serve as an opportunity for movement in relation to the degree of their restlessness.

Each person has a bowl in front of him. What do we put into the bowl—first—? Go through the whole process helping the children to direct the actions of baking a cake individually. Let's have group two bake a cake all together. Right in front of us is a very large bowl–this big–. We all stand around it in a semi-circle. Will those two other groups who are sitting watch and help us out. What do we put in first? This process is repeated, only this time the lilliputian exercise is used. Will two of you step into the middle of the cake and become the electric beater. The rest of us can turn the bowl. Now all together, let's pour the cake into the pan. And shove the pan into the oven, carefully. Two taps. Rest.

Evaluation and Planning:

Let's have some comments from the audience. Could you see the ingredients go into the bowl? *Response.* Could you see the bowl? *Response.* The pan? Did the hard work show on their faces? *Response.*

What shall we do while it's baking? Remember we have to do something quiet while it's baking or else the cake will fall. What can we do so the cake won't fall and still get ready for the party? *Response.* Decorate? Who bought the table cloth in group one? Let's all help everyone in group three. Everyone up to put the table cloth on. The other groups watch to see what we do and how we handle any objects.

Playing:

Give suggestions. First, the table cloth needs to be spread. Paper plates? At first, reaching for objects in the air is all right, but having established that group one bought the party supplies at the store, group one should continue to supply them. Somebody get the napkins, the forks, the spoons, the party hats. Place everything around the table.

What about the cake? Why don't we all take the cake out and ice it? Let's cool it first, and make the icing. Who knows how to make icing? This can be used as a large group activity or an individual activity, but everyone is involved. If it is an individual activity: Everyone find your space. If it is a large group activity: All those who are icing the cake make a large circle–all those who become the cake get together in the center. The rest of us make a large circle around them. Let's take the cake out carefully and move it to the center of the floor. Let it cool. How does the cake move when it cools? *Response.* Now let's make the icing. Who knows how to make the icing? Move to those who give suggestions and help them direct actions. Small actions should be done in front of the body while the "cake" cools and settles down. Then spread the icing on the "cake" group. Let's carry the cake over and place it on the table. Rest and sit down in your groups.

Planning:

What about the other decorations? Could one person at a time in group three add some kind of decoration to the room. Get help if you need it. Before you start let's have suggestions from the group. What decorations might we have? *Nut cups, streamers, hats, games, puppets.* Whisper each thing into their ears as they enter area, unless they are able to think of a decoration by themselves. Which of you who watched could go into the room to use the puppets and show us where they are. Who remembers where the streamers were hung? One child at a time from the other groups, one and two, is asked to enter the playing area and handle one of the decorations. Show us what it is by the way you handle and use it. Remember the weight and where you're placing it. *Response.* Good. According to the lesson plan procedure all the action should be revised through the children's answers as a result of the teacher's questions. What did we do first? *Got up, got dressed, ate, brushed our teeth.* What did group one do to get ready for the party? *Went to the store and bought the cake and ingredients and decorations.* What did we do next to get ready for the party? *Everyone baked his own cake.* What were the steps for baking the cake? *Measuring flour, baking powder, sugar, butter, and then stirring them together. Beating the eggs and combining them. Greasing the pan. Pouring the whole thing into the pan. Putting it into the oven.*

What did group two do to get ready for the party? *Set the table.* Where did they get their supplies? *From group one.* What did we do next to get ready for the party? *Everyone made icing and spread it on the cake.* What did group three do? *Decorate.* Let's start from the beginning and act out the whole thing from sleeping. Ready? *Response.*

Now we're ready to have our party. But we haven't discussed why we're having a party or whose party it is. Suggestions should be accepted that would appeal to most of the children's imaginations like those connected with fantasy characters rather than the personal friend of a few. There is also the logical reason for having a party which would be a celebration or surprise. These facts would be considered in a sequence story later but for now provide motivation for playing out the party only.

Let's start at the beginning. When would someone announce the idea about having the party? After we wake up. . .eat our breakfast. . .get dressed? Who's going to do that? Several might raise their hands. What are you going to say? *Let's have a party. We're going to have a party.* After everyone's dressed I'll turn the music down and beat on the drum three times. That's your cue.

Then what happens? *They go to the store.* How do we know? *Someone says so.* Who? *I will.* Let's have the same people be the cashier and clerk in the grocery store. What happens next? *Everyone bakes the cake.* How do we know? *Someone says so.* Who? The whole sequence can be reviewed here if it is felt to be necessary in order to include dialogue. What happens next? *Group two bakes the cake.* After this? *Everybody ices it.* Next. *Group three decorates.* When each group is doing its activity, what is everyone else doing? *Watching.* There are only two times when everyone is up working together, when are these times? *When everyone's baking and icing.*

What are the things we're going to add this time? *People talking.* Do you remember what signal I'll use for people to talk? *Three taps.* After what? After I turn down the music. So there's going to be music all the time. All those who are going to talk raise your hands. What are you going to say? *We're going to have a party. We have to go to the store. Let's all bake the cake. Group two bakes the cake. Let's all ice the cake. Group three decorates.* Who says the party person is coming? What are you going to say? *Here he comes.* Then what is everyone going to do? *Hide.* You are all so good to remember so much and help each other. . .so you can all go to the party. All these points can be placed in simple outline form on the board as indicated in the beginning.

Playing:

Let's begin with the music and play the music again at the end when the birthday person comes. I'll play the music all the time and between each part, turn it down, tap three times on the drum, as a cue for the person to say his part. And I'll do the same when the birthday person is supposed to come. The whole piece can be played through with the leader's help as the narrator or side coach. In a group discussion have leading questions to formulate positive criticism.

Evaluation:

What did you enjoy? What could be changed? Why? Where were you confused? Why? Variations and suggestions for change and extension can be brought out by the leader.

Replanning:

Who would like to narrate our story? Perhaps there could be several narrators. What main events would the narrator need to remember? I. Buying, baking; II. Baking, icing; III. Decorating.

How about changing groups this time? Whose suggestion will it be to have a party? After this, which group will go to the store? Who will be a clerk? A cashier? Which group will make the cake? Which group will decorate? Who will be the person whose party it is? What kind of person could he be? A magic person? Could we end it by having him take us to a magic place? *Where we'd all have a birthday.* Oh, that's a good idea. What would he say. *Come with me we'll all have birthdays today. And that's the end.*

Release:

Let's try an exercise to put into our story. Make a large circle. Every other person step inside the circle and sit down. The people on the outside give those in the circle room by stepping back. Those on the outside are the cake makers. As they put in their ingredients, those in the circle become the ingredients and show what you are in movement. Cake makers, will you say what you are putting in? As soon as I start to play the music will the cake makers begin one at a time to say what ingredients they are putting in and those underneath them who are inside the circle move either the way the music or the ingredients makes you feel. When we get to the icing makers let's do the same thing but switch groups.

There are many parts in this lesson which could be done individually. The whole lesson could be a culmination of several months of work. These patterns of organization can be repeated using different leading questions: anything which younger children would like to do on Saturday, going to the zoo, going to the beach, making a garden. Circuses and fairs have performance aspects that would be more difficult to try at first. Each part could be tried and then added onto as it is written, but the progression would have to be gradual. It is always necessary to plan a little while sitting down, using the two taps for a signal, acting this portion out, and sitting down again. Longer intervals of passive and active participation sustain the children's energy so they neither get too tired nor become too restless.

It is always possible to rework large group scenes such as tried in the cake making sections so that new arrangements are added.

"Look the Earth is falling in!"

Lesson 8 **THE HARE THAT RAN AWAY**

The main sections of the longer lesson plan included at the beginning of this chapter used many steps. Among these, the most necessary that the leader should work out in some detail are the steps of motivation (or warm-up) and stimulus (or body). The following outline includes important elements of the lesson which the leader should keep clearly in mind while working with the children. As has been mentioned, it is always possible to vary the lesson away from the structured form, once that form or structure has become established. The mistake is to have no form at all. In this instance many experienced teachers, as well as beginners, become lost.

LESSON PLAN FOR MIDDLE GRADE CHILDREN

I. Motivation—alphabet writing with the body

 A. Connect lines and spaces with emotion

 B. Connect lines and spaces to rhythm

 C. Connect rhythm and emotion to character

II. Stimulus

 A. Simple story acted out individually so that everyone is the same character in his own space, thinking about the connection of emotion and rhythm to character.

 B. More complex story

  1) Five different groups of characters each with a distinct rhythm

  2) Five different group positions on stage

  3) Five different group times for entrance

Motivation:
 Get into several circles or one large circle. Think of your body as a pencil and very quickly write the next letter of the alphabet using your whole body. I'll start. The instructor forms the letter "A". Continue with the alphabet until all have had a chance to do a letter.

Now write any letter and pantomime an action or thing beginning with that letter. I'll start. The instructor writes the letter "O". Then accompanies the letter with the action of eating an orange. Did I pantomime an action beginning with that letter or use something beginning with that letter? *You used something.* I'll do one more. Strike at a ball twice then three times and get angry when striking OUT. Was that using an object beginning with the letter or performing an action beginning with the letter? *Performing an action.* Who will start? *Response.*

Now look around the room and try to see as many different lines as you can. Is a line always straight? Can you find one that isn't? Is there one line in the room that you can show us with the motion of your body as you've been doing with the alphabet? I wonder if we can find the line in the room? Can you show us which line it is? Can we make that line? Can you show us again? Does anyone else have a line to show us? Now, could you go up to the object and make the line right in front of it? Can we make the line following him? Everyone turns toward the child to follow him in making the line. Think of this line being around your body. Now can you fill the space inside. All of us are enclosed in lines that make up a large box; let's all try together to fill the space inside the box. Fill only the space that isn't being filled. See how many different lines are being made. If I play this kind of music how would you make your lines? Play slow, sad music. *Slowly.* How would you walk? *Heavy.* How would you feel? *Sad.* Can you be sad with your whole body? What kind of line do you make when you're sad? How do you fill the space. What kind of line would you make with your body to this music and how would you fill the space? Play music which is light and staccato. *Response.* Let's sit down and rest. Would you listen right where you are with your whole body to this sound. Make noises on percussion instruments and after each one invite children to illustrate sound language with body language. Continue the same in the story. By getting up and sitting down could you make a line with your body to go with the sound? Sometimes we repeat lines that are the same. Like this / / /. How would you walk to this? What if we changed that slightly: / ♦ ♦ ♦ / ♦ ♦ ♦ / or / / / ♦ ♦ ♦ / / / ♦ ♦ ♦ . Would you walk? Hop? Or run? When we repeat lines in space, we have rhythm. Do you know the story of Peter Rabbit? What kind of rabbit was Peter? *Eager, curious.* Have any of you ever felt like Peter? How did you feel? How did Peter move? What did his mother warn him not to do? *Not to go to Farmer McGregor's garden, but he went anyway.* Where did he go in the garden? *To the lettuce patch and then to eat other vegetables.* As he was rounding the cucumber patch who do you think he saw? *The farmer.* And the farmer saw him and was after him. I'll be the farmer and all of you be Peter. Peter ran and ran and he ran right into a gooseberry net. He couldn't get loose and he thought his time had come. There he was stuck in the gooseberry net by the gold buttons on his blue jacket. And as Mr. McGregor was coming, a bird swooped down and helped to free him. He was off again. This time to avoid the farmer, he ran to the toolshed and jumped right into a can of water. The farmer was sure he had seen him somewhere in the toolshed and he looked all around. Suddenly Peter sneezed and Mr. McGregor was after him. He jumped out of the can and out of the window, and the farmer could not reach him so he went back to work. Peter was exhausted and wet and extremely frightened. He didn't know where to go. So he tried to find his way straight across the garden to the fence. There was a wheelbarrow which he jumped into. As he was looking over the wheelbarrow he could see Farmer McGregor hoeing. But beyond him was the gate. Peter got out of the wheelbarrow as quietly as he could. He ran as fast as he could right for some berry bushes which were at the side of the gate and slipped under the gate. Peter just kept running until he got home.

When Peter got home he didn't feel very well and his mother put him to bed and gave him some comfrey tea.

All of you were really playing the rhythm of the rabbit. I wonder if you could listen to these rhythms and name the animal it might be. Or perhaps you'd like to hear the story and then we can decide what rhythm the animals have. Frequently, after so much activity, the children would prefer to hear the story. Providing rhythms first is working in abstraction, but may be suitable for older groups. The following story is adapted from an Indian fable.

Stimulus:

And it came to pass that the Buddha came back to life as a lion. He wanted to help his fellow animals just as he had his fellow-man. There was much to be done; for instance, in one part of the forest there was a nervous little hare who was always thinking, "Suppose the Earth were to fall in, what would happen to me?" And she thought about it and thought about it. "Suppose the Earth were to fall in what would happen to me?" And one day she heard a noise. It was merely a fruit falling against the leaves. But she stood there and listened and because she had thought more and more about the Earth falling in, and also because she was nervous, she yelled, "The Earth is falling in." And she started to run fast through the forest. In the midst of her running, she met a brother hare, "Where are you running so fast,

Sister Hare?" But the little hare only said, "I have no time to stop and tell you. The Earth is falling in and I am running away."

"The Earth is falling in! MY!" And he repeated this to his brother hare, and he to his brother hare, and he to his brother hare, until there were a hundred thousand hares all saying at the same time, "The Earth is Falling In." Then the bigger animals began to take up the same cry, first the pigs, then the monkeys, and next the elephants.

The wise lion overheard them. "There are no signs that the Earth is falling in. However, they must have heard something."

"How did you find out the Earth was falling in?" he asked the elephant.

"I heard it from the monkeys," the elephant replied.

"Well then, how did you find out that the Earth was falling in?"

And the monkey replied, "I heard it from the pigs."

And the pigs said, "I heard it from the hares."

And the hares, said, "We heard it from the little hare."

Then the lion said, "Little hare what made you say that the Earth was falling in?"

The little hare said, "I saw it!"

"You saw it! Where?"

"Right over there. By that tree!"

"Oh well, come with me and I will show you how this happened," replied the Buddha.

"Oh no, I'm not going near there for anything," said the hare.

"But I will take you carefully on my back." And he showed her how a fruit had fallen against a leaf.

Then she said, "The Earth is not falling in." Both of them went back to the other animals and she repeated, "The Earth is not falling in."

And the animals began to repeat gradually one to another. "The Earth is not falling in," until the words became softer and softer. "The Earth is not falling in," and the words died away altogether.

Planning:

Do you remember the four different kinds of animals? Let's see if you can by listening to the drum. What would this one be? Tap the drum slowly. *Elephants.* Yes, elephants. Can the elephants walk over there to that corner? What is this animal? Constant staccato tapping. *Monkeys.* Good, monkeys go over to that corner. And this rhythm? Two taps and a pause as we suggested for Peter. *Rabbits.* All the rabbits hop over to that corner. And the last. Just listen. Tap two slow and then a sound made by the tapper dragging across the drum. *Pigs.* Pigs over there. Now we need a little hare and some brother hares. Hares stand in the center. And a lion. Lion stand deep in the forest over there. The story can be retold using the rhythm pattern to designate the animal. It might be necessary to review the rhythm patterns in succession. I want you to listen and whenever you think you hear your animal's rhythm begin to move to the center of the room and then back into the forest. Now this time I'll play two phrases of the rhythm which will take you to the center of the room, and if I play two more phrases that means that you leave the center and go back to the forest. Play alternately two phrases for one group, two for another. This will leave the two groups in the center together, until they respond to the next two phrases which takes them back into the forest. What happens when the rabbits meet the pigs? *They tell them the Earth is falling in.* And when the pigs meet the monkeys? *They tell them the Earth is falling in.* Who tells the lion the Earth is falling in? *The elephants.* How do you think the lion would talk? *With a deep voice.* How is this sound for his rhythm pattern? Tap very slow and loudly. Does the lion believe the elephant? *No. He asks them how they found out.* What do they say? *They say that the monkeys told them.* Then what does he do? *He asks the monkeys.* What do the monkeys say? *They say that the pigs told them.* What does he do then? *He goes to the pigs.* And then what do the pigs say? *That the rabbits told them.* What finally happens? Can someone finish the story for us? *The rabbits say that the little hare told them. The lion finds the little hare and asks her. She says that she heard the noise. When he asks her where she heard it, she points to a tree. And then he takes her over to the tree. Just then a berry falls on a leaf. The lion says that was the sound she heard. The Earth was not falling in. She says, "The Earth is not falling in." The lion takes her back to the other animals. She says "The Earth is not falling in." And all the other animals say, "The Earth is not falling in."*

Playing:

Now let's act it out. And when you hear the rhythm of your animal, then that's when you begin to move.

"The trip to earth had become real!"

Lesson 9 **A TRIP TO EARTH**

Motivation:

After making music on percussion instruments, invite children to illustrate sound language with body language. For example, in the comic strips sound and body language are almost interchangeable. One amplifies the other. A good way to accomplish this is through charades. The leader could begin by taking on the body position related to the sound during sleep. The action of sleeping is depicted by having both hands under and supporting one cheek while the head is tilted. The children can then supply the sound. This sound would convey snoring or the comic caricature of "Zz-zz." Show other examples. Then reverse the order; the leader provides the sound "G'rrr," and the children get into the position of a mad dog. The game can be extended by having them freeze as soon as they get into position with the first to freeze and appear kinesthetically involved to be pointed to by the leader. The designated child becomes the next to provide the sound as a stimulus for the others. The game could continue in this fashion, including variations as discoveries are made.

Stimulus:

I'm going to tell a story but I need your help. If I want lots of noise, I'll do this, move hands up, palms going toward ceiling. And when I want less noise, this, Hands, palms going down. I'll signal no noise by moving my hands away from each other, in a horizontal direction with palms facing the floor. Whenever I mention the scientists working in their laboratory mixing different chemicals, you can help by making this noise, "Blurp, blurp." So whenever I do this what do you say? Provide the action of pouring from one beaker or tube into another. *Blurp. Blurp.* And they pulled levers which went "klunk" and turned wheels which sounded like "errr-up." Now I'll do all these actions together and see if you can remember them. *Blurp, blurp. . .klunk, klunk. . .errr-up.* Any action the leader can create when he introduces sound can be used.

There's more. A large comet tore through the sky, "Whoosh," and landed, "Boom." The crowd heard about it and police came, "Ummmmmmm." A little mouse gets involved. "Squeek, squeek." Sounds of a party are heard.

Now we're ready. This is a story about a man who lived on the moon. He was so bored that he just sighed most of the time. He couldn't wait to go to Earth because he could see lights and flashes of color and even hear the sounds of music coming from the Earth. So he waited. Meanwhile some scientists were working in their laboratory pouring chemicals. *Blurp, blurp.* And pulling levers. *Klunk, klunk.* And working wheels on their computers. *Errup, errup.* They were looking for a way to go to the moon and had been experimenting for a long time with their inventions. Meanwhile the Man in the Moon sat and became more and more bored and envious of people on Earth. Suddenly a comet started to whiz through the atmosphere and the Moon Man just stuck his arm out and caught it and rode it all the way to Earth. *Whoosh.* And then landed. *Bang.* People who had heard what had sounded like a major explosion hurried to the scene. The policemen, *Ummmm,* came also. The constable insisted that the invader be locked up until further investigation could take place. And so the Moon Man was locked up in jail. He sat and sat and was so lonely until he heard a little mouse. *Squeek, squeek.* Something very strange began to happen. The Moon Man, true to his name, began to wane and become smaller until he became so small that he could climb right through the bars of the jail and escape. He went through a forest and saw the most beautiful trees and little animals with bright yellow wings. And then he heard a party. Lead the children in a party song. . .clapping in rhythm. It was a masquerade party. Someone said, "Look there's someone who came dressed as the Man in the Moon." Well this was what he had been looking for, and he felt right at home. But because there was so much noise at the party someone called the police. *Ummmmmmmmm.* So the Man in the Moon hurried through the forest, and when he came to the edge he saw a very strange looking old building. It looked almost like a castle. When he got to the castle, he walked down long corridors and looked in many rooms. There were two scientists doing experiments. *Blurp, blurp, klunk, klunk, errup, errup.* They told him they were building a rocket to go to the moon and asked him to climb in and try it out. They had been working on it for so long that they had gotten too fat and could no longer fit into it. He thanked them and said that was just where he wanted to go. The Earth was no place for him. And so he was off to his home. *Whoosh.*

Planning:

Let's use the center of the room to act it out. We need a Man in the Moon, scientists, police, constable, people, mouse. Several children can be used for each part. The "people" group can be broken down into various divisions, such as taxicab drivers, ice cream vendors, and newspaper boys. Where is the moon? The lab? The place where the Man in the Moon lands? The jail and the forest? Where should the people come from, police, ice-cream vendors, newsboys, general crowd? After designating places where the players are to be located, have those players take their places. The leader can begin the narration as a cue for them to move. I'll tell the story more slowly than I did before so that when you hear the cue for your part you'll have time to fill in with action just as you did with your voices. The Man in the Moon should use as much of the space around the center as he needs since he catches the comet and is brought to Earth. He can leave the moon, circle the Earth once or twice and land. Also, the people, as they are given their cues, leave the sides, circle around the center and surround the Man in the Moon. Then slowly go away to the sides muttering on cue. As soon as the forest is mentioned all of you at the sides who make up the forest, come out from the sides and turn into individual trees for the Man in the Moon to go through. Then the same people make up the party members, so change from frozen trees to happy, laughing people walking around, noticing each other, shaking hands, talking gibberish, singing and back again to the forest, when you hear the police siren.

The main parts can be joined together during the first time through. Details will be added in when characters are formed, such as the ice-cream vendor's cart and bell. One person needs to be given the line, "Look there's someone who came dressed as the Man in the Moon." Someone also can be cast as the informer who gives the cue for the Man in the Moon to leave. Children who are seated and not participating directly may be encouraged to make the cue sounds under the teacher's direction if necessary.

After the first run-through, a discussion should be held to clear up the direction in which people are traveling during the scenes and in the transitions between the scenes. For the second time through, the class may want to try the whole story by themselves without the aid of a narrator. After the second evaluation, recast, and attempt a third run-through without a narrator.

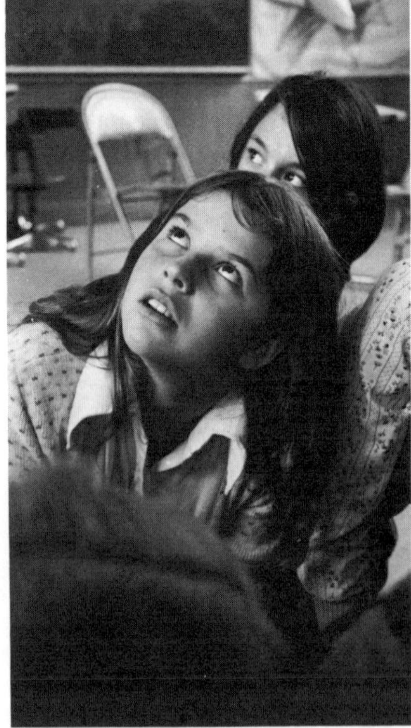

"They had heard a strange cry of which everyone else in the town was afraid."

Lesson 10 **HAUNTED HOUSE**

Motivation:
Close your eyes and listen to all the sounds you can hear. Try to identify those which are near and those which are farther away. Pause. How many different sounds did you hear? *Response.* Let the discussion include any possibilities the sounds may provide as a stimulus for movement. Another sensory warm-up for the development of concentration and imagination might explore the sense of touch such as Exercise 12 in Chapter Three, "See With Your Hands." Close your eyes and keep passing the objects whenever I say change. One half of you are people who are lost in the dark, and I want you to try an experiment. Demonstrate by having one of the children close his eyes and the leader make the sort of movement which would cause him to feel a slight breeze in the air around him. Could you feel or describe any particular kind of motion going on around you? *Response.* Divide the children in the room either arbitrarily or using gesture. This half be the lost people for now and find your space. The rest of you are spirits who move among and around the people. Move noiselessly because you are spirits. Each spirit move around the person so he can't hear you, but he can feel the air move around him. You don't need to touch him. Begin. In many cases the victim feels vibrations of movement and, without hearing or seeing, can describe the actual motions which the "spirit" makes. The anticipation of a new experience can enhance one's expectancies and help increase sensitivity to subtle vibrations. Remind them to relax and not "try" if they get discouraged and can't seem to notice any difference at first. The amount of concentration achieved in order to actually allow for this state of "openness" is worth discussing. When did you begin to feel the vibrations? Why do you think you began to feel something when you hadn't before? How were you different the second time in comparison to the first time? Let's change places and see what happens this time. Now let's sit down. What holiday is coming up? Several common holidays, such as Halloween, might be mentioned. From a number of replies the leader usually has the opportunity to select those which help to focus the lesson. Such a question also allows the sharing of ideas, possibility for action, and allows the leader to set limits. All right, let's take a trip to that abandoned house. What will we find on the way? *Alligators, rooms, cobwebs, ghosts.* With all those good suggestions I want you to listen to a record and let the music help to tell you where you are and what kind of place it is. The record chosen is the slow section of *Silver Apples of the Moon*, Part I; about one and a half minutes to not more than two

minutes is sufficient. If this record is not available electronic music which has an ethereal quality is appropriate. Can you describe what you saw? *Response.* See if you can put that all together in your own way. Find your space and move about in your own imaginary environment. *Response.* I see someone walking through a door, through cobwebs, a lot of slimy snakes. Whatever is commented upon by the leader can partly be based upon what was said in reaction to the children's responses from having listened to the music. Verification of the images by the leader encourages the group and individuals to strive to create and overcome their rigidity. What were some of the experiences you had? And where did you visit? By pulling out some of their comments, a setting or mood for the appropriate holiday can be established.

Stimulus:

Some of the experiences you're telling about remind me of a story that a friend of mine told about Halloween. A haunted house he knew about was near a cemetery. He and his friends went to the house because they had heard a strange cry which everyone else in town was afraid of. As they neared the house the moments between the cryings increased as though "it" knew of the approaching visitors. Suddenly it stopped, and the front door opened. A young voice started to talk. It was a young, weak, frail voice, and sounded like that of a young girl. She said that she had died when she was very young and her spirit had left her body after being placed in the grave. The problem now was that since her coffin had been left open, another spirit had inhabited or started to live in her body. When she had returned to her coffin, her body was gone. She had to come and live in the castle for the winter, because even though she was a spirit, it was cold in wintertime.

Since she had lived in the castle, some gravediggers had entered the castle and had opened a wall from which they had taken a hideous monster. The monster was hideous because it was neither man nor beast. She had heard the gravediggers talking about their reasons for moving the monster. It seemed they wanted to move it so that no one would find it, especially some professional body-snatchers who had heard about it. The men said that the monster had been a curse to the family who had lived in the house, and that the body-snatchers were being paid to bring it back to life. She asked us if we would bring it back from the grave outside where the men had taken it because she wanted to be sure that the body-snatchers would then come to this room, and she wanted them to help her find her own body. We agreed to help her so she gave us directions.

She said we must go through a passageway in the wall which led to a door. The door opening was outside but disguised by bushes on one side and a wall on another. The body was on the left of the door under a cement plank for which we would need a tool for lifting. The plank was between the bushes and the wall. She said we should come back the same way. After we had buried the monster's body in the wall, we should leave by going back again through the passageway so no one would see our flashlights leaving the castle in the dark.

She warned us to be careful in the forest because there were marshes, alligators, and poisonous snakes and spiders whose webs could trap us. She asked if we were ready.

Planning:

Now, who'll lead the way? Do we have our flashlights? *Response.* What about the crowbar for lifting the gravestone? *Response.* Is there anything we've forgotten? Will the leader show us where the passageway begins and ends? Stay behind the leader because the passageway is narrow. Where is the door at the end which opens onto the outside? *Response.* We'll all have to push together to open the door because it's very heavy. Who will be the spirit to show us where to place the body in the wall after we return? Are you ready? Wait for the music.

Playing:

Put the record on and then join them or stay to the side and narrate supportively. After they've reached the door and pushed it open, the following comments will help guide them: **You might need to use your flashlights so you can see the grave. Who brought the crowbar to lift the stone covering the grave? Some of you will have to hold up the stone slab while the others lift the monster's body out.** Turn the music up and allow the mood to dominate the imagination so that the rest of the obstacles like the door and the slab of stone over the grave, carrying the monster, burying the monster, and walking back through the same obstacles can be sustained. After this first trip, the return trip trip could be accelerated by having the leader repeat the spirit's instruction to hurry and leave the castle through the same passageway because she has heard someone coming. **Go slowly now that we are in the forest, remember to watch where you step. Some of you have a flashlight. Keep it focused on the ground so that we can avoid the marshes, alligators and spiders.** There are generally three levels of attentiveness for which the leader can guide the planning. Much concentration originates from belief, which in turn develops spontaneity. This session was partly planned before the journey took place and the rest was left to develop during the process of taking the journey. Every incident could be planned while the whole group is seated with the accompaniment of a map drawing, particularly if the group is very large and inexperienced. Within this structure, the leader could create spontaneous episodes for the children's immediate reaction. For example, an ending could be improvised by the leader's recognition of a Marsh King who suddenly rises up out of the forest, placing again his curse upon the castle and everyone who had been there. At the time of the evaluation, the motivation for the Marsh King's character could be discussed in relation to the rest of the story. However, children do not mind illogical sequences, and something as simple as his jealousy being the reason for his appearance would be acceptable. The details of his jealousy may (or may not) be filled in. A person to play the Marsh King should be chosen before a second replay and encouraged to handle all the suggestions in his or her own way. At this time the whole journey could be recast and replayed with the additions, changes, and the new ending.

Still another way to proceed on journeys is to discuss with the children the main setting, what they may find there, and let them go using some signal for their beginning and ending like the music or percussion instrument. However, this procedure is rarely wise unless the music is unusually appropriate and they are very involved and experienced. When children sustain this level of spontaneity, the true state of play is reached. At such a time, they can usually do without an adult, proceeding for at least an hour with only some gentle nudges or suggestions to get them going again.

This story may be replayed each time a new episode to the story is added. Additional episodes might include finding water for a town that needs a new source. A friendly monster who needs a friend can be at the bottom of the old well. Townspeople encourage the building of pipes in order to conduct the water after it has been tested. The monster has words of wisdom to bestow upon the town. . .saying that now the curse has been removed because everyone has worked together to restore the town. From a simple beginning children who become involved can continually create, restimulating their own imaginative resources. In this way, they can allow fantasy to accompany their decision-making and life affairs, eventually to provide motivation for curriculum objectives.

Lesson 11 **THE PROBLEM**

The overall organization of a lesson should include intervals of active and passive, or reflective, activity. The intervals of active activity can be more widely spaced as children mature, and may be separated by aural clues. Throughout this text, an emphasis usually is placed on the use of either percussion instruments or music accompanied by vocal explanation for this purpose.

To begin a lesson, a game structure immediately involves the child in action. For this reason the structure is most useful when children are pre-adolescent and tend to become self-conscious. The instructor will want to tailor the lessons to his class. If children need to be energized, then an active game like tag should be used. If they are a large class and their energy needs channeling, then a quiet game such as listening games or observation exercises should be used. (*Electricity* and Beckon are both examples of quiet games.) Other values of the game structure that have been mentioned include placing the individual player in competition with himself and in opposition to whatever impediment he is able to isolate. Total involvement by being able to identify with the other players becomes the value for the group.

The following lesson is an example of how each section is added by use of a previously introduced technique. The new technique is briefly explained, put into action, and then repeated. Children are intrigued by being able to use a new device, but paradoxically need the security of repetition.

Motivation:

We're going to use all of the space we need for a game of tag. Let's clear the center of the room and set our playing area within the time that we count down from 15 to 0. The leader can stand in the center close his eyes and turn, stop, point in a specific direction, open his eyes, to designate "it." Depending upon age, time of day, and other factors, the instructor may use vocal signals to vary tempo: slow motion, regular speed, "it" becomes blind, everyone who has been tagged freezes, the tagger freezes. If 15 or less are playing, the instruction to freeze or semi-freeze when tagged can be given. If more are playing, the same direction can be given after about half have been tagged. The game will be more focused and intense with these directions because being "it" will become more a matter of strategy than speed.

Dodge-ball, played with an imaginary ball, isn't as physically demanding as tag. The same directions for tempo changes apply.

When used as a warm-up and introduction, the game activity should last about five to seven minutes. Vocal direction needs to be alternated about every fifteen to twenty seconds to keep the game challenging. A useful method of bringing this introductory part of the lesson to a conclusion with a feeling of "finish" can be accomplished by having everyone move together in "slow-motion" to create a shape.

Stimulus:

For older groups, age 11 or greater, the lesson can then proceed by having the students count off and organize within their groups. **Think of a playground activity like jump rope or walking with a book on your head.** Choose two extremes that the group can identify with, so that they understand their range of choices are unlimited.

Playing:

You have forty seconds to decide. No planning, now! All right, begin. Everybody at once! After about fifteen to twenty seconds of the whole group playing, have all the players freeze. **This is group one, group two, group three. When I call your group by its number, continue your activity. When I call another group's number, everyone but the members of that group freeze.** Call quickly at first so they remain involved. The groups should be called alternately. After they understand the flow of this pattern, begin to give directions that will structure further their movement by images. **Group four–the ball weighs forty pounds.** Continue to call different groups alternately, changing directions as to the size, shape, substance, and weight of objects held as well as the kind of environment moved through.

The fine line between fun and absurdity needs to be maintained by the caller according to the extremes the group represents. If a child is greatly inhibited such suggestions can titillate his imagination. The same child might alternately become easily embarrassed and more inhibited or resentful if his feelings are not respected. For this reason the leader needs to be sensitive to each individual.

At first, a reminder that no one is watching because everyone is involved can help. Total involvement of everyone is a necessary pre-requisite for the step that follows. After about five to seven minutes of group movement, gradually lengthen the time during which the individual groups perform. If the whole group seems to be involved, direct the attention so that when a number is called for a smaller group to move, the others become audience. **Group four is on television and the rest of you are the audience.**

The calling needs to be continued, but in relation to the children's reactions. It must be remembered that playing games is a universal activity and once the transition into movement and mime has been made, a game can go on for as long as adjustment is made between periods of concentration and relaxation. To promote a positive group feeling provide some instruction that will pull the group together. Group two throw your ball to group four. The ball is very large and light weight. Group four throw it to group three. Everyone needs to get behind it because it needs lots of force to be thrown that far. It's become a balloon so group three hits it to group one. It takes another hit to get it there. Now it has helium in it. Someone from group one comes to grab the string quickly before it floats off. It's becoming even lighter. There's another string to hold it by. Someone has to grab that also. Now it's become much larger and so light two can't possibly hold it and the others find strings to help hold the balloon down. And now the balloon has turned into a large piece of silk from a parachute and everyone takes hold of their edge. What will happen when we lift the silk up? *It will float.* Why? *Because it's light.* Let's see if all together we can make if float. One, two, three, let go and run underneath. It's coming down and falling around us. Everyone sit down under it.

Motivation:

While we're sitting here be very still and close your eyes. See if you can imagine yourself outside watching a ball game. What kind of ball game is it? See the people and feel the air around you. Hear the noises and see the colors. Now, continue by yourself to let all these things happen to you.

Watch the group. If, after a few moments, they need a reminder, continue. Test your powers of concentration by seeing, feeling, or hearing whatever you can. Try to let at least fifteen seconds of undisturbed silence ensue so that there is a calm in the activity. All right, open your eyes. Does anyone want to comment on how they feel? This step is optional. If the group is small and they wish to respond, this would be the time for it. If it is a large group or they are new to the creative dramatics area, it is best to keep the exercises going or the lesson could get bogged down with talk.

Planning:

When you get back into your groups, I want you to think of some problem that you would have if you were at a ball game. You can be at the game, coming from it, going to it. What are some situations that you think of that could happen? Anyone? *Don't have enough money. Lost something. Ran out of gas. Had a flat tire.* Stay in your groups and decide upon your problem, what kind of game you are watching, and how you're going to begin. That's all. You have two minutes. This might stretch to three minutes as the leader walks around to attend to their suggestions and simple development of what later becomes a basis for a plot. Encouraging them to consider more of a problem in their plot is premature at this point, however, and restricts spontaneity. As the leader walks around, he should check on their problem, their sport, and their probable outcomes toward some conclusion. What is your sport? What is your problem? How are you going to begin? What do you think could happen?

Playing:

I want this group to begin its action all at once and continue as I call its number. The rest can be audience. Figure out what the problem is or what their sport is. Demand concentration on the part of the audience and a positive need for observing. You don't need to talk unless you want to, but keep it going until I call someone else's number. Get into your groups. Count them off again. Everybody begin. Since this was done before, the children will have adjusted to it.

I'm not going to call for your groups to begin action anymore. If another group is moving, it will soon stop. I want you to watch out of the corner of your eye to see when the group stops. Then you begin moving.

Group one, begin moving, taking up all the space. Now group one give up the space. As soon as group one does give the space, another group be ready to move. If two groups start, one has to stop. Let's try it. Think of it as giving the space to some other group; the other groups need to take it.

The give and take between groups in relation to space stimulates a unity and spontaneous interaction which intensifies both the performance and audience situation.

Lesson 12 **MOON MONSTER**

Motivation:

If you saw a monster in your cave, what would he be like? Could you show us what he is like? How does he move and walk? Could you describe him? *Response.* For several weeks some of you have wanted to go on a journey into space so I thought we could just transfer the monster into space.

What would be your reason for going into space? *Collecting specimens. On a scientific mission. To set up experiments.* What would you take with you? How would you talk to each other and communicate with the television announcer? Can we have a volunteer to show us? Be either the astronaut or the television announcer. What kind of clothing would you wear? *Response.* How would you walk in space? A volunteer? Two more? How was their walking the same? It showed that their bodies were light. Does anyone know why? Do you know how you would find out your weight on the moon? *Divide by six?* Let's all try walking like that. A demonstration lesson could take place if appropriate for this age group.

Find your space on the floor. Put on your space suit. Fasten yourself in. And let's have a countdown. *Ten, nine, eight. . .zero.*
(As announcer) Ladies and gentlemen, the space capsule had a successful take off. As yet their true mission is unknown. Of course they'll find the usual rocks and moondust. They'll search for minerals with geiger counters, but why don't you see for yourself. Let's switch onto satellite television and see just what is happening. We switched on just in time. Some of them have begun to land and are now adjusting themselves to their new environment. They seem to be having a good time getting the different feel of moon walking. Some of them are taking pictures and collecting specimens which will be viewed later. Let's see if we can intercept their communication channel and hear what they are saying to each other about what they are finding.

Nothing to report as yet. They'll be quite busy for a while performing all those tests. Let's leave them now and switch back to our main network station to find out some of the background on this mission. Some members of the group might be part of the audience, but even so they will be passively involved. The lesson could oscillate back and forth between narration of the activity, interviewing the astronauts, and interviewing the audience at the take-off.

All right, come on back and let's sit down. I noticed that you all had your tools and a bag for collecting rocks. What were some of the things you found? *We have brought back rock samples.* Rocks? What kind? To use in a pollution experiment?

There are two extreme reactions which can result from questioning too deeply: 1) A long involved reply which might need to be cut off by the leader in the character of the narrator; 2) The child might say that the answer was a secret, meaning that he is shy or doesn't understand the teacher's line of questioning. The leader's questions are used to further stimulate the imagination for creative drama and movement, and should not cause the lesson to become bogged down. **That's a good idea and can be used in the story.**

Stimulus:

This story is semi-science fiction. Do you know what might be meant by that? *Only part of it is science fiction, but what's the other part about?* Maybe you'll be able to figure it out. It fits together with what was said about pollution. That's not science fiction is it, because it's happening now? What is happening now became so bad that over the earth people were gradually falling over dead on the streets because of pollution and viruses and other germs which were taking over. Two scientists had been working for years in their laboratory trying to find cures for diseases, and they had become so deeply involved in their work that they had not noticed what had been happening over the earth. One day they looked out the window and were horrified by what they saw. School children could not breathe and plants could not grow. Something had to be done!

They took their telescope and scanned the horizon while speaking of what they saw to one another. And then they saw the most curious sight in the prisons. Deep behind bars, men were exercising, playing at sports, and enjoying themselves. The scientists tried to come to some understanding as to what the explanation could be. They decided to send two of these prisoners out into space on an experiment. The scientists decided that something had to be done for the people on earth, and since the prisoners seemed to be healthy, they decided to send them. They called the prison, and in no time the prisoners arrived. The scientists innoculated them with vaccine, helped them to make the necessary preparations, gave them suits, and explained to them their plan. They wanted the prisoners to make as many tests as possible and take samples from the moon so that these might be used in order to help the people on earth to live with the pollution problem. After the explanation, the prisoners seemed excited. So the scientists fastened them into the space capsule.

The scientists manned their computers and watched the monitor control board. The top of the lab opened up and the capsule rose. They were off!

On the way the prisoners were uncertain at first, but then they did enjoy themselves. They ate most of their rations and played with the handles and gadgets which looked interesting. When they arrived on the moon, they hesitantly got out of the capsule, feeling a strange awkwardness in their movement. They walked very carefully and cautiously. They also tried some of the exercises they usually did in the prison every day. On the moon the exercises made them feel as though they were dancing. They started to search for some of the specimens they were to collect, and while they were hunting, they discovered a cave. They began to go inside. They hadn't gone very far when they saw "it!" It looked very awesome and terrifying even though it was small. Since flashlights were weak they used a laser-beam instead. They knew they had to bring it back alive and so they took a box of crunchy cereal out, started eating it, and offered some of it to the monster. Then they shined the laser-beam in the opposite direction toward the exit and the monster followed, happily crunching on cereal.

They had no trouble encouraging it to come into their spacecraft. Once the monster was loaded there were several exciting moments. The craft was slightly heavier then before, and the astronauts couldn't get it going. They got out and pushed it. When they got back in they worked the controls until they finally left the ground. On the way the monster kept eating the crispy cereal which caused him to become thirsty. He required quite a lot of water, and as a result, he started to puff up.

The scientists brought the capsule right back down into the lab and, after landing, they helped the astronauts out first and then the puffed up monster was helped out. The scientists began collecting serums from the monster right away while the astronauts took off their suits. Time was running out. News had gotten out, and people were curious. The scientists and the astronauts placed the monster so the people who were coming up to the lab could walk around him and view him from all sides. He did seem friendly and, according to the tests that had been taken so far, he appeared to be non-toxic. Large needles to sample the monster were being prepared by the scientists while the astronauts diverted the monster's attention. The scientists were in their lab preparing the needles in time for the people to arrive; the astronauts prepared to blindfold each person and then lead him towards the direction of the monster. They decided to do this as soon as the people arrived and then the visitors could use their imaginations when they felt the monster. Each person saw whatever he wanted to see with his own hands. In their state of desperation, they might wish for almost anything. And they did say many wonderful things about the monster.

When the monster heard all these flattering things about him a curious change started to take place. It breathed and grew and grew and breathed. As it did, you may guess that it breathed in all the viruses and poisons that were affecting the people so that an almost indescribable change occurred. It started to rise and ascended half-way to the moon where it exploded sending all the viruses and poisons into outer space.

The scientists were giving the people their vaccine and they were happy to know that it had come from the monster whom they had grown to be very fond of. He had left his mark on the people and they had begun to change.

Planning:

Now, which part should we act out? *The whole thing. I want to be the monster.* We have to plan it first because it's a fairly complicated story. Which part have we already acted?

The moon landing. What happened before that? *The scientists.* Where were they? *In their lab.* What would their actions be? *Response.* What else? *They're so busy doing their regular thing that they forget about something else.* What is it? What's happening outside? *Response.*

Release:

Half of you get up and show us how you would walk and what you would sound like as a scientist. *Response.* How about the other half?

Planning:

Let's plan what we're going to do so we can act it. What did the scientists say about the people they saw? What instrument did the scientists use to see farther? *They looked through a telescope.* Whom did they see? *They saw some prisoners.* How could they make contact with the prisoners? *They could call them on the phone.* The teacher continues to re-relate the story, outlining the plot verbally and beginning to introduce action.

Does the monster want to come? *They use that cereal and the laser-beam and he comes right along.* After they get the monster to leave the cave what do they do with him? *Put him into the space ship.* And what happens? *He begins to grow.* How and why? *He's eating and then drinking water and puffing up.*

Release:

Let's all try it. First he's small and then he stretches up from the middle. Move your arms and legs out. Keep moving them so you take up room above, around the sides, and down on the sides, and around your legs. Down again and then collapse. You're sort of like rubber. Someone (or have several students) sit in the middle, and be the monster.

Planning:

After they get the monster to Earth and get the serum, where do they put it? *In bottles.* Why do the people come? *To get the serum.* What for? *So they won't be in such bad shape. . .coughing and polluted.* And do they want to see the monster? *Yes. But they can't.* Why not? *Because he's ugly.* But why can't they see him?

They've been blindfolded. Do they think the monster is good or bad? *Good.* Why? *Because he's going to cure them.* When you think that someone can help you, don't you usually like them? So what did the people say when they felt the monster? Think of something you like a lot. Say it with your whole body. Everyone reach out and think of feeling something that you know would cure you because you couldn't walk. Can someone tell us how he would feel about it? Concentrate. Maybe you can't say it because you feel too many things. You feel so many things you can't even say one of them. But the monster knew how you felt because he got so big. He was like a person who feels so good that he wants to explode.

Release:

Those of you in the center are the monster. The rest, start around to touch the monster and as you do the monster explodes in slow motion. All of you react in slow motion, watching all the pieces rise. Come on back and change. Other half in the middle. This time let's see the monster grow first and then the explosion.

Planning:

Let's act it. Where's the lab? The cave? What window do the scientists look out of to see the children? To see the prisoners? Where's the door the prisoners enter by? Will the people enter here also? Should the lab and the moon be in about the same place? Will you show me where all these things are?

Who will be the scientists? *Response.* Get in your lab. Monster? *Response.* Get in your cave. Prisoners—where? Children and people? First, what are the children and people doing? *Response.* And then all of you can come into the lab at the end. Where are the children and people at first? Show me. Where are the ones who are watching the television monitor?

Playing:

Scientists start working in your lab. **Begin.** This is a complicated story so the television narrator should prompt the first two times through. Vocal sounds can be added for the take-off and the explosion. Some electronic music can be played for the whole moon section to the end. Having particularly slow music towards the end would help to slow down the explosion as the people watch the monster join the elements.

It is valuable to have the children provide endings. During the evaluation ask them to explain how they would end it if it doesn't seem finished. If the narrator is used, then the ending could be developed from this technique.

"The jackel could not understand why the Brahman was so sad."

Lesson 13 **THE BRAHMAN, TIGER AND JACKAL**
(A fable from India)

Motivation:

Could you pretend to be an animal and then show us some rule you've broken or want to break? Think of an animal you could be. Begin moving your back, your head, nose, and neck like the animal would. As soon as you get the feeling of how the animal would move, begin to move from a crawling position into a walk. Think of a noise, or sound, the animal would utter. Communicate to each other that it's market day and time to eat. Now let's rest after our meal. Use two taps on the drum if needed.

Think of a key word related to the rule you would want to break. In your animal character, you might be able to take a short cut by miming that word and then showing us the action that the animal could perform if he were breaking that rule. For example, if the rule you wish to break is "No gum is to be chewed while in school," you might start by creating an enormous mound of gum, tearing apart many wrappers, chewing the gum by pieces, and spitting the pieces out to make a larger and larger mound which you could mold, or stick all over the desks, walls, and chairs. The leader should move while narrating. Think first if you wish and then move. Keep your animal character. *Response.* Two taps can be used. Do you think there would have been any difference between doing your mime as an animal or doing it as yourself? *I think being the animal made it more fun.* Why? *I wasn't afraid of someone finding out about what I did and punishing me for it. You could really get away with something because you weren't yourself.* It is nice to be someone or something else, especially an animal. Animals have more freedom and can do more since people don't take them seriously.

There's a type of literature in which animals take on the roles of human beings and can tell us things about ourselves. We are more likely to accept them than if other human beings were to tell us those same things, as in a Peanuts cartoon. Is the name of this type of literature on the tip of anybody's tongue? I'm sure you'll be able to get a clue as I give you a few of the details. When these short stories were first written in about 612 a.d. by a man they think was called Aesop, he wanted to teach a lesson. He wanted to give examples which people would accept and not be insulted by. So he decided to use animals in conflicts which would normally involve people. People could then accept the moral, but not identify themselves with the fault the moral was to correct.

For example, do any of you know the story called "The Ants and the Grasshoppers?" It's related to working hard and being prepared for what might happen to you. Do you know the story?

The ants worked during the summer when it's hot and the grasshoppers played and enjoyed themselves. When winter came, the grasshoppers had collected no food and were starving. They begged the ants to give them some food, but the ants replied with the moral: those who do not work but play instead, will have to live on their play as we live on our work. Have you heard of that? Any others? *Response.*

Stimulus:

There is an Indian fable in which the animals and objects talk, that tells us a moral in another way. See if you can find it.

A tiger was locked in a cage and in vain he tried to get out. A poor Brahman came by and heard the tiger struggling to get out. The tiger begged the Brahman to help him, but the Brahman thought better of this and said that the tiger would probably eat him if he were to release him. The tiger promised the Brahman that instead of doing any such thing, he would become the Brahman's slave.

The tiger wept and sighed and begged so much that the Brahman's heart softened and he consented to open the cage. At the tiger's release, he strode out of the cage and looked the Brahman over, laughing at him saying that since he had been cooped up so long he was indeed hungry and would have to eat the Brahman.

The Brahman pleaded with the tiger, but the best he could do was to get the tiger to abide by the decision of the first three things he chose to question as to the justice of the tiger's actions.

So the Brahman first asked a tree who thought the matter out and then replied coldly that as a tree he stood to supply shade to all those who passed, but for his efforts they tore off his branches to supply food for their cattle. The Brahman could not complain to him.

The Brahman felt very sad until he saw a buffalo turning a well-wheel. After the Brahman had explained his story, the buffalo said the Brahman was a fool to expect gratitude. The buffalo explained that when she used to give milk they fed her delicious cotton-seed and oil-cake. Now that she had grown dry, only refuse and fodder were fed to her.

The Brahman was even more sad now and asked the road's advice. The road thought the Brahman was lucky to have so short a life, for those who had trampled on the road left nothing but ashes from their pipes and husks from their grain.

At this the Brahman turned slowly, meeting a jackal on the way. The jackal asked the Brahman why he looked so sad and the Brahman told all that had happened. But he had to tell the jackal the story over again because the jackal couldn't understand it. Still the jackal could not understand; he just shook his head saying that perhaps it was going in one ear and out the other. What he needed was to go to the place where it had all happened and then perhaps he could judge.

When they returned there was the tiger waiting for the Brahman, sharpening his claws and teeth. The Brahman reacted in terror and his knees knocked together in fright.

He begged the tiger to give him five minutes so that he might explain the matter to the jackal who seemed slow in his wits. The tiger consented and the Brahman explained the whole yarn over again not missing a single detail, making his explanation as long as possible. The jackal's brain began to reel, and as he tried to retell the story it seemed to become all fuzzy.

At this the tiger became so angry that he threw up his hands and tried to explain it himself—growing all the time more and more heated and angry.

The jackal pretended to tremble in fright as he agreed with every word the tiger said. But as he tried to relate the story again, he became so confused that he just gave up and told the tiger to continue with his dinner for he would never understand.

The tiger said he *would* understand for now the tiger was in rage at the jackal's stupidity. He said he would *make* the jackal understand. To make this possible, the tiger identified himself, the Brahman, the cage, and even the jackal himself. Then he began again, but when he got to the first part and explained how he was in the cage, the jackal begged him to slow down. Then he asked the tiger how he had gotten into the cage.

The tiger started to explain this and found that the jackal was becoming confused again. Losing patience, the tiger jumped into the cage to demonstrate, screaming and roaring at the jackal, asking him if he understood.

Calmly the jackal replied that he did. The jackal got up and shut the cage door with the tiger inside, replying that matters would now remain as they were.

Release:
Let's all get up and move. How would the tiger have held on to the bars of the cage? How would he have walked around in the cage? How would the trees have moved? The buffalo? How would the Brahman have walked? At this point the tambour or drum can be used to suggest rhythmic walks. How would the jackal have walked and talked?

Planning:

It's more difficult to explain this moral isn't it? But if this fable teaches a lesson, who do you think learned their lesson? *The tiger.* What do you think he learned? *There's more to a person than what his actions tell you.* That's one way to say it. Any other ways? *Don't lose your temper.* Why not? *The tiger might have been able to figure out what was happening if he had kept cool.*

Did anyone have the ending figured out? *I knew that the jackal wasn't that dumb.* When? *When the tiger started talking because it was about the third time he had heard the same story and how could he be so dumb and still keep alive. Besides jackals are clever.* Does anyone know what animal a jackal is like? *Sort of like a fox or wolf.* That's right. What happened first in the fable? *The tiger was locked in a cage and the Brahman came by and saw him.* Did the Brahman let the tiger out right away? *No, because he thought the tiger would eat him.* How did the tiger get the Brahman to let him out? *He cried and begged and promised not to eat the Brahman and to be his slave.*

After the Brahman let him out, did he keep the promise? *No. He said he was hungry and would eat the Brahman.* Did he? *He said the Brahman could ask the first three things they met if the tiger was justified in eating him.* Whom did they meet first? *They met a tree.* What did the tree say? *The tree said he gave shade to all who passed by and they only tore off his branches. So the Brahman didn't complain.* Whom did he meet next? *A buffalo turning a water wheel.* What did the buffalo say? *The buffalo said he was a fool to expect gratitude. She said when she gave milk she got good food to eat, but since she was old and dry, she got garbage.*

What was the next object he came to? *A road. He thought the Brahman was lucky to have such a short life because his life went on and on and people dumped all their trash on it, and ashes from their pipes, and they walked on it.* How did the Brahman feel now? *Really sad.* Then what happened? *The Brahman met a jackal, who asked him why he looked so sad. So the Brahman explained everything, and the jackal told him to stop because he couldn't understand it. Then the Brahman told it over again and the jackal still couldn't understand it.* What did the jackal say? *He said it was going in one ear and out the other and that they should go to the place where it had all happened.*

When they got back what did they find? *The tiger was sharpening up his claws and teeth and getting ready to eat the Brahman.* How did the Brahman feel about this? *He was more scared than ever and his knees knocked together in fright.* What did the Brahman ask the tiger? *He wanted five minutes to explain to the jackal about everything.* **What happened then?** *The tiger said it was all right and the Brahman started to explain. But the jackal still couldn't understand.* **How do you know? What did the jackal do?** *He tried to tell the story in order to figure it out but he couldn't remember it.* **What did the tiger do then?** *He got really mad and started to tell the story himself. He got madder and madder and the jackal became more frightened.* **Was he really frightened?** *No, but the tiger thought he was.* **How did the tiger react to this?** *He got still madder and he started to act out the whole thing and introduced each character, and even the cage. Then he started the whole thing over and acted it out. He said this is the cage and I am the tiger, and I was in the cage. Then he got in to show him. So the jackal came over and said that now he understood.* **What did he do?** *He closed the cage door so everything would remain as it was before.* **How do you think the tiger acted then? Think a minute. Was he very angry or could he have been stunned or shocked?** *He could have been.* **And then the Brahman and jackal said good-bye to him and just walked away. How do you look when you're stunned or shocked?** *Your mouth sort of hangs open and your eyes are large and you don't move at all. Like you can't believe what you see.* **Good.**

Was the jackal really ever frightened do you think? *He was pretending.* **Since he was pretending, do you think he may have exaggerated his fear which made the tiger even more angry, because the more afraid the jackal looked, the more stupid he appeared? Have you ever been so frightened that you couldn't move or talk? How do you think the jackal might have sounded when he was trying to retell the story to the tiger to prove to the tiger that he was trying to understand. How did he talk? Can anyone start? I'll be the tiger. Now do you understand? I am the tiger and this is the cage, this is the Brahman. The Brahman came walking up. . .all right now, say something. Start the story for me.** *Response.* **Like this. This is the cage, and I was in it.** *I understand now. The Brahman came walking by.* **You were in the cage.** *That's right. Go on. You wanted. . .ah. . .* **Wanted what?** *To get out of the cage. Like this.* **Closes the door.** *Now I think things will remain as they were before.* **Good. Where should the cage be? Where does the Brahman come from? Next, the tree, then the buffalo, and the road? Where should the jackal come from?**

Playing:
    Cast the story. Any number can play any part at one time because the story needs dialogue as much as movement. The more who take each role at the same time, the more dialogue is encouraged in the group character. Two trees work well, three children could

be the road, one for the cage door, two jackals can amplify the ah's and stuttering. And two or three tigers can g'rrr louder. The children will want to replay it and exaggerate the characters still further after they change parts.

"As the judges chewed, an expression of delight and ecstasy over took them."

Lesson 14 **ROAST PIG**
(adapted from a dissertation by Charles Lamb)

Motivation:
Prepare highly odorous spices or foods which have been placed in containers beforehand. Blindfold half the group, and bring out jars or bottles of spices and strong but delectable smelling foods placing them in some order. Also provide a sample for each to taste. Each player should go through the line and be handed a container which he can smell and a sample which he can taste. The food should then be put away and each player should make a list of the foods he thought he tasted in the correct order. Under each food he should list as many adjectives as possible that more fully describe both the olfactory and gustatory sensations he received. The same arrangement can be repeated with different foods for the next group. If the class is small, the whole group can be handled at once.

This exercise is an experiment frequently used in science classes. Each group is allowed to taste the food, but only one group is allowed to smell it. The group who performs both activities is able to identify the foods with more accuracy, emphasizing the dependence of the gustatory sense upon the olfactory sense. In creative dramatics it could be used to introduce the following story or line of questioning: **Have any of you ever thought of inventing something–something that you needed because it would save you time, energy, money, or from experiencing boredom?** *Response.* **I wonder how things do get invented? I remember meeting the man who invented the price gauge on the gasoline pump. You know that when you get gas at a gas station there are two disks that turn at the same time and on one the number of gallons of gas was shown in tenths, while the other shows the price of the quantity of gas purchased. After** further verbalizing along this line, the group should be sufficiently stimulated toward activity to begin planning.

Let's see if you can all make your own invention so we can see how it looks and works. Remember all those funny machines we invented while doing the mime exercises? All right, get to work! The teacher may help the individual students develop an invention. **I can see that some of these inventions are alive and some of them are not moving. Some are so complicated and elaborate that I can't wait to see how they're going to be used.**

Depending upon the leader's preference, this warm-up can be extended or not. If it is, then the whole group can be broken into pairs by the leader. The inventor of each article should try to sell his invention to his partner. A group discussion could follow describing the inventions from the buyer's point of view. If time permits, the invention could be sold to the whole class or auctioned by the inventor himself or by his partner.

Stimulus:
This story is about an invention that came about by accident, and is one possible explanation for the oriental custom of roasting meat, instead of eating it raw.

Bobo was left in charge of his father Hoti's farm, and since he enjoyed playing with fire, it happened that one day the fire got out of hand, spread, and burned the farm down.

While he sat mourning the loss of his father's pig, there came an odor which was indescribably pleasant. As he stooped down to feel if there was any life left in the pig, the oily flesh burned his fingers so badly that he had to cool them by tenderly sucking out the oil. In this way he tasted it. For the first time in his life he tasted the pig. He did it again until, by slow understanding, he realized that the roasted meat was what he had smelled.

He fell upon the pig gouging out hunks and was stuffing his mouth full of the delicious tasting meat when his father returned. He barely felt Hoti's blows with the cane, punishing him for his carelessness and gluttony. Bobo only shouted with happiness for his discovery and described the succulent joys of roast pork to his father. His father began to inspect the evil food, and was soon overcome with the same desire. Both continued eating until the whole litter of pigs had been consumed.

Fires began to occur more and more often at their rebuilt cottage until the neighbors grew suspicious and had Bobo and Hoti called to trial in Peking. Evidence was given to the community. The judges of the crime decided that the pig's flesh should be used as evidence and they should sample it.

As soon as the meat was exhibited and placed in a box, each judge in turn sampled it. As they chewed and tasted, an expression of delight and ecstasy began to cross their faces. With the help of the head judge, Bobo and Hoti were declared not guilty.

Soon the judge's house and other prominent establishments in the town were burned. Insurance companies went out of business, and the field of architecture itself became nearly a lost art.

A few centuries later, some very wise scholar discovered that it was not necessary to burn down a whole house and all its contents just to roast or cook a pig, and a simpler method developed which merely involved placing the pig on a spit all by itself. That is how we have developed the art of roasting pigs.

Discussion:
Do you think this is a true story? *No.* Why not? Does it make a

good story? *Yes.* Why? *It sounds so exaggerated.* Do you know of any inventions which have come about through accidents? *The invention of rubber.* Have discoveries come about by accidents? What about the founding of America? Many stories can be used to examine the concept that exploring is often performed without complete knowledge of the results. Risks and chances must be taken if change is to occur. Naturally, as few risks are taken as possible. One of the reasons the story appeals to children is the extent to which people would go to satisfy an irresistable craving. Just as often, however, the creative process occurs when an individual works alone. At such times, the risks are to him alone, and he easily forgets his danger and becomes caught up by his discovery. One example is contained in the myth of Icarus.

The tongue-and-cheek quality of the story may also be compared by the leader to that of Twain, O'Henry, and Thurber. Are there any other stories that you have read which pretend to speak the truth, but are exaggerated? *Response.* What kind of story do we call these types? *Satire or tall tales.*

Release:

As soon as the music begins, I want all of you to become any kind of pig-like animal you can think of. The value of the previously introduced mime movement and warm-up exercises will be evident at this point. Make large, gross actions, using your whole body: rolling in mud, snorting. If the children are not at the point where such exaggerated movement is possible, then having them move in the character of fire or a burning building would possibly come first, to be followed later by a subtler animal interpretation.

Light a candle in order to gain the concentration necessary for the following experiment to be translated in terms of movement. Watch the movement of the fire and the melting, destruction, and change that takes place. What's left of the candle? Is it changed or destroyed? *Changed, because there's still carbon and water.* If one of you became the candle and another the fire, then how would you show this change in movement? *Response.* The fire continues. The candle does not disappear. It changes into another substance. Show us with your movement.

Can we have three groups of you: animals; anything that will burn such as houses, walls, and trees; and the fire. All those who are fire can place yourselves at regular intervals near the wall; all those who are fixtures and animals scatter over the floor. As soon as I start the music the fire begins to move and work toward the middle of the room. You'll have nothing more to burn after you meet each other in the center, because of the change which takes place. When that happens, fade out with the music. Play one or two minutes of the introduction to Stravinsky's *Firebird*.

Planning:

Come on back and rest. In the story do you think Bobo was hungry at first? *No, he tasted the roasted pork by accident.* Why did he eat so fast? *It tasted so good.* Listen to this rhythm. Tap on a drum slowly at first and then gradually speed up. Do you think you could eat in the same way, actually showing this rhythm? Do you want to try first with the drum, and then without? *Response.*

How do you think the judges would walk and how would they look at the boy and his father? *Suspiciously, eyebrows raised, like they were guilty.* When I start to tap the drum begin to walk. Remember you are an honorable member of society. Think of the robes you would be wearing.

Now, let's have a few judges, animals, objects, fire, the boy, and the father. Point these characters out. In other story planning sections, the characters were not chosen until the end. This helped the children to think in terms of the whole piece, not just their particular part. Choosing characters first will emphasize the child's concentration in terms of role development. If they have become accustomed to thinking about the story as a whole, however, there is no reason why they should regress and not continue to do this.

How does the story begin? *Bobo is left to take care of the farm.* How would we know that he was left in charge of it? *His father could leave and tell him to be careful.* Why would he tell him to be careful? *Because Bobo likes to play with fire.* What could happen? *He starts to play with fire.* Would he do this right away? *He could take care of the animals.* What would he do for them? *He could give them a bath. And he could feed them.* How would he begin to play with fire? *He could be heating something or making a fire.* Go on. *And then when the fire starts to spread he could become excited and just watch it.*

Does watching fire make anyone here feel that way about fire? Could you explain it? *It's exciting because it goes fast and it's like magic, because suddenly whatever was there is gone.* Oh, that's a fascinating way to look at it. So it's not destructive at all? *Oh no. It changes things.* That's what our experiment was about, wasn't it? What does Bobo do? *He just watches it.* Does he stand there or get excited or both? *Oh, sort of both.* Several of you show us how you would see the fire and the magic changes. *Response.* If the reaction does not show fascination with fire, some others should be invited to try.

Then what happens? Does he change? *He realizes what has happened.* How does his face look then? *Sad. Scared.* How does he walk? That's quite different. Why do you think he's scared? *He's scared of his father.* That's right. His father put him in charge and even warned him. But what other change takes place? *He smells something.* Does his face change again? And his body? Can those who haven't had a chance to be up show us the change from sad, scared, to whatever he feels when he smells something? *Response.* Does he find whatever it is? *Yes, the cracklings.* And what does he do? Show me, all of you. Then who enters? *Hoti, the father.* And what does he do? *He beats him.* What is Bobo's reaction? *Nothing.* Nothing? He does nothing but what? *Pours food into his mouth.* Pours? or stuffs? Let's have you two go at it. And you two be the father. Go ahead and what would you say? How would you feel if your son had let the whole farm burn down and was now stuffing himself with something repulsive looking? What words would you use? *Stupid, lazy, dirty! You're stuffing yourself and let the whole house burn. I won't give you any allowance for a month. A year!* Oh, he's angry isn't he? Has anyone else had that experience? Parents can get very angry. So can teachers and everybody and completely lose their tempers. Let's all try the father again to the drum taps. Ready? *Response.* Remember the two taps which are extra loud that act as an instant conditioner or should by this time.

What does the boy say? *He holds up the meat and wants his father to taste it.* How does his father react to this? *He's surprised at first, but then he starts to look at it.* And then what does he do? *Eats it also. So both of them are stuffing themselves.*

Who sees them? *The neighbors.* What do they think about it? *They think they're crazy.* Someone mentioned that the judges would be suspicious, how do people act when they're suspicious? *They're scared.* Remember that they're in a group and what would they do in this group? *Whisper and move together.* How do you think that the judges heard about the fires? *They saw them.* What else? What about the neighbors? *They could go tell them.* Where would they go now? *Run off to the judges.* Where are the judges? At a different place? Or could we have them be in the middle of the room?

If the judges were in the middle of the room then where would they come from? *Over there.* Where would the people come from? *From the other side.* And where would they go? To tell the judges? *Yes, they'd go to where the judges were.*

Playing:

All the people that are going to be the fire and objects which change, get up and be the gossips after the boy and father start eating? When they see the boy and father eating what do they do? Leave them, or take them to the judges? *Take them both.* Where will the judges enter? *From there.* What will the first judge say? *Who has the evidence?* Who does? *All the gossips.* Let's see them give the evidence to the judges and carry the boy and father in. This half be judges, you be gossips, and you be boy and father. Judges enter from there. Gossips grab the boy and father and meat. Carry them to the judges. Are the judges going to be in the middle or there? *In the middle.* Then the judges need to start walking in at the same time that the gossips get the meat and bring the boy and father. Ready? Go. *Response.*

Planning:
What does the head judge say? *Give me the evidence.* And they do. What does he do with the meat? *Tastes it.* And then what would he say? *They sort of like it.* What would he say? *Ummmm. Try some.* Who would he say this to? *The other judges.* So they do. What is the result? *They say he's not guilty.* Who says it? *The head judge. But they all say it as they pass the meat along and taste it.*

Where is the fire? Animals? The parts of the farm that will melt? And the boy at first? Where will the judges be?

Replaying:
I'll play the drum for the eating and the beating. When the music starts let's begin. For the second playing, slower movement and the subtleties of the gossips and judges eating with growing enjoyment should be explored.

Also explore the reasons behind fear and suspicion. If you saw some creature that you didn't recognize would you be afraid of it? What would you do? *Hide.* What if it didn't bother you, or even pay any attention to you? What would you want to do then? *Walk toward it and find out about it.* Can you show fear and follow it with a feeling of curiosity? Would someone volunteer to be the abominable snowman or a monster such as bigfoot? Half of you show fear as the creature advances and then change and become curious because he keeps walking on past you. Now the other half. Do you think people find out more through gossip or through finding out about the unknown for themselves? *Finding out for themselves.* Then why don't they? *Because it's harder.* Why is it hard? *You don't know what's going to happen.* What could happen? *Anything.* Can you compare it to something you know that would be hard to do or find out about because no one has done it? Any new invention or exploration in which the risk factor had not been weighed could be named.

Extension:
Next, develop the dialogue, particularly that of the judges and father. In both cases, they are authority figures. This would be a good opportunity for a rebellious child to let out stored up resentments in relation to such a type. The situation doesn't have to be similar, just the relationship. Most children are able to transfer their experience as victims or culprits into disciplinarians simply through imitation and enjoy the catharsis of emotional release. Another question to be asked in reference to the development of authoritarian anger is more direct and can be used along with the above question. Can you remember an occasion when you became angry at someone you were playing with because they broke one of your toys and you felt like beating them as Hoti did? Or did you want to punish them as the judge might have? Was the judge angry like the father? How was it different? What would he say after the gossips had told him about the situation? Would he be the one to tell the other gossips to check the evidence?

"They prepared to tie the boy to the tree."

Lesson 15 **JAVELIN THROW**

Motivation:

We're going to play a game called "Indian File." One group of you will go out of the room and line up. Be sure you remember your order in line. Then you'll run into the room in this same order. When you run in, make a large circle (or a figure eight). Run all around the room and out again. When you're outside again change and get your order in line all mixed up so the first person will be fourth, and the second person might be last. As soon as you reorder yourselves, run back in and line up so you're in a line facing us.

Those of us who stay in the room will try to put you back in your original order. This means all of us who are sitting and watching have to observe carefully when you first run in so we can replace you. Are there any volunteers to run in? Let's start out with nine the first time. Go outside and line up, being sure to remember your number in line. Perform the exercise.

Since that worked well, let's make it a little more complicated. This time when you run in, provide some distraction by each using different movements and perhaps making some extra sound. Also, don't remain in the room for such a long time. This time let's have ten volunteers. Come in when you're ready. Rerun the exercise.

Let's try it once more. Since those who had to reorder you were able to overcome the handicaps of distraction and larger numbers, everyone do something different this time according to a rhythm pattern that the audience will set up. Let's see if we can still handle ten because the audience is not just going to be passively watching, but will be involved too. While we're setting up our rhythm pattern by tapping on the desks or floor, take the time to decide generally what actions you're going to perform to the rhythm. Move differently from each other or alike, but be sure to move according to the rhythm pattern. All right, go outside and line up.

The leader may wish to establish a pattern by tapping on a drum or desk and then encourage others to join in when they feel the beat. The basic beat should remain consistent. Finish the game and have them sit down.

Could you close your eyes and imagine or bring to mind a particular kind of place you can describe and associate with the music that I am playing? Accept their responses, and in doing so accept anything which relates to primitive tribes, ritual, living on an island, survival, or ancient man. Encourage them a bit further. Using elements of their descriptions, the place then should be briefly described by the leader. This, then, is a primitive island that we rediscover. Close your eyes and visualize the place. Drums should be played by the leader.

What were some of the places you saw? *Response.* Suppose you were all alone on an island, what would be some of the things you would have to do for yourself? *Provide food and shelter, make utensils.* Let's imagine we're the last of an ancient tribe, making things to present at the harvest festival. Find some space and begin to make whatever object of art or utensil that is important to you.

I see jars, jewelry, woven rugs, and pottery. It starts to rain and you have to run into the storehouse. Don't forget your object. Oh, it's cold in here. I see the remains of a fire. Let's get it going again. *Response.* Now that it's going, we can see better and can show what we've made. How could you show us what you've made? How would you show the size? The weight? The shape? Its use? Everyone experiment in handling the object in space. *Response.*

The rain has stopped and it's very warm by the fire. Go to sleep. The music is turned on. It should have a primitive and intense quality. While you're sleeping a thousand years pass. As soon as the drum starts you wake up and find yourself on an island you've never seen before. You notice some words which are written on a stone which reads: Anyone who enters this village must make a sacrifice so that the vicious forces which once destroyed the village can be satisfied.

Let the object that you sacrifice be something that you value and try to show us what it is by the way you handle and use it. Perhaps you can start out by moving the air around you as if it were a substance, as you did before, until an image is formed from the shapes you make as you move your body. Continue to move by yourself or in relation to others, shaping the space and letting your body be moved by the space as well.

If your arms make a pattern, explore the pattern and the feeling your body has in relating to the pattern. The image of the object will come. Whenever you're ready, sacrifice your object in turn, then sit and watch the fire grow for a moment, then slowly die as a result of whatever was thrown in. *Response.*

Now everyone has made his sacrifice. The fire is out but mounds of earth are beginning to rise, and the story about what had happened to the ancient tribe of this land is being revealed to us. Let's sit down and hear the story about the island.

Stimulus:
There were once two tribes which were separated by a volcano

which rose overnight. One of the tribes lived near the sea, the other was in the hills. The chief of the tribe by the sea had a son named Sanno who was not a good hunter or swimmer and this son escaped over the mountain to hide his shame and not bring his father more embarrassment. For a time he became lost while on his journey but soon found his way to the other tribe who lived in the hills. Since the members of this tribe were mountain people, they worshipped the sun rather than the sea.

One morning, as they were performing their morning ritual of praying for rain by waving their arms up and down, the boy from the sea watched them while hiding in the bushes. He had never seen this kind of dance before and was intrigued by it because he thought it was something he could do. He remembered that all the children were allowed to do in his tribe was to dance in the water. When he tried to dance the water dance, a fear that he could not explain always overwhelmed him and he would sink.

While he thought about this, the dancers left. They had been circling a young girl who had been tied to a stone. During the dance several different men had gone to the edge of the clearing and had collected brush and sticks which they had placed around the stone. Now the boy understood. They were going to sacrifice her if it did not rain soon. Nearby, there was an old man who sat in a large chair covered by mats. Sanno thought he must be the king of the tribe because of his elaborate headpiece. This man then went over and placed his arm in a circle over the girl and left. Sanno realized that she was the chief's daughter. He leaped out of the bushes and began to untie her, thinking to himself that no matter where one would go, there would always be something to fear. If he were not the son of a chief, it would not matter that he was so afraid. In time he felt he could work to overcome his fear like the other boys. As he was untying her he spoke to her about this. He said that just because she was the chief's daughter, she should not have to die.

She interrupted him, saying that he should not be doing this because it would anger the gods, and now it surely would not rain. Because of his defiance, they would both be killed. Their fathers were chiefs, and they could not escape their fate. While she spoke, he finished untying her, caught her by the shoulder, and lifted her up, ready to run in the direction from which he had come. He realized he could not go back to his home. So he turned and ran toward the forest. Suddenly, those who had performed the rain ceremony blocked their path. They grabbed the boy, tied him to a tree, and quickly prepared the base of the tree with sticks.

In the meantime the old priest of the Sea people, who had journeyed into the mountains to die, had arrived at the clearing. He saw the young prince being tied to a tree. He quickly hurried back to the Sea people to alert them. As the Sea people started up the mountains, the Sun people were tying the princess back on her stone and raised their arms toward the sun repeating a chant by which to appease the gods. At the king's command they formed into a semi-circle around the boy and began to set the fire.

At this time, the priest returned with the Sea warriors. The king of the tribe also arrived, and upon his command ordered his warriors to throw javelins, aiming right at the feet of each of the Sun warriors who surrounded the tree.

As soon as this happened, the chief of the Sun people raised his arm to have the fire at the boy's feet put out. He ordered his people to pull the javelins out of the ground and return them to the Sea warriors. The Sea people broke the javelins in two, as a gesture of peace. Then the Sun chief ordered that the animal cord around the boy be broken and that he be released.

The king of the Sun people announced that he had recognized the mark of the family on the javelin, and that he accepted the Sea king as his brother. He also ordered his daughter freed because now that the two tribes could be friends, there was no need to fear the lack of rain or water. If the tribes could cooperate, their important resources could be shared. By command of the king, all raised their arms to the sky and bowed to this great victory.

Release:
Can we repeat the kind of Indian file game we played earlier as a ceremony to be done by a different group? Let's make a circular arrangement around the whole room. Those who don't participate in the game or ceremony should provide the beat. Volunteers for Indian file? *Response.* This time you don't need to know your numbers in line, just go off to the side and start moving your head, arms, legs, every part of your body to the beat, run out, form your circle, and keep moving to the beat. Then begin to move toward the center forming a circle. As soon as you are about 10 feet apart, we will help you freeze. Toward the end the tempo can be accelerated by the leader.

Planning:
Where does the action in the story begin? *When the boy runs away.* Are the reasons for his running away important to the story? *Yes.* Why did he run away? *He was afraid.* Does the story

deal with his fears or the relationship between the two tribes? *Both.* Does he show his early fears in the story or is he brave? *He's pretty brave. . .in the story.*

Since his early fears are not the main focus of the story or problem of the story, how are they connected with the story? *They get it going.* How? *He runs away.* Let's start there, and if we want to act out the beginning of the story we can go back. What is happening as he is climbing the hills or mountain? Something is taking place which he sees as soon as he arrives. It takes place at the same time as he is running away. What is it? *The men enter and are about to sacrifice the girl.* Where could the girl come from? *She is already there when the men are waving their arms up and down.*

If we start the story with the boy climbing, should the men be entering and the girl be there? *Yes.* Would she just walk on by herself or would the men bring her on? *I think they would bring her on.* What should their cue be for coming on? *When the boy starts to climb?* How do they move? *With their arms going up and down, like we just did.* What else do they do? *They need to get wood.* How many of them get wood, all of them? *Just a few.* After they've brought her in, chanted, and a few of them have brought some wood, then where do they go? *Back to the forest or wherever they came from.*

Who enters? *The boy.* He's been making his way up all this time. But now he's there because he sees someone else. *Her father.* How does he know that it's her father? *He's the chief. He can tell that by how he's dressed. Then he gets up and goes over to her and moves his hand over her in a circle. He knows that she's the chief's daughter being sacrificed for rain.*

What happens after the chief leaves? *The boy unties her and starts to run down the hill. But then he turns away because he can't go back to his father's tribe. So he goes in the opposite direction and those men come out and grab him.* Do you think they've been there all the time watching her? Or else how would they happen to return just in time? *They might have started to follow him when he went towards his tribe.* Probably. Why do you think that? *Because they were right there to grab him. He even bumps into them when he turns around to go the other way.* What happens to him next? *They tie him to a tree. Some of them go get wood. Some of them build a fire.*

Who sees this and what does he do? *The old priest. He goes down the mountain quickly to get the other tribe.* He can't just suddenly be there then if he has had to climb the mountain like the boy. So what should be his cue for entering. How long does it take him to climb the mountain? Longer than it takes the boy?

Yes. So all this time when he's climbing what is happening? *The boy unties the girl and the men have grabbed him and tied him up.* Should he enter when the boy has grabbed the girl? *About then.* When does he have to reach the top? What does he have to see? *He has to see them starting to hurt the boy.*

While he's going to get the warriors what is happening? *He can't get right back if it took him so long to climb up. It would seem silly to have him get right back.* Then a lot of preparation has to take place before they really hurt the boy. What are some of the things they could be doing after they tie the boy to the tree? How could this be stretched out? *The boy could put up a fight.* Good. They finally get him tied up but he keeps resisting so it takes them longer. What are all the things they can be doing about getting him tied up? Where does the rope come from? *One guy will have the rope and it will have to be uncoiled. A couple of others will take it and tie him to the tree. Some others can be getting wood. And others can be getting kindling.*

There's someone else who's in this part, but we haven't talked about her yet. *The girl?* What could she be doing? Would she just be watching? *I think she'd be crying.* All right. What would they do about that? Do you think she's brave and she might feel like crying, but instead would hold back her tears? *More like that. I think she'd be mad and try to be brave.* Sometimes when you're mad, do you feel like crying? *Yes, sometimes.* Is it anger mixed with being hurt? *Sometimes you're angry because you're hurt.*

While she feels this way, what could they be doing to her to make her feel even more angry and hurt. *They would be tying her up again.* And then because she's brave would she let them tie her up? *She'd go with them, but she'd sort of do this–shake them off.*

As they're tying her up who could enter and lead the last part of the scene? *The guy who's her father, the king.* How does he know what's been going on? *He's seen it.* If he hasn't seen it, how would he find out? *They'd tell him.* When should he enter? *When he hears all the noise and yelling made by the warriors.* What does he do then? Would he just sit down and watch or give orders? *He could give orders.* How would he give orders? Would someone volunteer to show us, or several of you show how the king would walk.

We want to stretch this scene. As the father speaks in gibberish, can you remember all the things that his commands are saying? *Tie them up.* Who's first? *The boy. Then getting the wood, the rope, and tying her up.* Is this all at the father's command? *Yes.* So when does he come out? *When he hears them yelling at the boy or just when they begin to tie the boy up.*

Will the father be angry with the girl? *No, because it wasn't her fault.* What wasn't? *Running away.* Why is she being tied up? *As a sacrifice for rain.* What gesture could the father make to show his faith in her after he's told them to tie her up? *He could point to the sky.*

When do the men come from the sea? *When all the Sun warriors surround the girl.* Then after they do this what could her father have them do just before the javelins are thrown? *Surround the boy.* What else might they do to the boy? Something that would make the Sea warriors want to save the boy and for that reason they would throw the javelins? *Light the fire.*

Would that be a good time for them to throw the javelins? *Yes.* Why? *It's exciting.* Why is it exciting? *Because it's the last possible time they have to save his life.* Where do the javelins land? *Right at the feet of the Sun warriors.* Why does the Sun king tell the person who begins to light the fire to stop? *Because he realizes his men could have been killed by the javelins and these Sea warriors are good fighters or else they wouldn't be able to come so close without hurting someone.*

How does the Sun king know that they are friends? *Like he said they could have killed them, but they didn't.* For what other reason does he know? *The mark on the javelin.* What was it? *A family sign.* What did he do and say as a result? *He said to his warriors to give the javelins back.* What did they do with them? *Break them.* What else does he say? *To let the boy loose and also his daughter because he recognized his brother and they will not need to sacrifice the girl. They can all get along if they can cooperate and learn to use the land.*

How could it end? *They could all listen to him and then he would talk to the sky and hold his arms up. They could follow him.* And then would they all freeze? *Yes.*

Where's the mountain? The sea? The clearing? The tree where the boy is tied? The place where the girl is? Where is the path up the mountain that the Sea people, the priest and the boy take? If they have to take a long time so it won't look like they live close by, how could they use this space? *Not use a straight path.* Show us! What would you call that kind of path? *Zig-zag.* Where do the Sun warriors enter? The king?

Who thinks they know the cues pretty well for the people to enter so they can give them a signal or help me? Will someone try? Why don't we all help do it? That means we all have to watch every minute.

Now we need some characters in order of appearance. That's a good way of remembering them. The boy? In this case it's better to have one boy until we recast. Mountain warriors? You mountain warriors remember you have three things to do. Produce the rope, tie him up, and collect the wood. How will you know which one will light the fire? *The king will tell him.* Girl? Priest? Sea warriors? The king who's the girl's father? The other king, the boy's father? *Should we talk?* You can use gibberish and talk if you want to.

Playing:
Begin tapping on the drum to provide beginning atmosphere. **Begin. Watch for your cue.** In the first acting out, maintaining the flow of the story will require concentration and some coaching preferably from the children themselves. On the second or third playing, the flaws in pace can be integrated by use of music and percussion instruments. The children will have a better feel for the need of these stimuli in reference to mood building. Questions need to be asked that emphasize timing and building.

Evaluation:
When do you think the story starts to become most exciting? *When the boy sees the girl.* What's the next exciting part? *When they meet the other tribe.* And next? *When they throw the javelins.* At each of these parts I'll beat the drums. How would they be played differently so that each part builds in excitement? *Faster and louder.* Will one of you build some excitement on these drums and then fade out? *Response.*

Are there any parts which you think could be stretched out? *When the boy's climbing. When the priest goes back to get the Sea warriors. And when they've moved back and away from the boy after they've tied him up.*

Instead of questioning the children on the entire story at first, the leader may wish to talk through sections and play each until the entire story is understood. Also, separate small groups might each play segments first broken down in outline form. Portions of the story may also be written on cards, including the number of the episode.

In this situation the type of music that does not build and is steady in intensity could be taped in advance and held ready for play during segments requiring stretching. Upon the replaying, character development could be explored and encouraged through the use of dialogue. When the boy sees the girl for the first time how do you think he feels? Why does he feel that way? What might he say to her about getting away? *Response.*

How old is the King? Is he noble or majestic? *Response.* Show me how he walks. *Response.* Is he sad? *His wife could have just died and so he is sad because now his daughter is going to die.*

What does the boy say to the girl? Can anybody put it into their own words? What does she say? If at first she believes in her tribe's tradition and he doesn't, how would you explain their different ways of thinking? *She's really superstitious and believes in the taboo.* Why doesn't he? *He wants to get away from all of that.*

"She lifted the lid just an inch, and swoosh, the top came open. . ."

Lesson 16 **PANDORA**

Motivation:

Let's make a big circle. Each of us has an imaginary box in front of us that is filled with lead. See if you can lift it. It's very heavy, isn't it? How do you show its heaviness? *Response.* Some of you were lifting a ten pound piece of lead and some of you were lifting twenty pounds. Now that we've been working so hard let's change our bodies so that they feel completely different. Just loosen them as if you were a willow blowing in the wind, or a rag doll, or a string puppet. All your joints are so loose that you can hardly stand up, like silly putty. Now let's look like we're lifting a heavy load but remain just as relaxed in your joints. Altogether. Lean over, bend your knees, get your arms underneath the box, and then instead of all the pull coming from the shoulders, get the force in your legs and come up under the weight. All right, again, the same thing. Repeat the above steps. Supportive comments are often needed for encouragement. All right rest for a moment. Most young children will have no difficulty with the squat position, but they will not be as ready to show the weight they are supporting. The older children by comparison, will find it more tedious to squat. Showing that they are supporting weight will be a more tangible reality and its firmness will show in their back and arms.

The secret is that we want to show that we are lifting a weight when we're really not. When we break this exercise down into some easy steps like we were doing, then it will look more real. Someone will really see what we are carrying. The teacher demonstrates. At first you bend over, then bend your knees until you are in the squat position. Now some of you can't get into this position because everyone is built differently. There are as many ways to do something as there are people to do it. As soon as you bend your knees reach down with your arms and begin to lift the box by lifting with your legs, not your back. Put all the strength in your legs and don't carry as much of the load through your shoulders and back. That will make your package look heavy when there's really nothing there. We're playing a trick on people. Because of the way we can move our bodies, we can almost be like magicians.

Now, I want two of you to lift a table that weighs 35 pounds. Keep the table between you. Are there any volunteers? *Response.* How high is it? And how long is it? How wide is it? Can we see the table? Almost. Now can you put it down very carefully in front of one of your friends? Now, will another student change it so that it becomes a pail half full of cement? You'll need some help won't you? *Response.* Notice that all the weight is between the two lifters. There are many ways to carry these objects. There's only one main rule and that is what? Can anybody remember? *Carry the weight in your legs and not your arms or your back.* Right. So you might limp while carrying the pail of cement if all the weight is between both of you. Whom are you two going to leave your cement with? *Response.*

I wonder if another pair can think of other ways to carry this pail of cement. Could you place an object between you that would equalize the weight more? *Use a board.* Could you show us how? That's like combining the carrying of the table and the pail of cement. The table acts as a pallet. Now leave it in front of someone else. You'll need the board because the pail becomes a chest filled with treasure. You'll need quite a lot of help from all of us. Some of us are tired so all those who haven't had a chance to carry anything can help. How are you going to begin, all at once or separately? *All at once.* Why? *Because it will be lighter if we all do it together and at the same time.* How do you know? *I remember from before, when we lifted a dead body and then the dead monster.* Good. Ready. Shall the rest of us count for them? One, two, three, lift! *Response.* Is the weight in their legs or their arms? Did they get the main part of their body under the box? *Response.*

Set it down carefully and keep that heaviest part of your body under the box as long as you can, then your back won't have to take the strain. Put it in the middle.

That's good. Are you tired? I'm tired just watching you. If we were paid by the hour for all this good work we've been doing, we'd have enough money to buy all that treasure. But maybe that's not treasure. I wonder what it is. See your own box in the space in front of you. It's rusty. It's an old chest. You feel it and it's rough where the rust is. There's some silver which is tarnished. You get excited about opening it because it looks so old. Is it heavy? It also has a bright gold rope tied around it. Maybe this means there is something important in it or someone has just recently put something in it. Try to lift it.

It will be hard to get the knot loose. What could you do to investigate further about what might be inside? *Knock on it, rattle it, listen to it, or open it.* We can't open it; it's locked. Let's try some of these other suggestions and see if we can hear something. Listen. There's something alive inside. All right everyone think of some way of opening your own box. But don't open it just yet. Just figure out a way you're going to open it. And what's inside of it? I want to see every step you go through to open it. The expression on your face will tell us what's inside. Can you talk with your face? Let's try. I'll start now to open my box and then whoever is ready go next, one at a time, so we can see each other. Here I go. First I have to undo the cord. Does anyone have a tool chest where they can get me a screwdriver? *Response.* Thank you. Now I can undo the cord and slip it off. Next the lock. Does anyone have a pin so I can pick the lock? *Response.* That won't work. What else can I do? *Saw it!* What else? *An ax. A bomb.* Good ideas, but that might destroy what's inside.

Have you thought about what may be inside your box? If you had your choice of the best thing you could think of, what would it be? Think about it. What's the best thing you can think of that would be in that box? All right, who's ready? *Response.* How are you going to open it? Can we tell how you feel about what's inside the box? *Response.* That's right, use your face. Can anyone tell us what emotion he used or how he felt? Have each of them open his box so that the others can observe and comment on what is clear and from having seen a positive example. If the class is large, one half will have to watch while the first half performs, and then exchange roles. If the class is too young to successfully become an audience, everyone will move at the same time under the leader's direction.

Having them look for a particular reaction from each person will encourage responses which are favorable. They should also be motivated to watch for ways in which their boxes can be opened. After this period of intense yet passive response, they will be ready to move.

Release:

Do you remember some of the emotions people showed in their faces? I'll be the first magician and change you into whatever character. Whomever I point to must then become the magician and remember to show the emotion you feel because of your character. Whoever I point to must then become the magician and change the rest of you. Then that person points to someone else. Here we go. I am going to change you all so that you will become little demons. Little demons! You are the most wicked of the demons. After a few moments the teacher points to a new student. Now you are the magician. And because of your power you can change us all into anything you want. *I will change you into vampires who have long hair growing out of your noses.* Quickly! Who did he point to? Change us before we are all destroyed. Change us into something good. *I am going to change you into angels with large white wings.* The game has many variations. It can be used as a warm-up for practicing spontaneous character changes. After the group seems to have had enough exhilarated movement, use a drum as it is needed. Two taps on the drum provides a signal to get them to react.

Stimulus:

Come back to the circle and rest. Those were very nice characters you thought of and your bodies were so expressive. I hope you can use some of those good characters in this story that tells about how all the pain and suffering on earth was created.

Many thousands of years ago all the Greek gods lived on the high mountain called Mount Olympus, in Greece. The name of Mount Olympus is how the Olympic Games got their name. Zeus was the most powerful of the gods. One day he was out riding his chariot through the sky. His half brother, who was part god and part man, decided to steal the fire from Mt. Olympus to take to the people on earth, because the people on earth lived in darkness. When Zeus returned and found out that the people on earth had received light and might be able to see what was going on up in the sky where the gods lived, he had Prometheus, his half-brother, punished. He had him chained to a rock alive and commanded two vultures to chew upon him continually so that he would always be in pain.

But Zeus still wasn't satisfied with this punishment. With fire the people might be able to learn about the wisdom of the gods and all the super powers they had for making the sun move and the stars shine. So he sent Prometheus's brother, Epimetheus, a beautiful young bride named Pandora. Pandora and Epimetheus had many happy days together. They ran in the woods, hunted, and climbed trees. And then Zeus decided to disguise himself as a poor man and visit them.

The poor man knocked on the door of their cottage. He asked Pandora if she would take a box he was carrying and store it for safekeeping. He said he would return for it later. He also said that under no circumstances was she to open it. And she promised she wouldn't. It was a very interesting looking box, old with tarnished gold bands around it, a large lock on it, and a heavy gold rope tied around it.

Epimetheus said that she had better stay behind with the box while he went hunting alone. She went outside and started to take a walk, but as she was walking she was unable to get her mind off of the box's contents. So she went back into the house to see if it was still there and it was. She went up to it and felt it and listened to it. She was sure she had heard something inside of it. So she knocked on it and listened again. Oh, if she might have just a peak inside! She could close it up again, and no one would know. So she started to work at the lock. It wouldn't give. She went to the cabinet where the tools were. She brought one out and tried again. This time she got the tiny boned tool into it and the lock snapped open. Voices inside the box were getting louder and louder saying, "Let us out. Let us out," and she was carried away with excitement. Now the knot had to be untied, and so she used the bone for that also. She slipped the cord off and the voices kept getting louder still. She lifted the lid just an inch, and swoosh, the top came open, and all the most hideous looking black devils clawed their way out, saying "Now we're free! We'll pollute the earth so that people will not be able to eat. We'll spread disease, envy, hatred, and suffering and death." Pandora tried to close the box, but the force of the spirits was so strong that she could not compete with them. Just then Epimetheus came running in having heard the great noise and seen all those swarming demons, he asked, "What have you done?"

There was still one voice in the box that called to her saying "Let me out! I am Hope, and I'll always be here to help."

Release:

Who were the demons? What were some of their names? What did they say at first? *Jealousy, envy, all the bad things, and disease, hatred, pollution. At first, they wanted to get out.* How do you think they moved when they wanted to get out, can some of you show us? And what were they saying all together. *Let us out. . .let us out.* Go on. *We want to destroy you. We'll bring on all the bad things and suffering.* And what else? *And we'll hurt you until you'll have nothing left.* Nothing, won't there be anything? What was left at the bottom of the box? *Hope! There will always be hope so there never will be death or an end to everything.*

Let's form a large box. First make a circle and step back about four steps. Show that you have a flat surface, which will be part of the box, in front of you. Place your hands, one after the other, in front of you. As you take a hand off the surface, bend your wrist and pull your hand off at the same time. Curve your fingers over your palm, moving them back until your fingers are bent back over your wrist. Then move your palm forward with the fingers following. Each hand should touch separately the flat surface in front of you. Let's have lots of wrist action, so that when you finally place your hand on the surface it looks flat. That's the secret. To make something appear with just the movement of your body when there's nothing there. That makes your body magic.

Now, shake your hands out. Half of you who want to be demons now get inside this box. Let's see the box. Where are the corners? Let's have four of you at the corners. Even though the demons are moving as demons, remember that they show the box also. Why? Do they like the box? *They want to get out.* What do they say and who are they? I'm beginning to see a box there. Change. Demons be the box and those of you who are the box become demons. Where's the box? What are those on the outside trying to do? *Open the box.* One of you find an opening. *Look, come here you guys. I hear something.* Take it slow. . .everything in slow-motion from now on. *Let's open it. How? Get a tool. Here. There. They're coming! We're coming to bring evil. They're ugly. Help!* And what else? *All of the bad things. Hatred and death.* Who's left? *I'm still here. I'll help. There will always be Hope.* It went very well in slow-motion. All right. Have a rest. Let's see if we can remember the story to this point so we can do this part again with some music and all the creatures moving in slow-motion.

Planning:
What did the old man say to Pandora when he brought the box? *Not to open it.* What was he going to do? *He'd come back for it.* Who else was there? *Epimetheus?* What did he do? *He said he'd go hunting. And Pandora should stay with the box.* Why? *Because the old man had left it in their house to keep it safe.* Then what did Pandora do? What was she thinking? *She went for a walk. She was thinking about the box.* What did she do? *She went back in to look at it.* Did she open it at first. *She couldn't. She tried.* What did she use? *She used a tool and got the knot untied. Then she got the lock undone. And the whole top started to come open.* What did she do then? *She couldn't do anything.* Why? *All these demons started to come out and they were too strong for her.*

Who were the demons? *All the bad things on earth like disease. . .and death. . .suffering, pollution, and hatred.* What did they say just before they got out. *Let me out!* And then what did they say? *We are going to bring all the bad things to the earth.* Can you think of an evil character who hates everyone because he or she is jealous and all he wants to do is to hurt whomever he can, anyone?

Release:
Remember the game we played? Why don't the demons play their parts by using that game. One demon will start out and say, "You are all Death. Everything you do or touch makes everyone and

everything fall." Then Death can say, "You are all. . ." What? *Jealousy. . .you don't want anyone to be better than you.* Go on. *You are all . . .Disease, you're all bleeding and have scabs.* Good. That's very convincing.

Planning:

Now who runs in because of all this noise? *Epimetheus.* What does he say? *What have you done? You're bad. You've spoiled everything.* He scolds her as if she were a naughty child. But then something interrupts them. *It's a little voice. It's hope. He says, I'm Hope. And I'll always be here to help.* What else could he say? *Don't worry. There's always hope.* What does he remind you of? *Like my grandmother. She says everything will be all right. All you have to do is not worry.* We need a little hope in this story don't you think? How should we end it? *The demons could float off as Hope comes out and they could get smaller and smaller and sort of die or crumple up.* What do Pandora and Epimetheus do? *They could stand and look at Hope. I think Pandora would cry or bend down. She would bend down and put her hands over her face.* That sounds just right. Let's try it.

Playing:

Where's the door to their house where the old man first comes? Who else goes out that door? *Epimetheus.* Where's the door that Pandora uses to leave the house to go to the garden? Show me how she's walking? *Response.* Does she hurry back in? *She does but it's hard to explain because she knows she shouldn't.* Can you show us? *Response.* Oh, I see, she walks away from the box, but very slowly because it's like she's being pulled back. She's very what? *Curious.* When have you ever been curious about a box you shouldn't open, but wanted to? *At Christmas.* That's it!

We've left out something important. Where's the box? If some of you want to play the box, how will the old man bring all of you in? Can he? Can he mime the box like we did at the beginning? And then when Pandora leaves for her walk, just after Epimetheus leaves, all of you can come together and form the box magically. Then when she returns from her walk she sees it and it's four times as much a curiosity and temptation to her. Her temptation equals the size of the box, almost. The box can form to the music when it starts. Come together in slow-motion so it's like a dream.

Who will be the old man? *Response.* Does he need a helper? *Response.* Who will be Pandora? She could have a sister who is visiting her. Let's see how that works out. Epimetheus? Demons? Box? Just one or two? You two be the part that lets the demons out, so they have something to push against.

Evaluation:
Do you remember the cue for the box to start to form? *When Pandora leaves for her walk.* The music will start then and the box part forms, and the demons get inside. Until then will all of you be an audience for us and watch how it goes? When we do it again we'll change parts. Begin with the old man coming to the door. Pandora and Epimetheus are in their house.

Playing:
After the evaluation, the story can be recast and replayed. The most important aspect to work on will be the mood affected by the demons. The suggestion can be made that the demons move throughout the story in the background to the music which is playing softly. There might also be more of a challenge or struggle between the parts of the box and the demons in slow-motion if there are more box members. The dialogue will be weak at first and might be improved by the addition of mood, narration and working more on the dialogue during the planning stage.

The mood aspect has been mentioned. Narration should be dealt with next. For this story it is possible for the leader to narrate from the beginning while the characters appear moving to the narration. Zeus can appear quite simply, by casually walking around and looking as if he is in control of everything. Then Prometheus can enter as soon as Zeus has left, carrying his torch, running around the room to suggest the distance to the place on Earth where he arrives with the light. He returns to Mount Olympus the same way. The light from Earth begins to bother Zeus which he can demonstrate by rubbing his forehead. He looks again to see a slight movement of bodies far away across the room, representing the "people" of Earth. He calls for his vultures who both fly in taking Prometheus by the arms, nailing him down, then continuing the scene by pecking at him, as he groans. Since the focus should return to Zeus and his decision to punish the people for their newly-gained light, the body of Prometheus can be carried off by the vultures. Zeus sends Pandora to tempt Epimetheus and wonders how they will carry through. This may be shown by his pacing back and forth. Like the "magician" in the earlier game, Zeus points to someone and creates Pandora. Together, Pandora and Epimetheus run, hunt, play other games, and then see a flash of light which signals the entrance of Zeus as an old man. The leader-narrator may then provide the speaking parts of the characters. Many exercises are included in this book dealing with the development of dialogue which can be used or included at this point if the students show interest in continuing the development of the story.

Lesson 17 **NORWEGIAN WINTER**

Motivation:
Can you think about the times in a nation when people become most united? Are these times of joy or sadness? *Usually sadness.* Why? What might have happened? *When someone dies. Or when there aren't many jobs.* Can you think of any times or events in history or the recent past when people worked together as a nation or as one group? *In the Civil War, or when it flooded.* Why did they remain together? *They had to.* Why? *They wouldn't be able to do anything unless they stayed together.* Can you imagine or remember a time like that? I'm not talking about something that happens which affects a few people, but an event which makes everyone's life change. This is an abstract area for most children because these types of situations may not have touched their lives. They need to be reminded of events that may have reached them vicariously, such as pollution, war, or the death of a leader.

Stimulus:
The following material can be used very simply as a basis for a plot from which the children can be directed to expand their own story or unwritten script. The leader may teach a series of events in history and the social sciences through this thematic approach, expanding it into related projects such as maps, graphs, fictional history.

This is a true story which happened during the Second World War. Through their courage some Norwegian children worked together to save their town's treasure from their enemies, the Germans. Their idea was to dig up hundreds of gold bars which were worth a great deal of money, find a way to quickly transport this gold to the river, and ship it off to safety. The children knew they had to do this. The gold represented power and money to buy more armaments. Most of their fathers were away fighting.

Release:
We have to make a lot of decisions about how we want to play this story. If it's snowing very hard and you can barely see another person, do you think you could pass bars of gold? Let's see how you would do it. Play the first two minutes of Dvorak's *New World Symphony.* As soon as the music starts you can all appear from the house. You can hardly see, the snow fall is so thick, but you must figure out the quickest way to pass the gold. Ready? At first children may need to listen to the music once with their eyes closed. Use of Exercise 39, Blind Group, also may be helpful in reaching a level of absorption for obtaining belief.

Planning:

See if you can hear a change in the music. What is the difference between the first part and the second? What was the first part like? The second? Does the first part suggest how the children would be walking? *It sounds like they're being careful.* Why? *They might be watched.* From where? *Anywhere.* So they can be seen. Can they also see around them? If they can be seen, where are the soldiers who are observing them? *Hiding.* So they're behind things? Where? *In the forest.* What might the soldiers be using to help them see that the children wouldn't have? *Binoculars. . .maybe guns.* If the children want to get their work done and possibly are being watched, what would they begin doing? Would they run right out and begin digging up the gold? *They'd be running and playing.* What are some of the activities they'd be doing? *Building snow men. Having snowball fights.* Would this give them more time to know whether or not they were being watched? Can a person be involved in one thing, yet be doing another at the same time? *Response.* Can you do that? How would you move? *At first slowly and then gradually speed up and begin moving faster.* What would you be doing at the same time you are playing? *Watching.* Would everyone be doing it at the same time? *No. Everyone would be doing the same thing but at different times.*

Playing:

Let's put the music on and as soon as you feel like it, begin playing. Take turns having a look around.

Planning:

When the situation seems safe what would you begin to do? What is your purpose? *To get at the gold.* Where is the gold? *Here.* When would you begin digging for it? *As soon as it seemed safe.* How could you keep from being observed? *Some of us would be building a fort in front of it.* As though you were playing a game of war? How would you transport the gold so that it would look like part of your playing? *On sleds, with someone wounded lying on top of it.* Would this take longer? *Yes.* As soon as you were sure that things were safe could you get down to business and really pass the gold quickly? *Yes.* How? *Make a chain.* How would you be more certain that everything was safe? *Have someone high up in the trees watching the area.* And who would be watching the lookout? *Another watcher standing between the trees and the chain.* Who's going to build the wall? Who will pass the gold? There! Who's the first watcher? The second? There! What happens first? *Everyone runs into the forest.* The events should be reviewed through the words of the children. They're looking and then begin playing. They start a mock war so they can build the fort. The gold is dug up behind it, the watchers take their places, and the gold is passed. **I'll play the music and I want you to begin moving through these events.**

Playing:
Children can move through the segments as in their normal play.

Planning:
Let's listen to the music and decide how to end it. When should we definitely begin to pass the gold? *When the music speeds up.* **Why?** *Because the watcher sees something in the distance and tells us to hurry.* **Would you have finished digging the gold up?** *We would stop for that day because we had been given a warning.* **What does the music suggest you do?** *Probably begin playing.* **What would those who had been digging up the gold do? What could happen as a result of the warning that would help to make the situation very dramatic?** *The Germans could come and be suspicious.* **How could this meeting become very intense, yet not include physical violence?** *The Germans might go very near the digging.* **Would they see it?** *No, I don't think so.* **Where's the gold now?** *It has been loaded onto boats.* **Who has loaded it? What's happening to it during this last scene that would help to complete the story?** *The boats could be navigated towards the sea.* **Can we play the whole thing through? Everything up to this part? Who will be the Germans? From where do they enter? What will they do? Where will they go? Who's passing the gold onto the ships and navigating? Everyone else do what you did before.**

By this time the children have been through simple enough
actions, feel confident about their responsibility, and are watching each other sufficiently to pass and take cues from one group to another. The music is an interchange between calmness, intensity, and back to calmness, helping to guide the overall storyline and relate separate actions to a dramatic structure.

The main action of passing the gold and the overall conflict with time is all that the leader needs to present; the music helps to sustain the children's seriousness. Some children might not introduce the Germans, while others may introduce them at the beginning, leave the children to their mock play, and return at the end.

If the leader continually emphasizes sensitivity to the environment, sensitivity to the music, and uses group signals to promote unity, then children will be more involved in form and tension and less in the antagonisms between rival groups. This theme provides the children an opportunity to develop the story in a different direction, amplifying it from a simple beginning. The potential for action and conflict is sufficient to motivate the children emotionally when they become inspired by the music and the germinating idea. If the teacher feels the planning becomes bogged down, he may introduce cues over the music. **Begin digging now.**

Once the children ask, *Can we talk?* (or) *Can the music be turned down so we can talk?*, a new level of involvement is reached, and the music becomes internalized, along with the mood and emotion.

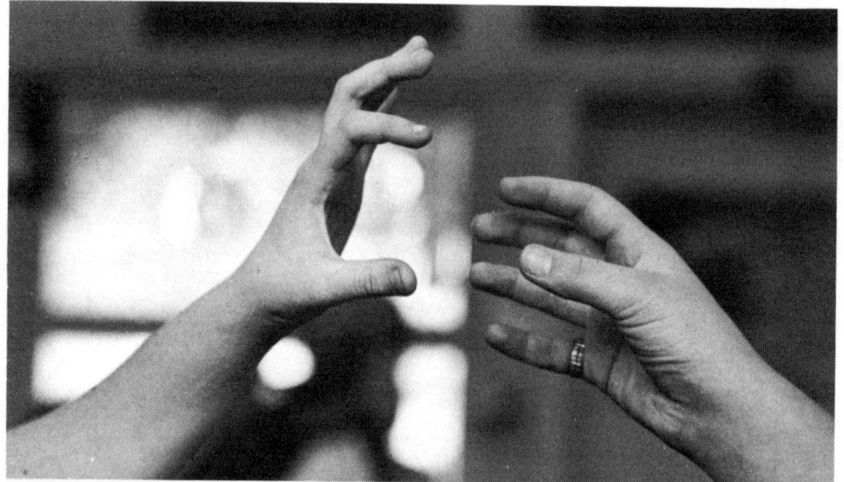

"Along came a spider. . ."

Lesson 18 **LITTLE MISS MUFFET**

In essence, this Mother Goose rhyme is a short play. The introduction, rising action, climax, and denouement are all included along with the protagonist (Miss Muffet) and the antagonist (the spider). It also contains action, the key element for creating drama.

Is this sufficient reason for using such a common rhyme? Is it long enough to sustain interest? Interest is coupled with involvement which is, in turn, affected by the conditions surrounding the material. When reflecting upon such a simple rhyme for action, if nothing else stands out, consider the mood. If it is sinister, mysterious, awesome, there will be a challenge in creating an aura of mystery surrounding the spider's environment that will overshadow the triteness of the rhyme. How the motivation is handled, either to enhance the material or to bring out new ideas which relate to the material, helps the children better understand new concepts.

Two possibilities for motivation which come to mind when relating this rhyme are: spiders and fear, and the identity of the mysterious Miss Muffet. Spiders evoke fascination from most people. Spiders abound with psychological meaning. Similarly, it is known that children made up these rhymes to stand for things they couldn't talk about openly. So who might Miss Muffet have been? It might have been the name of an undercover agent. One possible line of instruction stemming from this simple rhyme follows.

Motivation:
What are all the things we know about spiders? *Response.* What are some unusual things that maybe the rest of us hadn't heard about? *Response.* I wonder why people are afraid of them? Do you think people are afraid of them because of the way they walk? *Response.* How do they walk? Can you walk like a spider? *Response.* Does anyone know how they kill their prey? Has anyone seen them? *Response.* Can you show us? *Response.* Are there other things people are afraid of? *Response.* How do people act when they're afraid? *Response.* Can you show us? *Response.*

Stimulus:
There's a poem which some of you have heard and could even say for yourselves. The leader should recite the rhyme.

Planning:
Where do you think Miss Muffet and the spider are? In a forest? I'm going to play some music and see if you can be looking for a place in the forest to sit. When the music starts to fade sit down. Who do you think Miss Muffet could be? How do you think she

would be sitting when the spider entered. *Response.* What would he be doing? *Response.* Would one of you play Miss Muffet, and one of you be the spider? *Response.* Let's all do it. Get together in pairs. Count off, randomly grouping them as they are standing, or have them group themselves. Placing students into pairs and small groups is delicate, particularly during the late elementary years when they tend to form cliques. This is one of the main problems which should be dealt with in the exercises. Decide who will be the spider and who will be the victim in your groups.

Playing and Release:

This time as soon as the music starts, enter, sit and eat or do whatever else you think. Next the spider music will start, but the spider doesn't enter until the music begins to fade. *Response.*

Evaluation and Planning:

Let's all sit over here. How can we end it? *Response.* What do people do when they're afraid? Think of a time when you were most afraid. Can you remember what happened? And what you did? *Response.* Let's try some of these things. As soon as I start the drumbeat or the music, begin to walk as if someone were following you and you don't want to seem to walk too fast or else they'll walk faster, nor do you want to walk slowly or they might catch up with you.

Evaluation and Planning:

Did they catch up with you? It didn't look very convincing. I want to try a trick, but you have to concentrate. Start walking as before when the music starts and as soon as the volume goes down, look up in that corner as if something is about to happen and freeze. As they are walking the volume should go down. Then make some startling noise which frightens them. What happened? You were scared because you didn't expect it. Why didn't you expect it. *I was thinking about that corner you told us to watch.* Change roles and let's do the same thing to the music. Let's see what "Miss Muffet" will do this time. Play the same music. Response.

Evaluation:

Have them sit for discussion: There were all kinds of different responses. Some of you stood still and some ran. Can you remember a time when any of you were too afraid to move? *Response.* How about a time when you ran? *Response.* It's difficult to act as if you're afraid without a reason. I wonder if you'd be able to act out some of these situations you've been

talking about with your partner so that we could almost guess the reason for your fear. Half could volunteer while the other half watched or a few would volunteer at first. Playing emotions in a vacuum is embarrassing; some cannot create sufficient motivation to be believed. The reasons for these feelings should be discussed. **Did you feel embarrassed?** *Response.* **Why didn't you?**

Parallel examples of dramatic conflict could be offered as a bridge into current themes in history, literature, daily experience—once the theme is isolated. (Indian raids, territorial expansion, particular episodes which are frightening). For some, the rhyme might imply irrational fears; if the spider is a black widow, and poisonous, the action might denote bullying—a big force pushing a little thing around.

The topic of fear denotes a spectrum of erratic, deeply embedded dramas over which many blank tapes (old memories) are replayed. The construction of a situation by the class from a focus question and some extension into deeper dimensions of the topic 'fear' would result in emotional purges, loosening many antagonisms and emotional blocks.

Lesson 19 **TOWN PLANNING**

Using index cards to instruct children about their responsibility in relation to action, character, and place works well if the leader presents a problem situation with which the children can identify. Items can be alternately collected by the leader and selected by the children. The division into smaller groups for guidance in decision-making and action-taking should be formed under some common affiliation. The leader needs to direct the overall activity as narrator, role-taker, or both. In this manner, the leader can facilitate the groups in many ways (as, for example: a reporter, a radio announcer, a television interviewer, or a panel director) and gradually, by introducing more facts and drawing out opinions, either initiate conflict or prolong tension until some crisis is reached and a decision is made. Within the larger framework each group will receive direction, while within the smaller groups each individual acquires character qualities to help him toward some culmination.

Topics about everyday life can be developed and examined. A brief and varied collection of news items from the media can often become favorite subjects for which a format should exist. The following example is a problem area which has been explored using this format:

PROBLEM: the main reason for a town's development and growth no longer exists and a new type of industry must be sought. Signs around the room provide environments in which this problem may be discussed.

Union Hall	Environmentalists	Businessmen	Cultural Center
loggers	scientist	councilperson	actress
fishermen	architect	tourist guide	poet
truck driver	teacher	advertizer	ex-builder
tractor driver	builder	engineer	college student
		store owner	architect

Each group has a particular point of view upon which they base their arguments: The town cannot continue to grow if the largest industry becomes jobless; the present industry will soon ruin the town by its lack of planning; the town's resources must be sold, making money to create new industries; the beauty of the environment will no longer exist if growth continues in the present directions.

Emergency situations can serve to increase the intensity of the experience and can be inserted or included within (or become) the main problem. The following are examples of such complications: a forest fire, flood or tornado occurs and animals and people need to be saved; the changing circumstances in life-style have become a life and death matter and people must adjust although political and economic imbalance continues. Complications offer a wide range of choices and can be presented by different methods to older and younger groups. More direct and personal approaches should be used with younger children. A leader's beginning statement might attack the problem directly. **This problem has occurred just recently, and I can't understand it. I'm not even sure that anything can be done. If we were to try to do something about it, what kind of person do you think you could be?** The leader should continue to facilitate the group's direction. They may discover things together or be divided into smaller groups when the leader signals.

With older groups more information may be supplied at the beginning so they have a definite direction and continue to solve problems under the well-timed guidance and intervention of the leader. A conditional situation could be introduced by using the so-called *Magic If.* For example: **What if all people were required to serve the country a certain number of hours a week according to age and ability, but for no pay? How do you think this would affect the country? What jobs do you think would need to be done? What jobs should be done?** In this manner, the cognitive domain may be the realm used as a basis for gaining factual data, while the affective domain can be utilized in guiding the selection of data according to a combination of the values of the student and his role.

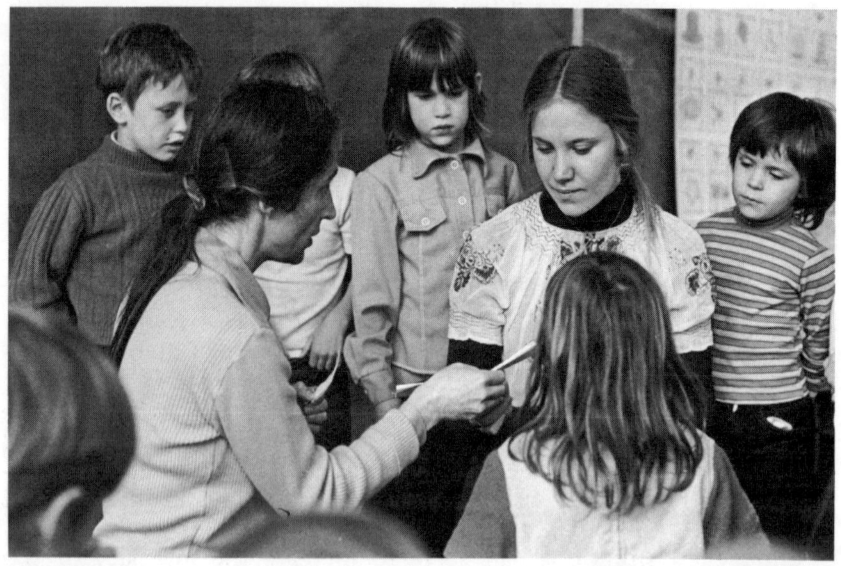

"It is alright to be sad. . ."

Lesson 20 **ROLE-PLAYING**

Any number of people can be cast in role, remaining mute, semi-mute, or separate in order to maintain aesthetic distance. The children will reduce the distance as they become involved and begin to ask or answer questions about the role-takers. A situation is set up in which the children are needed and are asked questions regarding their observations of the role-players, either directly or indirectly.

An example of a situation in which younger children might participate at will could be presented and guided toward an understanding and awareness of other people's feelings.

A young, foreign-speaking girl was sad throughout the past week due to a number of circumstances: a letter received from home and a related incident about which she has refused to speak. These details are not important in themselves except that they provide a way for the children to identify with the "foreign" girl.

After the girl is introduced as someone who likes children and works with children, the problem of her sadness may be presented to them. Through the leader's questions, the children find a way to make contact with her. After the children play games, pantomime animals, and play instruments, they find that their visitor reacts to little except those actions which include birds, bird-like motions, and bird songs. Meanwhile, a circle can be made around the visitor as she alternates between watching them and taking out a few props. These props include a book with a bird drawing, a white feather, and a letter with a picture of a bird, map, cross, and a hunter. The props serve to provide a mystery to be solved if the children want to put the facts together; a scenario could exist. The more important objective is for them to empathize with her sadness and to feel an increasing identity by being needed.

The vistor may then become aware of the class, draw a map on the board, and beckon the children to follow her. After a journey is completed around the room, she can put out her arms to stop the children. Bending down as if to enter a cave, she crawls into a darker, low-ceilinged space. The children wait for her to come out, and lift whatever was lying in her cupped hands into view. The leader continues guiding the children through direct and indirect questions. The object might turn out to be a dead bird, which they feel needs to be buried. They pantomime instructions for the visitor to bury the animal. She follows their instructions and ritualistically performs the burial. She seems relieved that the task is over and guides them back around the room and places them around a scarf that she had used to symbolically cover the grave. To end the scene, she appears happier, waves good-bye, and leaves the room.

The leader then guides a discussion through the children's answers to her questions. **Do you think she was happier? I wonder why? Do you think you helped her?** After some ideas about the children's relationship to the visitor have been expressed, the scarf is pulled up, and the leader asks if there was really a dead bird buried. The children probably will agree, at least verbally, that they have been playing, and that it was part of their involvement in helping the visitor.

The most important idea to be expanded upon is that the children had some affect on their visitor's feelings, by sharing in her drama. Related topics in order of importance are: people are sad sometimes and we can help them; it's all right to be sad; people are sad when something they love is hurt. The fact that the visitor's sadness might have been caused by a dead bird which hadn't been buried seems to be closer to the children's experience. This might be brought out by the leader at the end of the session by saying that they had thrown a dead bird away in the garbage where the visitor worked. The children immediately become involved in their own stories about such happenings, more interested in their own experience than in the visitor's. There might be little need to connect the absence of a burial with whatever motive accompanied this theme. Helping children to empathize with another person's feelings has many facets. It might be proven to the leader that they need more time to explore their own experiences before they can jump into another person's situation. For other children, empathy is immediate.

The role-playing format may be used as a stimulus to involve the children in imaginary or curricular themes. Both themes may be considered at the same time, allowing for varied degrees of aesthetic distance. Using an inductive approach, the aesthetic distance depends upon the leader's use of questions in relation to the children's rate of discovery. In each case, the leader should have researched and planned with general and specific objectives in mind, but at any moment should be prepared to insert the children's own contributions to the situation.

Two examples of formats are:

A tableau of a historical scene can come to life, each character being a specific person from the past.

An unusual, futuristic invention from which ideas develop concerning man's potential evolutionary form: scarves covering antennae lead to discussion of a new type of sensitivity.

"I take thee Rosalind, for wife." — Shakespeare

"Every dog must have his day." — *Swift*

5: IMPROVISATION

Among the most rewarding moments in the lives of many teachers is watching children's acceptance of each other's ideas while at spontaneous play. There must be an established flow among them at such moments for the experience to continue with benefit. It seems as if their bodies are moved by an unseen, collective director. The group can move in and out of character, time, and space, and advance through a plot or series of episodes only as long as there is cooperation and trust within the group.

Suddenly, however, something happens. The group discovers that someone is watching. A choking, halting, and stumbling begins. The collective director returns to each individual body, and the children no longer look out of the same eyes. The flow is broken; they become self-conscious, separate, different. As a result, they frequently feel unhappy, bad, or ugly. This process is one of the reasons why neither children nor adults can *play* before an audience. Developing the facility for seeming to play is why improvisation and creative dramatics are so valuable.

Our changing world makes it vital that people be capable of expressing themselves in both mind and body in order to prepare for and to accept the future and its new life styles. All that is known for certain is that change continues. Work in school that was once done to fulfill a utilitarian end now cannot be done for that purpose. Through creative dramatics and improvisation, one may learn to say with full authority, "I do not know what I am looking for, nor must I find it to keep looking. I shall continue looking because I am in contact with what I am becoming. I am growing and using the fullness of my inner resources. I can look far into the distance without the hindrance of social inhibitions clouding my vision." The fullness of discovery and its resulting confidence produces an expansion of awareness that allows room for the energy and excitement that comes with play. Improvisation provides the stimulus to generate the spontaneity that expands the stunted imagination.

Today's work for the future is to stimulate the inner resources leading toward sensitivity and understanding. Exercises used in beginning improvisation are intended to develop group feeling as well as to exchange creative energy in movement and sound. Release of energy through sound often occurs in the form of speech.

The awareness that allows members of an improvisation group to become flexible enough to enter into relationships and share space frequently begins with the same kind of exercise found in creative dramatics. The exercises included in the section on Abstract Mime in Chapter Three may be used as a preparation for those contained in this chapter.

When using improvisation with either children or adults, they must willingly *cooperate* with each other, understand the need for *trust* between group members, and readily *support* each other with ideas in rehearsal as well as performance. Ideally, to do the exercises in improvisation, most members of a younger group should have worked together in creative dramatics, so that exercises which focus on improvisation will continue the same disciplines. If this is not the case, improvisational exercises should be accompanied by ample discussion, movement, and warm-up sessions. Readers should refer to suggestions given in Chapter Three for use of the exercise section.

As the terms are used here, *improvisation* differs from *creative dramatics.* It should be remembered that the natural result of improvisation is a seemingly effortless performance, whereas creative dramatics exercises are designed for use in progressing through stages of growth. Performance, therefore, becomes secondary in importance. Although both improvisation and creative dramatics use the same exercises and techniques, the method in which they are used is different. In improvisation, more background in technique on the part of the player must be expected, more maturity is required, and self-discipline must be taken for granted. At first, both improvisation and creative dramatics require many simple movement exercises. Such exercises become a catalyst for engendering group excitement and relationships. Little need be said about the use of space in improvisation because use of individual space already should have become established in creative dramatics.

Beginning improvisation rehearsals frequently consist of a round of movement exercises stimulated by narration, music, speech, and enactment of familiar stories. After a few rehearsals, including warm-ups and movement, character development should be emphasized.

Many areas in the group rehearsal should be directed. The use of voice, movement, trust, sensitivity, grace, plots, character, and form are but a few of these areas. However, give and take among actors remains of fundamental importance. It is important to emphasize aspects of human nature more by developing broad character types which become clearly identifiable than by performing clever plots with preplanned jokes. Emotional release, resulting from character identification, may then create a more lasting impact.

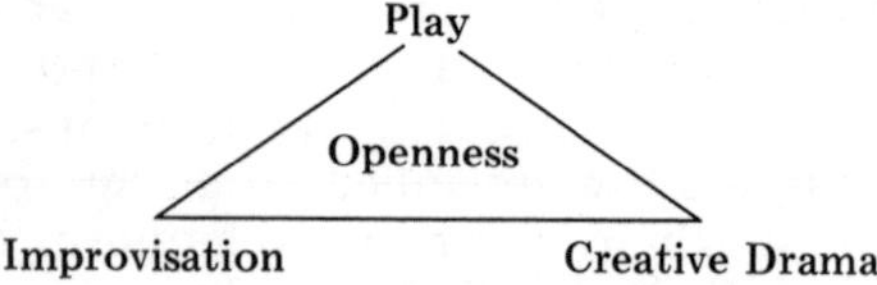

Recreational Values of Improvisation. The process of play, creative drama, and improvisation requires a surrender to childlikeness and innocence. This ageless innocence provides an openness that may help the players use their own life experiences.

Before children are able to make up their own story material, they must be strongly guided. Much of the learning process is a result of self-expression. Their values constantly take shape and form, but unless they are expressed in play, movement, or speech, they may go unheard or unknown, even to the child himself. The child absorbs what he needs, and there comes a time when he must demonstrate the mixing and distillation of all that has been fusing inside of him. Using stimuli for developing story material has been discussed previously. The children's own ideas help uncover material concerning the children's values and beliefs.

In drama, a child should first be asked to begin expressing his feelings concerning everyday situations and using faculties which reinforce those basic experiences. He should gradually grow more secure by repeating similar experiences or connected activities that channel his responses. The leader must attempt to deepen the child's internal responses by probing constantly, with increased intensity. The repetitive methods usually relied upon for early childhood teaching must be balanced by such probing. With both internalization and a balance between the methods used, the child may become receptive to ideas outside his own realm.

By comparison, older people may become separated over the years from their true feelings. Adult feelings frequently become very complex, while attitudes and opinions become vehemently rigid; they may be adamantly opposed to this or that viewpoint, give someone else's reasons why, and remain closed forever to anything new. Through improvisation such rigidity may frequently be reduced.

Many of the improvisation exercises included are catalytic and encourage an openness to one's own, internal "drama." When either a child or adult is functioning at his peak in the drama situation, he should be able to respond. Projections from one's past may be highlighted in a therapeutic form and developed internally.

From Creative Drama to Improvisation. There are many steps in the process from a young child's dramatic play to polished, performed, improvisation. This chapter is a natural progression for students, ranging in age from twelve years to adult, who have been previously involved in creative drama activities. Although similar exercises are used to prepare individual actors for performance, they are selected with specific goals in mind. Such goals are chosen, not just to stimulate the player's individual and group growth, but also to obtain aesthetic form for entertaining an audience.

In the process of creative dramatics leading toward improvisation, the group must be viewed as an orchestra in which the instruments glide, flow, and weave together. The group becomes a combination of all the interwoven elements included in improvisation. As in creative dramatics, script, props, costumes, make-up, and scenery need not exist. With improvisation, however, the emphasis is usually on quality performance and rapport with the audience. At this point, the true theatre situation may be tested: actors and audience are involved, together, in play-creation and responses. In contrast to many other theatrical situations, the art of improvisation must reach a peak of spontaneous harmony in which the audience's suggestions, combined with the actor's synchronized movement, compensate for lack of theatrical and technical trappings.

Theatre includes all of the performing arts and is thus unique. Improvisation, similarly, is the most unique form of theatre. Theatre reflects life, regardless of its style or form, and most often communicates through the use of words. If the words are empty or if there is no way to define a pattern for what has been attempted, critique becomes difficult. For this reason there must evolve a procedure that the group follows to enhance planning and inter-action. Exercises and scenarios are included to aid in planning the improvisations. If the audience realizes that a *bit* is an improvisation, they should view their contribution to the final result as an integral part of the improvisation. Likewise, unless a skillful *entr'acte* is planned, there should not be a long pause between taking suggestions from the audience and performing the piece. The brevity of planning allows only enough time for the actors to decide on the elements each is to portray. Techniques to hasten the planning process are discussed in the scenario portion of the chapter.

Like the creative dramatics exercises contained in Chapter Three, improvisation exercises can aid both the group (in becoming more unified and establishing its identity) and individuals (in acquiring the skills necessary to develop character, settings, emotion, speech, plot problems and solutions). These exercises should not be construed as complete stories unto themselves; rather, they provide basic building blocks to aid both the individuals and the group in their develop-ment. The exercises stress the key points of improvisation: character, traits, emotion, problems, groups, tension, and solution. Each player may lead the group to new discoveries. Some of these attempts may founder and fail, while others will evolve into complete scenarios. As members of the group become more used to their developing roles and better prepared to rely upon their partners, the group may move from rehearsal improvisation to performance.

The Scenario. Children can enjoy building their own improvisations in the same manner as adults. Playing familiar stories helps to stimulate the process of drawing fantasy situations to the fore. Viola Spolin and Peter Slade have contributed much to this area. In *Improvisation for the Theatre*, Spolin introduced the *game approach* to exercises. She provided a needed focus in the area of concentra-tion, giving children a personal objective, yet allowing more freedom for the relationships which must occur in improvisation. In this process, games become a catalyst for involving groups in movement, speech and situation.

In *Experiences in Spontaneity*, Slade aided group involvement in dramatic situations through a process he called the *ideas game.* In it, members of the group suggest objects or characters from which the story-teller selects three or four. The story-teller then narrates a story weaving these four elements together. In most cases the story contains a single character; the group, in the guise of this character, collectively performs the story or journey.

As an experience in theatre, such activities are exciting to an audience, for the objective is not to entertain through the usual memorized and planned script. Both Spolin's game approach and Slade's ideas game require the structure of a story form.

Improvisational Exercises. The exercises contained in this chapter are extensions of the creative dramatics exercises included in Chapter Three. The first section includes several types which can be used in quick succession to check the new group's potential capabilities. A selection of warm-up exercises that prepare the body physically and emotionally are contained and will aid in alleviating embarrassment between members of the group.

With the leader as a director, each person performs exercises involving each part of the body in his own space. A good beginning exercise might have the members of the group stand so that when they reach out with their arms parallel to the floor, they can turn first to the left, then to the right, making two partial semi-circles around their bodies. Although they are standing, every part of the body should remain relaxed. Have the students slowly reach over their heads, looking up, then melt down, as if forming a pool of butter around their feet and continuing to melt until the body is a part of the pool. Have them try it several times, until the action of melting becomes comfortable, and the students know what part of the body will support their weight. After completing this exercise, have the students rise again slowly. The body should remain poised and loose. Often, a quick shake with lots of sound serves to loosen the body and set the scene for whatever is to follow.

Other warm-ups may be useful. Rolling the neck around in one direction, then back around the other way with the shoulders and jaw relaxed, can be a comfortable beginning for uniting the group. Following this, the shoulders should be rotated forwards and backwards in a circle without movement of the torso. Next, extend the arms at right angles to the body with the palms upraised, parallel to the body. The stretching muscles are felt from the underarm, through the wrists, and into the tips of the fingers. Turn the hands around the wrists in one direction and back around in the other. Then move the torso and chest horizontally across the hips from right to left holding the hips stationary with the palms of the hands.

Next move the hips from left to right under the torso. Finally, roll the hips in a circle, first going in one direction, then the other.

To loosen the legs, first lift the heel of the foot and roll the ball of the foot around in a circle. Then step on the ball of one foot, lower the foot to its heel while raising, at the same time, the ball of the opposite foot. Alternate these positions. Gradually lift one foot above the floor so that the thigh is raised, then arch the foot at a greater angle to the floor while making the transition smoothly to the other foot. The player using this stationary walk may exaggerate his motion by using the facial muscles, bending the body forward, and varying the space between the feet. After taking the step by placing the toe down and lowering the foot to the heel, the opposite foot should be brushed back. The back foot moves forward and another step is taken. This walk provides a loosening exercise for the ankles, and it may be used in comic exaggeration at the discretion of the player. Exercises such as those described above may also help train the actor to use each part of the body distinctly. Each body part has potential for expression, and when the whole body is involved in movement, even the fingers can become characters.

The exercises which follow explore the elements of Improvisation. As used in chapters Three and Four, bold type indicates dialogue from the leader to the group or individuals, for example, **Everyone form a circle.** Italic type indicates the responses of group members, for example, *Let's try it in mime!* Medium type indicates instructions for the leader, for example, Have the group move to the music.

Improvisation Exercise 1 **JOURNEY THROUGH SPACE**

A physical workout, such as presented in the general exercises, may aid members of the group in relaxation. It also may be helpful if the lighting is dim, and slow, soothing music is played for a few moments. Sit or lie down on the floor and close your eyes. Keep your eyes closed and begin a journey by traveling through your own body. Go inside your brain and sweep out all the thoughts. Relax your jaw, the back of your neck, and your shoulders so that all your energy runs out of your body and through the floor. Your hips, thighs, and legs sink to the floor. Let your feet flop over. Remain there for just a moment. Don't think. All the energy that was once in your body is gone. You're completely relaxed. Your body feels very light, as though you are floating. Each part of you is being held up by a draft of air that supports your whole body, as it glides across space. Currents of air allow you to fall and rise. You feel as though you can go anywhere. You drift through the air, looking down on miles and miles of landscape. As you view the scene below, decide where you want to land. Now, gently float down to that place. Stay there a moment feeling the earth that is underneath your body and supporting you.

The leader may wish to stop the exercise at this point, particularly if the group begins to get restless. As the group becomes familiar with relaxing exercises, they may be extended for longer periods. In continuing, the background music might be changed to a type of electronic music that is even in volume and tempo, to help change the mood. Move at the same pace as the music and my voice. Begin to get up very slowly. Imagine that there is a magnet in line with the center of your body, on a level with your stomach. You are being slowly lifted off the ground by the magnet. Now there's a tight cord being pulled around your wrist and your ankles. You feel as if you were being taken prisoner but it isn't painful at all, it's more like an adventure into which you're being pulled. You sit up and attempt to pull yourself up by reaching for the many dangling ropes that are hanging down. Each rope on which you pull comes loose. Keep trying. Finally you lift yourself up. Now begin walking. Your feet are being pulled along by the same magnet.

You have trouble getting through large hunks of seaweed. They're suddenly growing all around you. Flies are biting you. You must keep walking or you will sink in quicksand. You begin to walk very quickly and soon become free of these obstacles. Suddenly, you can't see anything; even your own body has disappeared. You are enveloped in a cloud. You feel your way through the cloud and keep going, wondering if you'll ever get out. Feel your way through a passage so narrow that you couldn't have passed with your body. You continue moving through the air, which has made you invisible, and you move very buoyantly because lightness begins to feel good. There's a great force pushing you through a narrow passageway. You feel the pressure against your head and shoulders; your arms and feet are cutting through the air. Your body has materialized again. It presses against the currents of air which throws you into a spin. You fall to the ground. Right in front of you there is a maze. You think about whether you are going to enter it. Some of you do. Some of you watch while others slowly sink into the grass.

Moving the entire group by means of narration allows them to react to an imaginary realm of elements, colors, and forces. Within this fantasy environment, their bodies may be reshaped by forces which challenge them to conform to unexpected laws. The new experiences offer the exhilaration of floating, the feeling of being twisted by a resistance to obstacles, the pleasurable emotional release of pain and joy. The opportunity for muscular changes also arises, enabling the actors to stylize human and non-human characters.

After acquainting the group with space, movement may be further developed by telling a story in which dialogue and movement can be supported by the narrator. Simple stories which are well-known can be retold. The players provide the action and dialogue. Many of Dr. Seuss' stories are particularly suited to this purpose. Aesop's fables may also offer a secure structure in which movement and speech play an important part.

Narration, such as that contained in the above exercise, is best used with smaller segments of larger groups. The leader may move from one group to the next, leaving some in a semi-freeze position. Moving small groups in and out as parts of a larger orchestra also prepares the players to move to a story form. Groups of characters may then encounter new situations, creating tension and the ultimate resolution of a story plot.

Long or short stories may be outlined on the board and acted either from memory or a quick review. The players will enjoy themselves because the outlined scenario provides a loose structure, yet no mistakes are possible.

Improvisation Exercise 2 **ACTING TO THE MUSIC**

Listen to the music. Play a portion of Debussy's *La Mer.* What are all the things that could be going on if you were in a large sailboat during a storm at sea? Take the sail down. Lower the lifeboats. Get the life persevers. Try to stay on. Swim. Now, let's listen again and decide the order of these events according to the music.

Regardless of the particular piece of music chosen, plan events with the class after the music has been played. Alternately, the players may think and react to a leading question. If, for example, Stravinsky's *Firebird* were used as the stimulus, the following might be suitable.

If there were a fire and all of you were asleep in an apartment house, what would be some of the steps you would go through? *Wake up. Smell the fire. Call the fire department. Call other people. Gather belongings. Escape.*

Play the music quietly in order to allow comments and questions. The music can also suggest a theme and action to be carried out by the group, without comment or question. Allow such plots to develop, aiding the group if the progress becomes bogged down.

Improvisation Exercise 3 **FOLLOW THE LEADER**

This exercise can be presented in several different ways. Appoint a leader to direct the action in each group. As he moves, he leads the members of his group in an action, activity, or pattern. At successive signals, other leaders may be chosen to lead groups or can assume leadership as they become motivated. Groups may also be called by their numbers to move at different times by the leader.

Other variations of the above exercises include having the groups give and take movement, or moving two groups in mirror (or opposition) relationships. Setting any of these patterns into a thematic structure becomes the choice of the group. Themes may range from literal ideas, such as seasonal change, to a more symbolic process, such as creation and destruction.

Improvisation Exercise 4 **SEEING LINES AND SHAPES**

Each person becomes involved in creating a distinct movement using the imitation of forms in the room as a cue. After a few minutes, look at the actions chosen by those near you and choose one to imitate. Approach that person so the latter knows his action is about to be copied. He must find a new action by imitating someone else. Continue until everyone has exchanged an action.

Other movement exercises which follow may be used to exchange leadership and help the whole group become involved; they also may be used to develop speech.

Improvisation Exercise 5 **NEWSPAPER HEADLINES**

Divide the students into small groups with not more than five in each group. Have each group choose persons, places, and actions stimulated by newspaper story headlines. Examples include:

Violence is All Around Us
Next Time, Why Don't You Try That Old Bicycle?

> Weight Watchers Announce New Program
> The "Test-Tube Baby"
> You Think You Have Problems?

Have all groups begin their improvisation at the same time so that everyone can become involved in a situation. After their involvement becomes spontaneous, call the number of one of the smaller groups, semi-freezing all other participants. Give each group a few moments to perform spontaneously before an audience without having the whole responsibility of carrying out a plot. Continue calling group numbers more slowly, so that each performs for a slightly longer time. Finally, allow each group time to provide a resolution to its problem.

Improvisation Exercise 6 TENSION LINES

Each group is given a single line of dialogue from which its members build ideas for a sequence of actions. Lines that might instantly suggest tension include: **Let's get out of here, I think I hear them coming; I lost the key, I'll have to go back and find it; We don't have much oxygen left; Be very quiet when you cross the creek; I see a light; Do you think we should go in?**

The same organization as described in the preceding exercise can be used. Have the student leader call groups by number so that they give and take by moving and speaking. If the leader feels the groups are confident, allow them to perform individually so that the conclusion may become more meaningful.

Improvisation Exercise 7 JOIN IN CONVERSATION

Two people decide upon a topic of conversation and begin speaking. As soon as others guess the subject of the topic, they join in. Those who begin the conversation may challenge those who join by asking them questions. The answers must fit the context of the conversation. If the answers indicate that they do not know the topic, the leaders may decide whether they shall be allowed to remain in the conversation. Three chances to enter the conversation should be given; if, by the third try, they still haven't guessed the topic, they may not try again. This restriction will serve to reinforce careful listening.

An example of a simple topic is bird watching. A more difficult topic requiring character development is "Who will pull the light switch so everyone may go to sleep in the toy factory?"

Improvisation Exercise 8 **PROBLEM SOLILOQUY**

Each person thinks of a solution to his character's problem. Several solutions may be presented in a soliloquy so that tension becomes a part of the process of decision-making. This tension may lead the students toward further complications of plot development.

Those kids are always laughing at me. They think I'm some kind of freak, just because I've got blue hair. What's wrong with blue hair? In the sunlight it looks silver. Some people have to dye their hair different colors, but mine's just naturally blue. I could change it and be like them. Then they wouldn't always be hurting me.

Other members of the group listen for opportunities to strongly empathize with the character. A discussion can aid the development of beginning situations in improvisation.

Another possible resolution might be, *I won't change it. That means that I'd have to go somewhere else. There's the guy everyone calls Monster, cause he's a bully. I think I'll find out what he's like.*

The scene might continue, showing the problem character involving other players as characters.

I can't help it if all I want to do is destroy everything. I'll go to a store I know of. It's a large toy center. They have so many toys that if I could destroy them I would destroy everything. I could have had this whole toy store, but it was too much. I was afraid of it. There were stairs that went to the moon and my own space satellite. What was I going to do with it? It wasn't a store, it was real. Then this urge came over me to smash it all up. But I didn't smash it all up because I knew that whatever I did wouldn't make any difference. Some machines would just make more, and I started to think "What would I do?"

As the character addresses one of the toy characters, they may have a suggestion and become involved.

Improvisation Exercise 9 **PROPS**

Have the students identify with any of the props found in the middle of the floor. *I am a box. The first thing I remember was a stream of bright sunlight in the junk store. Someone found out how to open me, and the rays of sunlight felt warm inside.*

The player may also talk to the prop as though it were a character in a relationship. *You are mysterious. You don't seem to have any obvious use. Perhaps you have some secret use. That must be, for anything so plain must have a secret. I hear you talking.*

The leader should keep these short monologues in mind as the group develops a scenario built around a common problem. Complications that develop the action may be based on this problem.

Group the players into couples. Have each pair relate, using speech, in any of the following ways: as props; one as a character the other as a prop; one as a straight man and the other as a prop.

One player at a time identifies with a single prop in such a way as to speak for it.

Improvisation Exercise 10 **A CIRCLE OF PROPS**

The players are seated in a circle. There are many different prop objects inside the circle. They include: a net, a ball, a stuffed doll, a cane, a box, styrofoam pieces, foam-rubber shapes, a shawl, a glove, a mask, a wand, a fan, and play-money. One at a time the players enter the circle and handle each of the objects. The players also may be encouraged to use speech, creating characters who use the object. The player using the object should move as the character would, and must think about the relationship between the character and the object. **What does the object mean to the character?**

Pass the object to someone else who takes on new character qualities inspired by the object. The players may need to exchange objects to suit their character. Continue passing the objects around until each person in the group has been involved in a character. **Maintain your focus by means of the object.**

Another variation of the exercise is to imagine the character and pass it from one student to another with the object.

Now I want to bring this speech to a conclusion by offering a hand-made net to this old gentleman who has protected us from the zulus in the mountains throughout his lifetime. With this magic net he can become independent and allow them to become independent. The others in the group now take on tribal character walking as zulus as the little old man guides their actions. The group may be guided through even larger environments. *I have to find my way through this mountain. I hear drums beating on the other side where everyone is being held captive.* Using simple string or percussion instruments, accompany the improvisation.

Starting from simple stimuli, a group can spontaneously interact, passing leadership by passing a prop. The leader can use any number of verbal directions to create the plot. The group should continually be channeled into movement before the leadership is passed on.

Improvisation Exercise 11 **CONVERSATION GETS PLACED**

A conversation between two people begins. As soon as either party mentions a place, the two act as if they are in the location mentioned. Their reactions should be a result of conditions set by the locale. As soon as the place is mentioned the person who first started the conversation leaves and a new player enters. Two are always conversing at a time. When conversation begins to flow without inhibition or complusion, more players may participate.

Improvisation Exercise 12 **FREE ASSOCIATION**

Have everyone lie down and relax. For a warm-up each player chooses a color and an object that is associated with that color. (Two examples are green grass and grey sky.) Continue the warm-up adding a verb.

Next, the first player chooses an object, and the second player chooses a color that he immediately associates with the object of the first player. The next follows with a color association, so that a chain is constructed: green, pillow, red, fire, orange, flame, blue, dish, etc.

After this word association has been played around the circle, the first person in the circle makes up a three word series including color, object, and verb. (For example, black, prison, crumbles). The next person makes a word association to the verb (crumbles).

The leader should keep track of the direction in which the associations lead. If a pattern develops which challenges the group, the following questions can be asked: **Who do you think this story is about? What is happening to them? Where are they?** Together, an outline for an improvisation is developed.

Improvisation Exercise 13 **EXPANDING COMMUNITY**

Each player chooses a character, a trait, and a problem or complication. He joins with a partner and begins a conversation based upon these factors. The whole group should begin as couples, then together add movement by walking around the room. **Maintain a lively dialogue as you move. If you encounter other individuals, concentrate on the relationship with your partner no matter what spacial intervals exist.**

When the couples have moved all the way around the room, they change partners, each keeping his own identity. The process of relating may thus speed up. Continue rearranging the pairs. After this has occurred two to three times, have the students meet in larger groups. Place the emphasis on give and take and instant readjustment to character indentification and overall intent.

Improvisation Exercise 14 **THE PANELISTS**

A topic that may include a slightly bizarre twist is chosen by students acting as panelists. The students should tend to exaggerate character qualities in relation to the topic. Many topics can be discussed. A few examples include:

A man's father died leaving him a million dollars in the will to set up an organization whereby animals would be clothed.

Witchcraft has been practiced for centuries and a church where people are given auto-suggestion has been organized.

A children's TV show in which the panelists are the guests or become children who run the show.

The winners on a quiz show.

A teen-age bop show.

A foreign film producer with some of his crew.

Sportsmen being interviewed about their future career for TV commercials.

Improvisation Exercise 15 **IDENTICAL PROBLEMS**

Give each person in the group a problem. Each student will have several unknown partners with the same problem. Motivate them to go from one person to another in character to seek out these partners.
Examples of problems include:

You have a rock in your shoe, but you try not to limp.

Lint keeps sticking to your body and you struggle with the feeling that you need to scratch.

You can't see very well, and you keep blinking.

You think you are a member of royalty, and you keep posing.

Improvisation Exercise 16 **THE CIRCUS**

The leader introduces a circus, or sideshow. Between each announcement, members of the group arrange themselves so that they become part of a tableau in the described scene.

This is one of the most fantastic exhibits or collections in the world. Here is a sample of the "missing link"—a carcass which has been preserved for thousands of years. A cobra from faraway India. And Indra of the East with her four arms. A lion and his tamer—as you see they don't get along too well. The Laughing Girl—Lucy

Mae—her laugh alone, if you listen to it long enough, will keep you laughing so you can't stop. And now, the tight-rope walker will walk the wire blindfolded—he has a headache tonight and feels the blindfold will help his concentration.

Improvisation Exercise 17 **MUSEUM**

This exercise can be run the same way as Improvisation Exercise 16, The Circus.

Come along folks. Let's leave time behind. We see the pre-Cambrian age along with the twenty-first century, all housed together. Notice the strata of pure-volcanic lava; anything could grow here and it does. Here is an organic geranium. Here we have the fossilized sea horse, the largest of its kind. Here is seaweed, food for the future. Ah, a model of the pterodactyl—that bird who long ago flew right out of the sea and ventured upon the land as the dinosaur. Here is a model of the tarantula, in its actual size when it crawled from the sea. Here is a replica of the primitive family who still lives hidden in many parts of the world.

Now from one extreme to the other: this machine has changed all that—the atom splitter will provide power for the future. Here is modern art—Blue Boy sitting on a tomato soup can, and the Mona Lisa sneezing.

Improvisation Exercise 18 **EMOTIONAL RIBBON**

Divide the large group into smaller groups. Have them choose a series of emotions to play, for example: envy, confusion, shock, and compassion. Next, have them fit these emotions into a situation.

A simple example, using the above, could be the following: The players visit a person who seems to have everything. By asking questions, they find out this is not true. The shocking part is that the person is a slave to a system that is completely repugnant to him. He cannot escape his role in society.

The emotions may guide the scenario. Such emotions also can be organized in an arbitrary fashion and related to a simple journey or environment.

Improvisation Exercise 19 **BEASTS**

Becoming an animal character is the most expedient way to take on unfamiliar and zany characteristics that can be transferred to human characters. A group of eccentric animals can be the guests at the most socially accepted places of interest such as a cocktail party, where talking can become a combination of babble and gibberish. Other familiar environments may also allow for conventional chatter: a march, parade, rally, a schoolroom situation, a basement sale, or a restaurant.

Everyone sit or lie down, become quiet, and think about the animal character that you can see or feel in your body. Think of and feel those special qualities which the animal has. Begin to move like the animal moves. Feel that part of the animal which generates the most energy and begin to move in that manner. Let that energy help you to walk and move like the animal. Remember to allow for noises or speech. What other physical trait distinguishes your character and causes all other qualities to fall into relationship with it? What emotion do you feel? What part of your body seems dominant? With these elements in mind, walk as a person keeping the animal qualities. Go shopping at a basement sale. Some of you may become the sales people. You may use either noises, gibberish, speech, or a combination.

Any other environment may be set up just as quickly. After a discussion about how the exercise worked and felt, another environment can be chosen, providing more structures.

Improvisation Exercise 20 **USING THE TELEPHONE**

For a performer who is hesitant to speak and needs only a little prompting, using a telephone materializes a buffer so that long pauses of "a-a-aum" do not suggest nervousness. He can instead be silent. For the single telephone speaker silence simply means the other person is talking.

One warm-up telephone game begins with a player who reports some incident to a neighbor. The neighbor may repeat the story to another friend, leaving one element out and adding something new in its place. This continues until everyone in the group has had a turn. The story is usually quite changed by the time it reaches its originator and may be used as another beginning.

A calls *B* to ask if *B* can go somewhere (to the show, for example). *B* doesn't wish to go and makes the excuse that it's necessary for him to get permission. His request, of course, is denied and there is nothing to be done until *A* begins to implore *B* to use pressure tactics. From here the situation becomes free to take its own direction.

A calls *B* to explain that his plans have changed because *A* can't go. The real reason *A* can't go is because he has been asked by *C* to go somewhere at the same time, and *C* is preferred to *B*. Of course, to make the problem more difficult *B* offers many alternatives which simply make *A* rationalize even further. From here the situation can take many turns.

Improvisation Exercise 21 **OBJECT RELATIONSHIP**

Look at any object for several minutes and ask yourself questions about it. Where did it come from? From what material was it made? How was it made? How is it used? How does it feel? Where is its emotional or physical center? Who or what is its companion?

The leader can continue to ask random questions of different members of the group. Each will answer as his chosen object and the answers will follow no consistent pattern. The purpose of having individual players each concentrate on the different objects, or any object they independently choose, is to give them a tangible center of focus. They can concentrate upon this focus while the leader simultaneously elicits feedback for use in putting together a story.

Receiving clues from the group which are used by the leader to make up a story becomes a valuable device; because the individual's ideas are used, the group feels that, in part, the story is theirs. The leader may make up any story structure, remaining flexible enough to include the player's ideas but retaining a simple structure which may be easily acted out.

Have a discussion with the group, asking such questions as, **Who is our main character? Where is he going? Why is he going there? What happens on the way? Who helps him?**
The following story structures are the simplest that the leader may use to make up a story quickly that is flexible enough to include additions from the group.

A single character takes a journey while the remaining players become obstacles or part of its environment. The structure also may include a helper for the character. Another variation may include a fuller development of the supportive characters.

The other main structure includes antagonistic forces in addition to the above. When performing for young children, it is wise that the antagonistic forces be merely suggested by an atmospheric presence rather than by embodiment in the form of characters. Additional plot material may be added by harnessing forces to bring about a transformation of the antagonistic force.

Improvisation Exercise 22 **TRANSFORMATIONS**

Transformations occur whenever magic is used. Such character changes should be *produced slowly* through a conscious use of bodily and vocal techniques, as though the player was climbing out of one body trapping and into another. The readjustment from the old body into the new may be best emphasized if the player carries out the movements and mannerisms of each character as he moves back and forth. The character's shock of becoming different may be communicated if there is a definite transition or a contrived difficulty in making the transition between the characters.

Take on the qualities of two distinct characters, first one then the other. Next, provide a transition between them so that it seems as if the player is donning the costume and apparel of his character. Finally, perform the transitions in slow motion making a *jump pivot* to complete the transition.

Usually small mannerisms and vocal changes grow from larger body movement. Even the mental attitude of the character may be partly triggered by bodily reinforcement. If the player can isolate character elements, these may be combined so that the vocal qualities of one character are used with movements of another. Whichever wins, be it stiff-legged soldier or wiggly nose, it will be victorious in determining the personal mannerisms and, ultimately, the identity of the character. To aid the process the player can think of himself as a battleground for rival character traits that would impose themselves upon his undetermined personality, winning a new convert for life.

Improvisation Exercise 23 **TALKING OBJECTS**

Inanimate objects are sometimes left in a room by themselves without the presence of main characters. Plot information and suspense frequently can be provided to an improvisation through the relationship of these objects. In many folk stories, these objects provide conflict by dividing into groups.

The following situations are examples of this. Many examples have been included here because the use of inanimate objects may be widely varied. They may be used as props, characters, character and props, scenery, scenery and character. They also offer a refuge for the shy and unsure person who, nevertheless, wishes to become as much involved as possible.

The articles in the wizard's icebox are complaining that the wizard hasn't been ethical and they want to undo him.

There are different kinds of trees talking in the forest. They are in disagreement over the various forms of magic each can use to save the situation.

Articles in a store are talking to each other about being bought.

Clothes waiting in the dryer at various stages of dryness talk about their owners use and abuse.

Medicines in a medicine chest comment on their uses and users.

Objects in a deep freeze are beginning to thaw because the plug has been pulled.

Environments also may be created for players as the objects change from their early forms into caricatures, swelling with interesting material to advance the plot.

A city containing tall buildings, trees, street performers, a fountain.

The inner workings of a machine, computer, television, an imaginary machine.

Underwater plants, fish, and buried materials.

Improvisation Exercise 24 **SOUND GIVE AND TAKE**

Percussion instruments may be helpful in performing this exercise. The group forms into two lines of couples, one member of each couple in each line facing his partner in the other line. The player in one line knows the sound or noise his partner is going to make so that when he faces away from his partner, he can move spontaneously whenever he hears this sound. His partner plays the sound, making the "puppet" perform. The "puppets" become like a moving orchestra and must listen carefully in order to coordinate their motion with the sound. The sound may be produced vocally or with instruments. There is greater difficulty hearing or distinguishing the differences among the vocal sounds, and the two lines at first may need to face each other.

The silent movers may next lead their vocal partners by moving first as a cue for sound. Unusual environments and atmospheric conditions may be suggested by the sounds and the corresponding movement of the player's bodies.

Have the group consider a story sequence to be developed out of words that are selected from motifs in folk literature, representing archetypes upon which to associate. Stories with penetrating and ritualistic themes may be developed using the following motifs: underwater kingdom, mirror, death; sky-chief, wisdom, and fall to earth. These words have also been used as suggestions for stimulating a dramatic collage: grave, haunted house, fear; cave, treasure, dragon.

Scenarios. A symbol is any object, act, or word embued with varied levels of meaning, direction, or energy. There are many kinds of symbols: those which are cultish or esoteric; religious; and those which Carl Jung called archetypes. He spoke of archetypes as being universal to human nature and products of a realm uniting all universal or shared truths. Some examples are: The Wise Old Man, the Earth Mother, and the Hero.

The use of symbols are often necessary when we refer to intuitions and feelings that cannot be explained literally. If we think of lines and shapes symbolizing man's feelings, it is not difficult to understand how dance or drawing originated. After children have been captured by a certain mood in music, it is not strange that they immediately name common images or kinesthetic sensations such as a flickering light, going upstairs, an old house, a graveyard, while retaining a supernatural mood.

The symbol is sometimes referred to as a motif when it is universally applicable, such as running in place without making any progress or being trapped by a crowd; both are signs of anxiety. A concept for the individual, who is linked together with other individuals by collective symbols, can be considered in depth when motifs are emphasized in literature. If a quick list of such motifs were collected, many common associations could be made. Similarly, when a broad enough story framework is created by the leader, many of the children's ideas may be included. Also single ideas can be expanded upon and placed in a story framework which continues to be developed by a collective creative imagination.

A collection of motifs which occur in a cross-section of both adult and children's literary genres is listed below. (Through the process of improvisation and mime each of these categories may be transformed into another.)

Things	Characters	Places
shoes	birds	mountains
light	small animals	river
sword	magician	road
tree	snake	water
ax	an important person	locked room
key	an insignificant person	soil
lock	persons with extreme	cave
dream	qualities:	ocean
crystal ball	• who lack identity	
crown	• who carry a strong	
mirror	sense of identity	
heart	• who carry a superficial	
map	sense of identity	

Motifs tend to be concrete and more applicable to personal experience than an archetype which is more universally conceived.

A change in archetype characters can be observed over the centuries in literature for adults as well as children. Greek myths and other religions of antiquity placed superhuman powers upon gods who possessed favored characteristics and usually their powers were never questioned, particularly when they distinguished between good and evil. The gods breathed life into the superman or hero who had to prove his powers against mighty forces in nature (usually portrayed in the form of unrelenting epitomes of hideous evil). The line between good and evil was clearly drawn for the superhero and has been perpetuated throughout history by the binding compulsion to fight a foe.

These heroes turned into the common man when folk or fairy tales were introduced, and a variation on the theme of good versus evil became a welcome relief. Good sometimes was a bumpkin or pride-ridden fool who somehow learned his lesson. The humble, persevering, and devoted were transformed by magic realization, instead of having to prove themselves through the brute force as the hero. Lessons were learned and animals talked. When the magic changed, however, mystical experiences occurred and dream-like changes of size and shape became elements in fantasy.

One type of fiction is so wide in thematic content that it can be said to include all of the above characteristics as well as those in the infinite realm of space. This form is known as *science fiction*. Science fiction bridges the gulf between adult and children's literature due to the characteristics which both share—archetypes. It can be seen that the hero-dragon archetype is symbolic of an adolescent's fight against either too strong an identity, or the need for an identity with a parent figure causing anxiety and external and internal aggression.

Alan Toffler, in his recent book *Learning for Tomorrow*, explained why the literary area of science fiction becomes a catalyst for exploration in the affective domain—the area in which values and philosophy for individuals are considered.

The transformation of a child's inner nature also may be manifested by intense concentration and imaginative discoveries. Both may be achieved when the leader establishes a question-answer relationship with the children to establish story framework. The story is enacted not for its own sake, but for the recreation of psychic energy derived from the children's answers. (This process of renewal is necessary for continued growth into maturity.) The inner wanderings that occur in dreams, myths, and fantasies provides collective reality and meaning for the individual, permitting growth through drama.

The following scenarios show how some of the exercises contained earlier in Chapter Five have been used as components in the improvisations. Not only did the exercise expand out of need, but they evolved into scenarios during rehearsals and were redesigned in the attempt to build workable structures. As has been pointed out, these structures are not as important as the individual actor's emotional belief in his character. However, having several workable structures into which the audience's ideas for characters can be "plugged" enables the actors to take less time to outline a plot. They may thus spend more time on character development and synchronization of exits and entrances. In this manner, the transitions between scenes becomes smoother and the player's attention more lasting.

The scenarios which follow were all developed from suggestions by child audiences. They have been chosen because they reveal particular features of scenario development.

Scenario 1 *THE PUPPETS*

An artist creates two ________. He becomes so enthralled with them that they begin to take on human capabilities. A publicist hears about it and, through the enchantment that he adds, helps the artist to complete the task of creating the two ________. They are sent out into the world to take part in new experiences, such as eating in a restaurant, walking down the street, and so on. For some reason, perhaps because they enjoy being human, they present a threat. The law threatens them, and they decide to return to their original form.

These characters are flexible enough in function to be interchanged with those offered by the improvisation group. As a result this scenario may be used many times in rehearsals, each time with a completely new theme and different characters. In one rehearsal, for example, the "artist" might become a Buddhist monk giving a "novice" freedom to experience the world of Maya. Telepathy between the two may cause the monk to feel the pain of the novice's suffering.

Scenario 2 *THE BALLERINA*

All characters want to be like A. They get into a discussion and A leaves. They visit a wise ________ to find out where A could have gone. She suggests they return to their original location and A will be there. When they do this, they find A. They tell A about their wish. A tries to teach them but realizes it is impossible. She encourages them to reconsider, and suggests that because they are unique she could never be like either of them. They are surprised by this new insight and so return to the wise ________ who agrees.

The above scenario may be used in a performance. In replaying, the impact and spontaneity is frequently not as great as they were in the original form in which the characters are energetically and intuitively developed.

One example of the scenario in use might portray the following characters: a ballerina, rose, tin-man, owl, ostrich, and fountain.

All the characters want to be like the ballerina. They get into a discussion and the ballerina leaves. They visit the wise owl to find out where the ballerina could have gone. He suggests they return to their original location and the ballerina will be there. They do and find her. They tell her about their wish. She tries to teach them, but finds it is impossible. She encourages them to reconsider, and she suggests that she could never be like any of them because they are unique. They are surprised by this new insight and return to the wise owl who agrees that they are all unique.

Scenario 3 HANDLING OF CHARACTERS

Animal characters are mentally more neutral than are fairy tale characters such as witches, dragons, or princesses. The physical qualities of animals can be exaggerated, however. A long-term goal might be to reverse many commonly-accepted, socially-approved stereotypes, inspiring greater humor and self-acceptance. The incongruity and anomaly needed as a basis for humor might be provided, for example, by an ecologically-minded cowboy who puts his cattle to sleep by singing their praises and blowing smoke from leaf-rolled cigarettoes.

Animals may be used to explore the human counterpart if the following characters are given: a coach, a mouse, a pig, and a hen. This improvisation is called "The Big Time," and is based upon the problem that the hen can't lay eggs and becomes worried. The doctor on the farm is a pig who encourages her to change her diet. This doesn't work so he tries other remedies like fixing her plumbing and taking an inventory of her habits.

In the meantime, a mouse and a car-racing coach are driving there. The coach tries to get the mouse trained for Grand Prix racing. The mouse, however, only wants secure retirement for his old age. They stop by the farm to get gas, and the mouse feigns illness to get out of the racer and adjusts the car so it won't run.

The coach explains to the pig that the mouse has an asthmatic condition and hasn't been able to sneeze. The pig takes a feather from the hen and all three then go over to the mouse. The pig holds the feather under the nose of the mouse who immediately sneezes.

"It worked," exclaims the pig. "Your feather cured his disease."

"Now I can lay eggs," the hen says, running into the henhouse.

"It's all psychological," reveals the pig.

The coach asks about the mouse who keeps sneezing. The pig says the mouse will just have to give up the track and live out here in the country. He'll never drive again.

The coach leaves by hitchhiking away, because the racer won't start. As soon as this happens the mouse stops sneezing. "You're right; it's all psychological. As soon as my coach left, I got well. My racer needs to be fixed. I'll give it to the coach. I won't need it anymore." They catch the coach a short way up the road and he drives off with the pig who has always wanted to see "The Big Time."

Like "The Big Time," "The Birthday Party" is a simple plot in which neutral characters may be used. Animal characters with human qualities such as those demonstrated in most fables and many folk-tales might be used in this scenario since its action does not depend upon eccentricities in the animals' characters. Individuals could specialize their actions on rodentism or felinism, within a simple scenario. The scenario itself could be broadened; the "birthday" might be changed to the premise of "waiting for a special occasion."

__________ is to have a birthday. His friends can't decide what to get him, so they get together and think of the thing he likes most, a __________. They decide to take the __________ away from him so that when he gets it back, he will be happier than he could ever have been with something new. The plot includes his reaction to losing __________, his reaction to getting it back, and when they tell him what really happened, he can't believe it and walks off. (Many other endings are possible. Use a Market Place scene to provide an extension.)

The next scenario may be used both in rehearsals and in performances. In an improvisation based upon this structure, a scene may be improvised after the relationships have been decided upon. A third scene should develop around the relationship between characters from each of the two previous scenes.

Two different characters are given to two different couples. Each couple must develop a relationship, first with itself, then with the other couple.

A robber and a parrot. The bird finds the robber a job so he no longer needs to rob.

The vaccine and the germ. The vaccine changes the germ so the germ doesn't need to stay alive by eating people. The germ and the robber meet. The robber suggests to the germ that it could eat some of the plants in his garden in order to help him weed. When this happens a kind of fungus is discovered which has curative qualities, like penicillin.

The leader might ask each student to bring his own character to class. Each should give a description and reasons for having chosen his character. Next, the characters may be joined into couples. After their relationship in a couple is improvised, two couples may be grouped. One possible result of such an organization plan might lead to the following scenario:

A cactus plant and a horse are the characters. The horse finds the cactus dying of pollution, and the plant begs the horse to find her a new home. In a second pair, the characters might be a manhole cover and a cop. The manhole cover decides to come loose in order to attract attention. It does, and a cop stumbles into it.

The two couples join together to explore relationships in which they all may share. The horse gallops up to tell the cop his problem of having to find a place for the cactus. While the cop is thinking, he imagines stories about the Wild West of long ago; he is also standing over the manhole cover and overhears a gang of smugglers operating in the sewer. The cop realizes that he can get a reward for his discovery of the gang. He also knows that if it weren't for the horse, he could not have been at this place to make the discovery. He begins to listen carefully to the smugglers' plan. Since the criminals have located an open space, they have decided to hide their loot there. The cop gives the horse the directions for finding this haven, and the cactus and horse gallop away. A resolution follows if appropriate.

A different theme that reflects loneliness might emerge if the cactus and horse are replaced by a crippled man and a butterfly. The butterfly is lonely and discovers the old man. She begins to visit him every day. One day, she loses her way because the season is changing and winter is about to begin. The old man goes outside to find the butterfly and on his walk, is overcome by the storm. The cop finds him and helps him home. He tells the cop about the butterfly. Meanwhile the butterfly has become very sad and talks to the manhole cover. The manhole cover promises to attract the cop by getting some of his spider friends to make a strong thread that will loosen the manhole cover. The cop sees this and comes over to put things in order. When the cover tells him about the old man, he remembers him and struggles through the storm to unite the butterfly and its friend.

Developing Improvisation Structures. Point out the three main ingredients of an improvisation: problem, tension, resolution. Have each player choose a character keeping an emotion and/or character trait in mind. The character can be human, animal, or inanimate. List these headings on the board. Have the whole group fill in their suggestions under the appropriate headings. The excitement of the plot and the connection between the problem and the resolution is provided by tension, sometimes referred to as a *tension builder* or *stretcher.*

Scenario 4 THE LOST SHELL

The turtle lost her shell, and she can't cope without it. The trees and animals overhear and transform themselves in order to be helpful. They lead the turtle to the mountaintop, where the witch is using transformed members of the group as millwheels in order to pulverize the turtle's shell. She hopes to bring destruction to the village. The characters who are leading the turtle utilize their power to change their transformed members. Together they recover the shell and destroy the witch.

In the scenes between the forest and the witch's torture dome in which the turtle's shell was hidden, the actors may gracefully organize themselves into a pathway leading from one environment to the final scene as the witch is caught in her own destructive device. The switch from forest to the witch's mill of destruction completely changes each time the actors leave the forest with the turtle and re-enter, as the mill wheel accompanies their ominous turning with crunching sounds. As the actors change the scene back and forth, they quietly resculpture their bodies. Everyone moving upon the floor should appear to have full confidence in his spacing and design.

The turtle may walk with the forest elements, leaving the forest at one exit and returning on the other side. Between leaving and returning, however, their journey should be completed. When the witch enters, the pinnacle of evil has been discovered. Through the powers of nature, the forest elements cause the witch's defeat.

Scenario 5 THE PIG AND THE GORILLA

The characters include: a gorilla, pig, shower, basketball player, and a forest of noodles.

The basketball player is in the shower talking about how awful it is to keep losing; their team must do something. Meanwhile, a pig and a gorilla are in their natural habitat and are enjoying themselves, but decide to go out to seek adventure. They go through a forest of noodles and come to a school, where they find some children and a ball. They begin playing with the ball and are showing their abilities at just the time that the basketball player wanders onto the court. He asks them to join his team but first they must be clean and shaven. After they have been cleaned, the game begins. Both the pig and gorilla seem to have lost their vitality because they've been forced to conform. They decide to go back through the forest of noodles and they regain their strength, their hair, and their dirt. Each variety in the forest of noodles could react to the pig and gorilla as if to advertise their qualities. (Chinese: egg; Italian: tomato; American: Apple Betty; Japanese: seaweed; Hawaiian: pineapple.) Each is able to perform a different miracle. After a great feast, the gorilla and pig return to the game and win against the noodles who have become players. The noodles decide that it is better for them to be a noodle forest and be eaten than to be basketball players and lose.

Scenario 6 THE NERVOUS WITCH

Characters for this scenario include: a witch, a spider, a bat, and a skunk. The witch can't perform magic and, as a result, has no friends. A spider, who crawls out of the faucet, suggests they go back to the 1600's in his time machine. When they do this, they find a skunk and bat, who are flying around in a medieval castle missing their witch who died. They realize that they can't scare people until they find a new witch. The witch, however, remembers that none of her spells will work unless she is back in the 20th century, and all four decide to return to the present in the time machine. They have three chances to get into the 20th century. The first time, the controls jam and force them backwards in time, where they see dinosaurs. After freeing the controls, they go quickly forward, arriving in the future and seeing robots. Finally, they return to the 20th century and the witch recalls that she never did know any spells. The bat and skunk help her remember some spells that their old witch knew. A magic word takes them into the future. At first it is dark, but the bat can "see" for them. The smell at first is overwhelming, but the skunk can overpower it. They enter a new future which they describe optimistically.

For transitions in the above scenario, the players may wish to stretch the story by using the time machine.

Scenario 7 TWO SCENARIOS

In the following two scenarios, the characters given by the children dictate the plot and journeys which are developed. Both scenarios may be best used on the occasion when they are planned then repeated. They do not lend themselves particularly well to being rewritten for use with other characters. The first scenario is called "The Monster Convention." Its characters are: a dragonfly, monsters, and a scarecrow.

The Scarecrow can't scare anyone because she is too afraid of everything. To overcome her problem, she decides to go to the monster convention, where all the monsters assemble to vote for their president. The scarecrow enters and they make fun of her because she has come to try to be a monster. They tell her to go out and bring something back that she has scared. On her way to do this, she meets a dragonfly who tells her that he used to be a dragon, but because he didn't believe in himself he has become a dragonfly. The scarecrow returns to the convention and says she's ready to be initiated into the monster club. A package arrives and the monsters all become frightened. The scarecrow opens it. Meanwhile, the monsters all have run away. The scarecrow finds the box empty and claims she has now overcome her fear. All the quasi-monsters return in the form of a dragon. The dragonfly speaks from within, saying that he has grown back to his original size because he helped the scarecrow. The scarecrow departs, riding the dragon.

An Indian, gill man, skeleton, buffalo, witch, and buzzard make up the characters for the scenario called "The Indian."

The Indian builds a totem pole to appease the demon witch and goes to sleep. Each part of the totem pole comes to life in his dream. The gill man speaks of water and its cleansing effect; the skeleton, of the souls of the ancestors and all their wisdom; the buffalo, of the strength and life sustaining importance his herds have had on the land. During this time, the Indian reacts in sleep to their speech. He wakes after much restlessness. The totem characters tell him they will lead him on a journey to the demon witch and help dispell the evil effects of her poisoning of the earth.

Meanwhile, the demon-witch and her helper, the buzzard, are in the process of taking up evil deeds that will bring misfortune to the world, and realize that the group is on its way to destroy the witch's power. She imposes an obstacle on each member of the party and is defeated in each case. The buffalo overcomes the wall with force, the gill man drives back the river with his fishlike capacities, and the skeleton leads everyone through the tomb of dead souls (where the buffalo gets lost for a short time).

They finally get to the castle of the witch and bury three objects in the earth to appease the evil forces and help them destroy the witch. The gill man had collected some water, the skeleton a bone, and the buffalo some hair. After covering these objects with dirt the castle disintegrates and the witch is turned into a statue atop the buzzard's shoulders.

Scenario Outlines. The creation of many of the preceding scenarios has been based upon charts which the leader and players prepared on the board. The charts developed by the groups were called *Versatility*

VERSATILITY

character	trait	emotion	problem
egg	sore toe	ecstatic	accident-prone
pencil	jerks	nostalgic	too naive
raincoat	repeats words	hopeful	tragic flaw
pinball machine	blows up	outraged	impotent
penguin	compulsive	quick temper and cools	domination
eagle	radiates		breaks law
headache	eats		vanity
	itches		selfishness

Charts. Perhaps the traditional scenario plot structure should be briefly reviewed at this point. Through use of the group-developed versatility chart, a brief plot-scenario outline could be expanded to explore various elements of improvisation. New categories might be used at each session. In the chart below, only three items were chosen for expansion. These elements were problem, tension, and solution. In use, each element considers plot, but not in the repetitive activities sometimes referred to as stretchers that usually make up the bulk of the plot.

The first items on this chart were handled in previous exercises dealing with character development. With the understanding of these categories, the chart was filled in with about ten items under each category. Groups were formed and each player made his selection of a character, trait, and emotion individually. The problem, group, tension, and solution were chosen from the board by the group and developed into an improvisation.

Several players spoke adamantly about the need for emphasizing values that could be either accepted or rejected by the audience and remain entertaining. The problem of the disparity between values in society and those emphasized in schools and families were also discussed. The question was asked, "If the existing entertainment medium is an outgrowth of society's frustrations, how is our audience to absorb any spiritual nourishment for their needed growth?" In response, the group explored the possibility of using universal concerns of mankind rather than present-day pedestrian conflicts as the basis of their improvisation. They continued in this way to gather material from archetypes found in mythology, a practice which opened the way for more imaginative scenarios. Scenarios representative of themes from the 'collective unconscious' serve any list of characters that the audience may offer during warm-up.

CHART

group	tension	solution
water pools	suspense	freedom
weather	forbidden	peace
jungle growth	chase	acceptance
ghetto	doom of evil	helpful
harbor-rats, ships, gangsters	sudden transformations	tolerance, self-control
mysterious plants	journey	**new understanding**
"little people"		love (vs. hate)

Endings to improvisations are often weak and may become either forced or nonexistent. After discussion about the pros and cons of rehearsing endings, a category and list was added to the Versatility Chart; this chart collected a new category whenever necessary. The problem category was also reconstituted.

As a result of adding endings and problems the following scenarios were effectively performed and were presented several times with the addition of new characters.

Vanity

1. A *gazelle* admires herself in the mirror.

2. Her acquaintances tell her they can't be really friends of hers because of her vanity.

3. *Two* of them decided ways in which they will take her mirror away. One wants a chance to see himself—the other may make a noise to startle her so that she will leave her mirror. Since she is listening, she has overheard their plans and the attempt is foiled.

4. She leaves and the third *one* decides to steal the mirror while she is bathing. Since the *gazelle* doesn't hear this plan, it works.

5. When the *three* get the mirror, they begin looking at themselves, and they become vain. They decide to break it.

6. Those left on stage (scenery) pick up the pieces, and all become vain.

7. One lonely, (ugly, scrubby) bush can be left crying out of loneliness that a mirror is no substitute for *friendship*. Or, finding a mirror left, he can yell at them saying that they are all as separate and alone as the gazelle and the pieces of mirror. Tears and water have a cleansing affect which can transform them all.

The Fuzzies
(see also Lesson Five, Chapter Four.)

1. People are happy in the town, giving and receiving *fuzzies*.

2. A *magician* complains that people are too happy and he can't sell any more magic potions to cure them.

3. *He* announces to the *townspeople* the *fuzzies* are going to run out

if they keep giving them away.

4. *People* spread the word, become afraid, and begin to hoard *fuzzies*, even steal them, which makes them unhappy.

5. Now the *magician* is happy and can perform his works of magic.

6. The *fuzzies* have died and someone new comes to town who is unaware of the new policy. He has brought *fuzzies* with him and gives them away making the people happy again. The decision is made that since giving makes people happy, they should be able to give *fuzzies* away.

7. Someone gives the *magician* a *fuzzy*. He experiences happiness and is left alone on stage.

The Monkey's Heart

1. A greedy *gypsy* demands that her *helpers* get her a *monkey's heart*.

2. They journey through difficult "*scenery*" and bribe an *Ogre* in order to continue their voyage.

3. When they come upon the *monkey*, they *bribe* her also so that she will come with them.

4. They retrace their steps, tell the *monkey* the purpose of their trip. The *monkey* says that she has left her "heart" in the tree.

5. They wait for her. She doesn't return, but yells to them that she also has a brain. She reminds them that they also have hearts and brains. The idea entrances them so that they tell the scenery, "making up stories" with their newly discovered brains.

6. They expect that the gypsy will be angry. Instead, being so "scattered" or "irrational" in her desires, she's forgotten about them and wants something else. When they remind her that she, too, has a brain and heart, the idea of having something of her own can work some change on her.

APPENDIX

This abbreviated chart relates the steps in the affective domain to the exercises in Chapter Three. It is in the area of the affective domain that the process of creative drama is most completely contained. The exercises range from the practice of simple awareness to the fullest integration of a personal philosophy. The cognitive domain relies on the collection, ordering, and selection of data and is useful as a matrix upon which the steps of the affective domain are based. For example, in the exercise Space Has Size, knowledge about conditions in the world deepen the awareness and importance of the principle of physical space:

COGNITIVE

    general

The world may reach a population of 10 billion before 1980.

    detail

There is not enough food for 10 billion.

AFFECTIVE

    general

Enough space is important for life.

    detail

The space I use is important because it represents me.

In the chart are major items in the cognitive domain. The last two are most basic to completion of one process of individual growth and, in a similar matter, the holistic approach to education.

Cognitive

Knowledge
Comprehension
Application
Analysis

Affective

Receiving
Responding

Valuing

Organization
Characterization

Synthesis
Evaluation

From moderate awareness to active awareness. Eliciting response permits levels of involvement toward greater depth.

Senses, Involvement 1-17
Space 18-21
Imagination 22-29
Plots 30-36

Acknowledgement of values, commitment to values, and the development of a value system upheld by continual challenge.

Character 37-47

Putting together separate elements to form a whole. Using the total body medium in order to unite the drama and reach a level of discovery about life.

Judgments based on external and internal criteria enables the learner to continually make new discoveries.

Mime 48-61
Abstract Mime 62-69
Speech and specifics 70-87
Improvisation

GLOSSARY

Affective domain the area of learning dealing with awareness, development of values, decision-making, and including the emotions as related to experience.

Antagonist the negative force in a plot.

Archetype a universal model culturally common as the stories of creation and overwhelming forces of those persons who have fought personal limits to enliven and make valid a renewal of human nature into eternal forms, ie. hero myths, including the Trickster, and "the eternal feminine."

Beckon a children's game. One child with eyes closed stands in the center of a circle of children. The leader is a member of the circle and points to someone in the circle to move toward the person standing in the center. The latter points in the mover's direction before being tagged by him. If he is tagged, another mover is chosen to advance toward the center. When the center person points correctly, someone new is placed in the center.

Bit a small scene in a theatrical performance.

Casting a step in the process of creative drama in which the leader engages children in a role or character either through dialogue, action, or referring to them indirectly as being in a particular place.

Catharsis an emotional release.

Center a physical or emotional body placement of energy from which an actor moves for character identification.

Charade a description of a concept without verbalization.

Cognitive domain an area of learning based on a collection of facts and information from which to form opinions and build concepts.

Commedia dell' Arte a spontaneous, stylized theatre presentation which originated in Italy. Can be compared to creative dramatics in the use of an unwritten script.

Concertatore the director or leader of a Commedia troup who would give the main outline or scenario to the actors from which they would improvise.

Creative dramatics a process of growth in which children are doing and being; improvised drama which receives its impetus from a myriad of stimuli and conforms to many structures developed over a time period.

Creative play a step in the process of creative drama in which children have played through a story or event many times and are able to repeat it for a performance. It may be written down though it is not memorized.

Cycles play performed during the Middle Ages, related to a Christian theme.

Dramatic play the step before the creative drama process. An essential beginning for a natural progression in creative drama, a step in which children interpret their environment usually physically at first until the understanding has been internalized and can become symbolic.

Equidistance each child is aware of having and needing enough space around himself to move in a large group without interference.

Eight to eleven inhibitions in relation to creative dramatics activities have started and more time needs to be spent on exercises in involvement and the senses. However, if creative dramatics has begun then children are at their most energetic, expansive, responsive, and perceptive stage.

Electricity a game in which students either tap hands or hold hands in order to pass a shock by pressing the hands of the person on the left, if the shock is received by the person on the right.

Emotional memory a term defining recall of an experience using an action to inspire an appropriate emotion or feeling.

Entr' acte a short scene, used as a transition piece, to give the actors time to apply the audience's suggestions to their scenarios.

Evaluation a step in the process of creative dramatics when children who are more experienced can verbalize ideas related to their interactions.

Five to nine an age when children are most receptive to creative dramatics involvement and its introduction will greatly influence their later growth in depth of thought and feeling.

Game involvement of a group in a structural activity which is performed under a well-defined set of rules.

Game approach the use of Viola Spolin's point of concentration inherent in games.

Gibberish a production of vocal sounds using nonsense in order to contribute to language flow and tone color as related to meaning and body movement.

Given circumstances the time, place, and situation in the plot of a play affecting the actor's creation of character.

Group characters children combine in a way to form one animal, object, or person.

Ideas game ideas dealing with characters, setting, and actions are asked for by the leader from the children and a story is created.

Imaginative play a step in the process of creative drama in which children are involved in one group activity toward a common goal which is more free-flowing and less structured than a game.

Introduction the first step in the creative dramatics session which a visiting leader would be more likely to use than the children's regular leader or teacher. The visiting teacher builds the trust needed to help the children feel at ease and considers the safety of the physical surroundings for use in drama.

Jongleurs minstrels, actors, musicians, who had many performing talents. They usually traveled from village to village during the Middle Ages.

Jump pivot a 180 degree turn which a player makes when changing character.

Jung, Carl a Swiss psychiatrist who made a collection of several thousand dreams from which he discovered common features he called archetypes.

Lazzi set pieces of comic business which remained unique to each actor in Commedia and for which the actor became well-known.

Lilliputian exercises handling objects as if one were very small and the objects by comparison are large. Used to extend movement.

Locomotor movements running, jumping, skipping, walking, leaping, hopping, movements which allow a physical distance to be covered.

Magic if a way for an actor or player to establish belief or a connection between himself and the motivation and action of a character by asking, "What if. . .?"

Motivational activity the step in a creative drama session which establishes the children's incentive for what is to follow so they become involved and interested in the next step or stimulus.

Mime a term used to describe stylized wordless gestures that are classic and traditionally accepted.

No play a stylized Japanese play requiring slow movement, masks, stylized actions, and usually enjoyed by upper classes.

Occupational mime referring to ordinary everyday tasks shown in action without the use of the stylization of classical mime.

Pantomime a description of an action without verbalization. (Pan, a Greek god of nature.)

Planning a step in the creative dramatics session when the leader guides children to form their playing by asking them questions about the events, the setting, the characters, and may include casting.

Play see dramatic play.

Plots the outline of happenings which gives a story action and suspense.

Protagonist the positive force in a plot.

Purging a release of emotion in an effort to cleanse.

Release the step in a creative dramatics session which occurs after children have been non-active and need to put ideas into physical action.

Replaying the step in a creative dramatics session during which the children play, add on, and refine what has been played before.

Scenario a shortened story line sometimes broken down into outline form.

Science fiction a genre of literature dealing in futuristic ideas extending from the laws of science. Borders on fantasy fiction in which magical changes may take place.

Sense memory a term defining the recall of an experience using the senses.

Signal a cue which is explained at the beginning of an activity. It may be in the form of music, a drum, the voice, or visual.

Simon Says The leader directs a movement while the children follow. For example, "Simon Says to touch your head," and the group follows the leader. If the leader leaves out "Simon Says" and only says "Touch your head," traditionally anyone following is considered "out" or next to lead. In this book "Simon Says" is merely used to get the children involved.

Slade, Peter author and pioneer of children's drama in England.

Soliloquy a dramatic monologue delivered to oneself, as if one is thinking outloud.

Spolin, Viola the author of *Improvisation for the Theatre.* Uses theatre games to develop spontaneity and involvement in improvisation.

Stage picture a group tableau or a still pose which the leader calls to establish form.

Stimulus the impetus around which a theme and action form for a creative dramatics session. It may be a story, an idea, picture, a piece of music, an object, a person, a place, or any combination or these.

Stills a momentary freeze position quickly called by the leader.

Story dramatization a step in the progression of creative drama in which children play complete story.

Stretcher this element may be a journey, a time machine, talking props, a market place, a chase, or an expanded part of the scenario in which many adventures take place and happenings build suspense, providing further conflict and meaning to the resolution.

Talking chorus in Greek drama, the unit of actors who provided narration and important background information for the development of the plot.

Tension builder see stretcher.

Theatre Italien the theatre in Paris where Commedia was performed.

Through line of action the actions that an actor concentrates on when developing a role. Each action must have a purpose and be logically connected to the character's overall objective or goal.

Trait a characteristic which may be physical, mental, emotional, or psychological. Helps expand the character's uniqueness.

Twelve to fifteen many children will not choose creative dramatics as a form for self-expression due to inhibitions and as a result many exercises need to be used for involvement.

Ward, Winifred author and pioneer of creative drama in the United States.

Way, Brian the author of *Development Through Drama*, a book on children's drama; and the writer of many children's participation plays.

Zanni the clown or buffoon character. Could be laughed at because of his exaggeration of reality and pitied because he was the butt of the jokes.

BIBLIOGRAPHY

Brown, George. *Human Teaching for Human Learning*, New York: The Viking Press, 1971.

Courtney, Richard. *Play, Drama, and Thought*, London: Cassell and Co., 1968.

Dorson, Richard. *Folklore and Folklife, an Introduction.* Chicago: University of Chicago Press, 1972.

De Mille, Richard. *Put Your Mother on the Ceiling*, New York: The Viking Press, 1973.

Slade, Peter. *Experiences in Spontaneity*, Longmans, 1968.

Spolin, Viola. *Improvisation for the Theatre*, Northwestern University Press, 1963.

Tyas, Billi. *Child Drama in Action*, New York: Drama Book Specialists, 1971.

Way, Brian. *Development through Drama*, Longmans, Canada, 1967, 1970.

MUSIC

Copland: *Music for Movies*, **background**.

Grieg: *Peer Gynt Suite*, **background**.

Mussorgsky: *Pictures at an Exhibition*, **background**.

Vivaldi: *The Seasons*, **background**.

Beethoven: *Pastorale*, **climatic**.

Berliotz: *Symphony Fantastic*, **climatic**.

Grieg: *Peer Gynt Suite*, **climatic**.

Holst: *The Planets*, **climatic**.

Stravinsky: *Firebird Suite*, **climatic**.

Villa-Lobos: *Little Train of the Caipiria*, **climatic**.

Luening: *A Poem in Cycles and Bells*, **eerie**.

Mussorgsky: *Night on the Bare Mountain*, **eerie**.

Saint-Saens: *Danse Macabre*, **eerie**.

Subotnick: *Silver Apples of the Moon*, **electronic music synthesizer, eerie**.

Copland: *Appalachian Spring*, **historical**.

Copland: *Billy the Kid*, **historical**.

Gould: *Spiritual for Orchestra*, **historical**.

Dukas: *Sorcerer's Apprentice*, **magical**.

Mussorgsky: *Dawn of the Moskva River*, from *Khovantchina*, "Prelude to Act I," **magical**.

Rimsky-Korsakov: *Scheherazade*, **magical**.

Tchaikovsky: *Midsummer Night's Dream*, **magical**.

Copland: *Dance Symphony*, **lyric**.

Debussy: *Prelude a l'apres-midi d'un faun*, **lyric**.

Dvorak: *New World Symphony*, **lyric and climatic**.

Ketelby: *In a Chinese Temple Garden*, **lyric**.

Tchaikovsky: *Romeo and Juliet*, **lyric**.

Bizet: *Carmen*, **processional**.

Borodin: *Prince Igor*, **processional**.

Rosini: *La Gazza Ladra*, **processional**.

Beatles: *Magical Mystery Tour*, **rhythmic**.

Breuer: *The Moog Synthesizer*, **rhythmic**.

Ketelby: *Jungle Drums*, **rhythmic**.

Mac Dermot: *Hair*, **rhythmic**.